The Observer

ALASTAIR SAWDAY'S
SPECIAL PLACES TO STAY

EUROPE

SPECIAL PLACES TO STAY
WITH COURSES
AND ACTIVITIES

A selection from our much-loved series on
France, Italy, Portugal, Spain, Ireland and Britain
- in association with The Observer.

EDITED BY JACKIE KING

Design:	Caroline King
Maps & Mapping:	Bartholomew Mapping, a division of HarperCollins, Glasgow
Printing:	Canale, Italy
UK Distribution:	Portfolio, Greenford, Middlesex
US Distribution:	The Globe Pequot Press, Guilford, Connecticut

Published in 2003 in association with Guardian Newspapers Ltd

Alastair Sawday Publishing Co. Ltd
The Home Farm Stables, Barrow Gurney, Bristol BS48 3RW
Tel: +44 (0)1275 464891 Fax: +44 (0)1275 464887
E-mail: info@specialplacestostay.com Web: www.specialplacestostay.com

The Globe Pequot Press
P. O. Box 480, Guilford, Connecticut 06437, USA
Tel: +1 203 458 4500 Fax: +1 203 458 4601
E-mail: info@globe-pequot.com Web: www.GlobePequot.com

First edition

ISBN 1-901970-34-5 in the UK
ISBN 0-7627-2964-3 in the US

Printed in Italy

A WORD FROM ALASTAIR SAWDAY

Is this book a 'first'? Pregnant with ideas and opportunities, it gives you hundreds of places to stay in six countries. I had no idea that our Special Places could do so much for travellers! We have always sought out the most appealing places and people, but the range of interests and activities within these pages has astonished even us. You may never need another holiday brochure. Read on…

The list is long and fascinating – and exhausting: beach riding, pottery, organic vegetable growing, fly-fishing, archery, aromatherapy, falconry, wind-surfing, writing, wood-turning, parachuting, French, Irish dancing, yoga, Alpine flora, ballooning, flamenco dancing, geology… and much more. You can drive a carriage, a horse, a quad-bike, a canalboat or a canoe. You may learn to make stained-glass windows, flower arrangements, furniture, corn dollies, jam or just dinner. Play jazz, golf, the guitar – even polo. Your mind, your body, your heart, your spirit – all can be nourished by Special Places.

Our ability to launch this remarkable book has been due in no small way to *The Observer*. They spotted its potential for their wandering readers – who tend, I suspect, to be independent in their travelling habits. These places – and the fascinating, bizarre, energising, life-enhancing things you can do in and around them – will, however, appeal to you all. No more excuses for not doing what you have long wanted to do. Go forth and release those arrows.

Alastair Sawday

ACKNOWLEDGEMENTS

Jackie King put this book together, with her enviably calm professionalism. Jo Boissevain has been in solid support and her sharp eye and creative input are much valued. Julia Richardson masterminded another complicated production project. Then a team of helpers rallied around to tackle the detail: translations, chasing photos, correcting errors, talking to owners in several languages and generally dotting a lot of 'i's. So we owe much to many people, most of whom are listed below. It has been a joint effort to be proud of, executed with a natural kindness, efficiency and generosity of spirit that I have learned to expect from the people in this office. I must also mention the easy relationship we have had with Lisa Darnell of *The Observer.*

Lastly, we owe much to the remarkable people who own and run these special places, courses and activities. There are only rare limits to their kindness and generosity. They are the key to the huge pleasures you will derive from this book.

Alastair Sawday

Series Editor:	Alastair Sawday
Editor:	Jackie King
Editorial Director:	Annie Shillito
Production Manager:	Julia Richardson
Web & IT:	Russell Wilkinson, Matt Kenefick
Assistant to Editor:	Jo Boissevain
Editorial:	Sarah Bolton, Emma Carey, Roanne Finch, Jessica Hughes, Laura Kinch, Susan Luraschi, Jose Navarro, Philippa Rogers, Danielle Williams
Production Assistants:	Rachel Coe, Paul Groom, Bethan Thomas
Accounts:	Bridget Bishop, Sheila Clifton, Jenny Purdy, Sandra Hassell
Sales & Marketing:	Julia Forster, Bryony Johnstone

WHAT'S IN THE BOOK?

CONTENTS

1-48 italy

See back of book for complete index of courses & activities.

• Though we have inspected all our properties we cannot check out all the courses, activites and people who lead them; our role is to put you in touch.

CONTENTS

49-108 spain

See back of book for complete index of courses & activities.

• It is vital you check whether instructors are qualified and whether full insurance cover is provided – what are the credentials of that riding school in Castilla? Make sure you are covered for taking part in adventure or outdoor sports.

CONTENTS

109-126 portugal

See back of book for complete index of courses & activities.

• Assume rooms have en suite bath or shower unless otherwise mentioned. A 'private' or 'shared' bathroom means that it is not en suite.

CONTENTS

127–208 france

See back of book for complete index of courses & activities.

- Meals must be booked in advance at B&Bs, and it's safer to do so elsewhere, too.

CONTENTS

See back of book for complete index of courses & activities.

• Most hosts - though not all, so check - are happy to liaise between you and the courses or activities listed under their entry. (Not all courses and activities are on-site.)

CONTENTS

- We give the room price, not the per person price, and breakfast is included, unless we say otherwise. Meal prices and prices for courses are per person.

INTRODUCTION

Each of the properties chosen for this book already appears in
one of our Special Places to Stay guides – 13 titles that cover
Britain, France, Italy, Ireland, Portugal and Spain. We've chosen
over 250 that offer courses and activities, either on the spot or
nearby. All of them are close to interesting and beautiful places
to visit and all have owners who are passionate about their area
and eager for you to discover its treasures.

You should know that, although we have not 'road-tested'
the courses and activities, we have visited every single entry.
We've met the owners, seen the bedrooms, tested the beds,
noted the bathrooms, strolled round the gardens and grounds –
and eaten and slept at many. We think all these places are special
in some way and hope that our write-ups will help you choose
the right place in which to spend your precious free time.

How do we choose our houses and hotels? Those who are
familiar with our Special Places series know that we look for
comfort, originality, authenticity – and owners who are willing
to go the extra mile. If there's a glorious view from a bedroom
or terrace, or a glass of *grappa* on arrival, so much the better.
We reject the banal, the insincere and the anonymous; even
in our larger hotels you will not find yourselves treated as a
mere 'bed night'.

Many of our owners are talented, generous and eager to
share their interests. And we know that a great many
of you like to combine learning with leisure. This guide is
for you. Our hope is that it will forge new interests and
friendships, and bring like-minded readers and owners
together.

A fascinating range of properties lies within these pages, from
the manses, cottages and castles of the British Isles via the
alberghi and *agriturismi* of Italy, to the *herdades*, *hosterias* and
haciendas of Portugal and Spain. The B&Bs we like are those
where the art of hospitality is practised with kindness and good
humour, while our hotels tend to be smallish and owner-run.
We have quite a range of self-catering places too, so you could
choose from a sumptuous manor sleeping twelve, a slick city
bolthole or a medieval tower for two.

INTRODUCTION

The anonymous hotel chains have no place here, nor do star ratings, which we feel can limit and mislead. Our aim is that you glean from the write-ups what the owners (or housekeeper or staff) are like, and whether this particular Special Place is the best possible one for you, your toddler or your teenager.

Where to stay? Here is a brief guide to the different types of accommodation available.

B&Bs

You are a guest in someone's home and, although your hosts will, naturally, go out of their way to look after you, there is an element of fitting in with their lifestyle. However, the benefits are many. Not only do you have access to up-to-date local knowledge on the best pubs, restaurants, markets, shops, walks and places to visit, but many of our hosts offer unexpected extras. Some will happily babysit your children (or your dog!), others will send you home with armfuls of cuttings should you discover a shared passion for things horticultural. Lifts may be offered to the nearest coastal path or station, picnics may be rustled up at the drop of a hat. And perhaps, at the end of a busy day, you'll be offered a glass of home-grown rioja before sitting down to a meal cooked specially for you.

Hotels, Inns & Other Places

In most you can rely upon all sorts of indulging extras: all-day access, daily cleaning, room service, a bar, a minibar, along with separate tables at breakfast and satellite TV.

Inns and, to some extent, restaurants with rooms, tend to be busy in the evening, perhaps with music and extended opening hours – it's part of their charm. Those wanting peace and quiet should take this into account.

Many hotels are properly geared up for courses. Cookery is a well-established favourite but there are lots of others, too, from windsurfing to wood-turning. The chances are that these courses will be shared with more participants than those run by B&Bs.

Self-catering Cottages, Gîtes, Apartments & Villas

Self-catering properties suit the independent-minded. You can get up when you please, prepare your own food, chill your own wine, turn the music up loud, let the children scatter their toys, curl up with a book in front of the fire. There is absolutely no need to worry about anybody else.

INTRODUCTION

Some of our self-catering properties have owners who live nearby; others live far off. If it matters either way to you, check when booking (though there will usually be someone you can turn to should you lose your key). You might like to ask, too, if other folk may be around – B&B-ers, perhaps, or those renting other gîtes – to share the pool and barbecue.

There is obviously less of a sense of being looked after in a holiday home. But you trade this for the delights of privacy and independence.

Types of courses

You are spoilt for choice – from mainstream cookery, wine-tasting, horse-riding and painting to the less predictable *submarinisimo* and balneotherapy; our owners have come up with a tantalising range of sporty, spiritual and creative things to do. But bear in mind that these tours, courses, sessions and lessons, many of which they run themselves, are their recommendations, not ours (and not all are on-site). Though we have inspected all our properties we cannot check out all the courses and all the people who lead them – our role is to put you in touch with each other.

It is vital you check whether instructors are fully qualified and whether full insurance cover is provided; what are the credentials of that riding school in Castilla? Do you need to take out your own insurance? Make absolutely sure that you are covered for taking part in adventure or outdoor sports. And do check out other course details before you sign up. Does "All About Truffles" in the Vaucluse involve enthusiastic participants snuffling around in the undergrowth, pig in tow… or watching a truffle slide show indoors? The same goes for flamenco dancing, breadmaking, medieval cookery: you may have got excited about castanetting, chopping and kneading the morning away only to discover that you have booked yourself into a series of 'onlooker' sessions instead.

Most hosts – though not all, so check – are happy to liaise between you and the courses or activities listed under their entry.

Courses range in length from one hour to seven days. Some courses give dates, but this book lasts two years, so, again, check. Prices, where given, are per person unless otherwise stated and may include full-board, half-board, no board, a picnic… or the activity may be entirely free!

INTRODUCTION

So, do your homework first and take the right gear (are those watercolour paints provided?).

Maps & finding the right course

Go to the maps at the front of the book, find your chosen country and area and look for the entry numbers nearest. You'll find an alphabetical list of courses and activities at the very back of the book, too, colour-coded by country.

Internet

Our web site www.specialplacestostay.com has online pages for all the places featured here and in our other books, with updates and links to owners' sites and their more detailed information on their properties.

Rooms

We state whether rooms in hotels, inns, B&Bs etc are doubles, twins, singles, family rooms, triples or suites. Extra beds can often be added for children, usually with an extra charge.

Bathrooms

Assume rooms have an en suite bath or shower unless another arrangement is mentioned. A private/shared bathroom means that it is not en suite.

Prices

We give the ROOM price for two people sharing, unless we say otherwise. Not all entries have single rooms so the single rate shown may be for single occupancy of a double room. Breakfast is included unless otherwise stated, and meal prices are per person.

Because this book lasts for two years we've given prices as 'From...' unless there's a range. Differences in prices may be due to seasons, room size, style or comfort. Always check before booking. Note that British hotels often quote prices excluding VAT (17.5%).

Prices in Spain are exclusive of EVA (VAT) at 7%. When prices for Spanish rooms and/or meals include the tax, we say so.

All prices are in euros (€) except for those in Northern Ireland, England, Scotland and Wales which are in pounds sterling (£). A currency conversion indicator is given on the inside back cover.

Prices for self-catering places are per property per week, unless otherwise stated. We give a range from the cheapest, low-season price to the highest, high-season price. High season includes public holidays. Some owners request minimum stays.

INTRODUCTION

Breakfast

Unless we say otherwise, a full, cooked breakfast is included in the British and Irish hotels and B&Bs, though in London some owners will give you a prodigious continental breakfast instead.

Coffee with croissants or brioches is the norm in France and Italy. Many Spaniards breakfast on patés and olive oil, perhaps with garlic and tomato. Your hotelier may assume that you prefer a more northern-European offering; do check. Note that the Spanish eat much later than we do: breakfast often doesn't get going until 9am.

Dinner

You'll find some wonderful cooks in this book, and not just at the bigger places. The home cooking in B&Bs – often shared with your hosts and other guests – can be an unexpected treat, whether it be sublime dining under candlelabra or simple but delicious dinners at the scrubbed pine farmhouse table. Produce will often be local or home-grown. Meals **must** be booked in advance at B&Bs and it's safer to do so elsewhere, too.

Again, note that the Spanish generally take lunch from 2pm and dinner is rarely served before 8.30pm. The Italians, too, eat later than the northern Europeans.

Facilities

If it is important to you that your B&B has a TV, or your holiday home a dishwasher / microwave / CD player or barbecue, check with the owners first. Most self-catering properties will have laundry facilities, though not all.

Symbols

Our symbols are defined on the inside back cover. Two are expanded upon below but check anything particularly important to you.

Children

The 🧸 symbol is given to houses and hotels that accept children of any age. Some owners may offer to babysit (or find you a local sitter). Don't assume though that all the toys, sterilising equipment and high chairs that you may need can be provided. If an owner welcomes children, but only those of a certain age, we have put the lowest age limit on their entry.

Smoking

The 🚭 symbol means that you can't smoke anywhere – and that includes hanging out of the window! British B&B owners will often give you an ashtray (and an umbrella) and let you explore their garden if you so wish. Hotels have smoking areas but bedrooms and dining rooms are usually smoke-free zones.

INTRODUCTION

Be aware that few southern European places are complete no-smoking zones. If it matters to you, ask.

Payment

The most commonly accepted credit cards are Visa, MasterCard and Eurocard. American Express and Diner's Club credit cards may be refused as they involve higher commissions. B&Bs are likely to prefer cash or, possibly, a cheque. See our symbols.

Deposits & Booking

Expect to pay a deposit – even in B&Bs. If you cancel you may lose some or all of it unless your booking is re-let. Check the exact terms before booking. Some places, particularly city hotels, will only hold even a confirmed reservation until the early evening; ring ahead to let them know if you are planning to arrive late. Check-out times vary – again, check.

Tipping

Leaving a tip is the norm in Spain. For lunch or dinner 5%-10% is fine. Taxi drivers don't all expect a tip.

In France and Italy almost all restaurants include a 15% service charge; in bars it is usual to leave a few coins of your change. At larger hotels in France €2 is customary if luggage is taken to your room, as is leaving the small change from your bill if you paid in cash, and €1-€2 a day for the chambermaid. Taxi drivers are rarely tipped.

In Britain and Ireland tipping is normal in restaurants and taxis (around 10%). Owners do not expect tips, but a letter of thanks is always appreciated.

Phones

Mobile phones won't work everywhere so buy a phone card on arrival, available from tobacconists and post offices. Hotel phones can be expensive. Cafés often have a phone for which customers pay the money used, counted on a meter.

Most continental mobile numbers begin with a 6.

There will be some changes to phone numbers in the Republic of Ireland (Eire) during 2003 which will affect area codes 04, 05, 07 and 09. Call +353 1 671 4444 for number change information.

We have included the country codes in the listings so when calling abroad you simply prefix with 00 and omit any bracketed zeros. When phoning within a country, substitute the first two digits (e.g. 44 for Britain, 34 for Spain) with a zero.

INTRODUCTION

Using the car

Don't forget your driving licence; it is an offence to drive without it and, if you hire a car, you must show it.

In Ireland, as in Great Britain, driving is on the left. The upper, off-motorway speed limit is 60mph (100 kph), and 30/40mph through villages and towns. Road signs giving distances may be in miles, or kilometres.

French speed limits are 130kph (80mph) on motorways and on national trunk roads 110kph (68mph). Other open roads: 90kph (56mph); towns: 50kph (30mph). Road police are rigorous and demand on-the-spot payment of fines.

Consider taking...

• Electrical adaptors: virtually all sockets in France, Italy, Portugal and Spain have two-pin plugs that run on 220/240 AC voltage. Americans also need a voltage transformer. In Britain and Ireland the voltage is 220AC.

• A universal bath plug in case yours is missing.

• Ear plugs could be useful for a light-sleeper driven mad by late-night Vespas in Italy or barking dogs in rural Spain.

Problems, problems

We have only around 100 words to tell a story; if you find anything in our books misleading we'd love to know. And do discuss any problem with your hosts at the time, however trivial. Owners always say "if only we'd known" when we contact them on readers' behalf after the event.

Subscription

Owners pay to go into this guide. Their fee goes some way towards covering the inspection and production costs of an all-colour book. It is not possible, however, for people to buy their way into the book.

Environment

We try to be as 'green' as possible. We lend bicycles to staff and provide a pool car. We celebrate the use of organic, home-grown and locally produced food. We are working to establish an organic standard for B&Bs and run an Environmental Business Trust to stimulate business interest in the environment.

We also publish *The Little Earth Book*, a collection of essays on environmental issues. A new title, *The Little Food Book*, is another hard-hitting analysis – this time of the food industry. To try to reduce our impact on the environment we plant trees: the emissions directly related to our office, paper production, printing and distribution have been 'neutralised' through the

INTRODUCTION

planting of indigenous woodlands with Future Forests. We are, officially, Carbon Neutral.

Disclaimer We make no claims to being objective in choosing our *Special Places To Stay*. They are here because we like them. Our opinions and tastes are ours alone and this book is a statement of them; we hope that you share them.

We have visited all of these Special Places and have published the course and activity information given to us by our owners. We have made great efforts to check all our facts/dates/prices/courses but we haven't test-run the activities ourselves – much as we would love to.

So we can make no claims for the courses or the credentials of the people that run them. But we do know and trust the owners that have given us the information. This book puts you in touch with those in the know, so use it as your springboard. Ask all about the things that are important to you before you go, and you'll get more out of your holiday than you ever imagined.

And finally... We have done our utmost to get our facts right but apologise unreservedly for any mistakes that may have crept in. Sometimes, too, prices shift, usually upwards, and 'things' change. Please tell us about any errors or changes.

We value your comments. They make a real contribution to our books, be they on our report form at the back of the book, by letter or by e-mail to europe@sawdays.co.uk. Whether you choose to just 'be' in our Special Places, or to 'do', have a wonderful holiday.

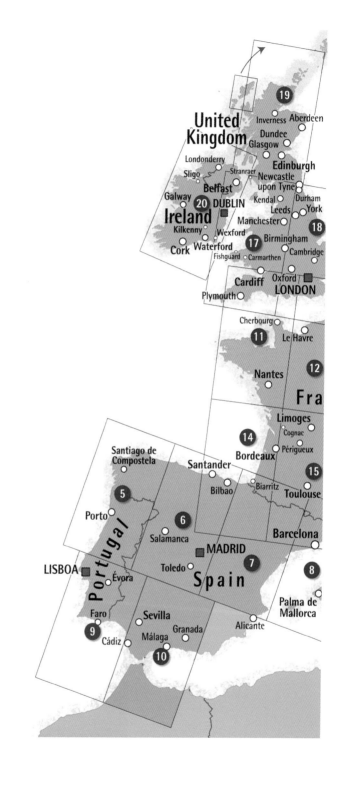

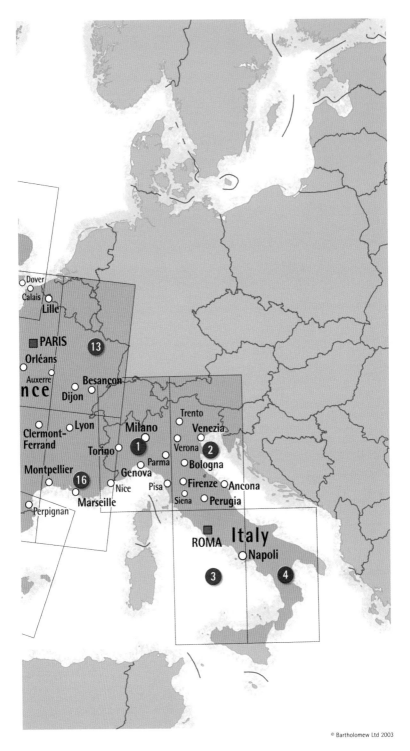

A guide to our map page numbers

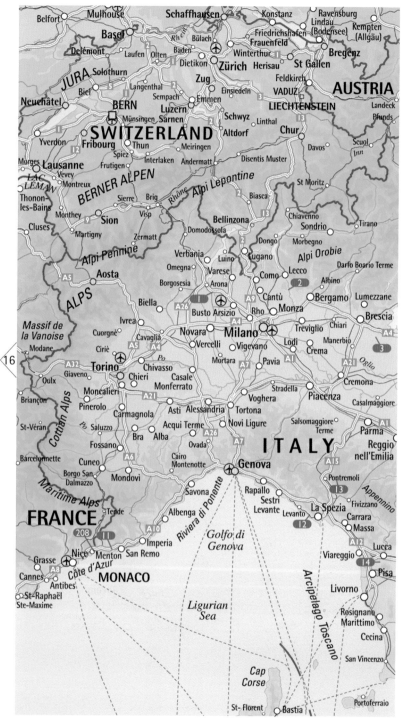

© Bartholomew Ltd 2003

Map 1

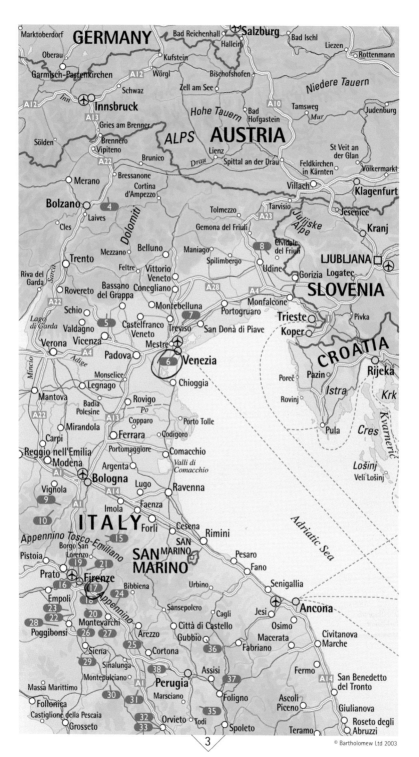

Map 2

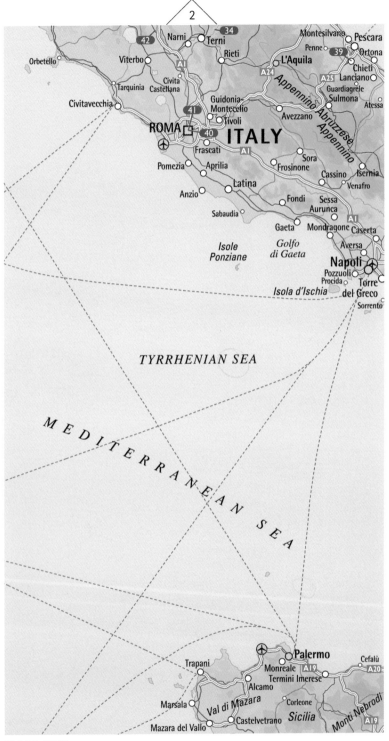

Map 3

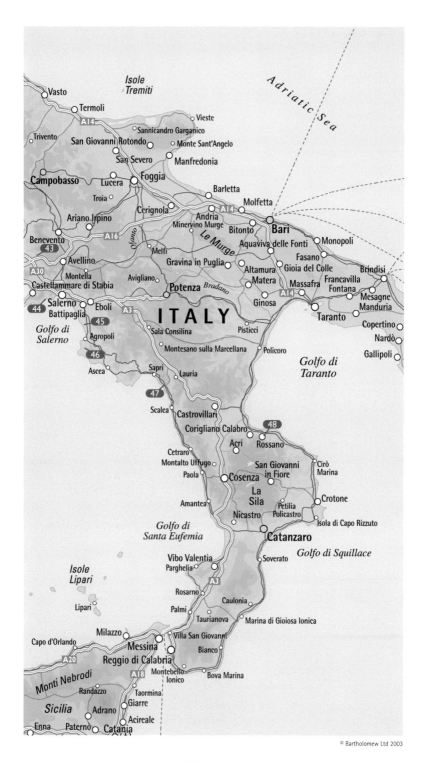

Map 4

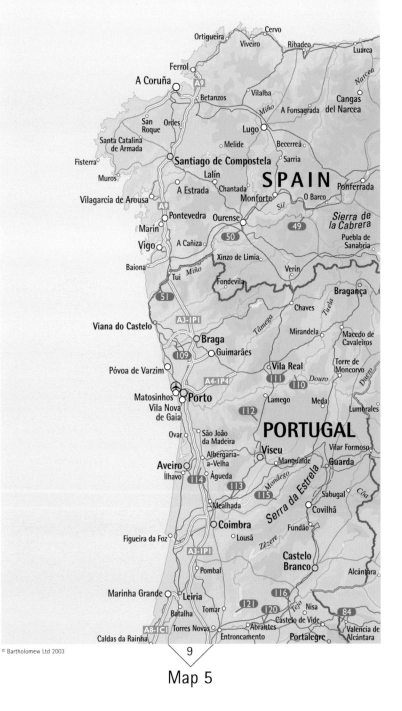

Map 5

© Bartholomew Ltd 2003

MAR CANTÁBRICO

Gijón-
Xixón
Avilés
Posada
Salas
Oviedo
Mieres
Pola de Siero
Pola de Lena

Ribadesella
Torrelavega
Santander
Santoña
Laredo
Castro-
Urdiales
Algorta
Bilbao
Barakaldo
Llodio
Durango
A8

**CORDILLERA
CANTÁBRICA**

Reinosa

Miranda
de Ebro

**Vitoria-
Gasteiz**

Ebro

Villablino
A66
La Robla
Guardo
Aguilar
de Campóo
Briviesca
Nájera
A68

**CORDILLERA
CANTÁBRICA**

León

Saldaña
Osorno
Melgar de
Fernamental
Burgos
Sierra de la Demanda

Astorga
Sahagún
Lerma

Truchas
Valencia
de Don Juan
Benavente
Palencia
Pisuerga
Aranda de Duero
El Burgo
de Osma

Sierra de la Culebra
Medina de
Rioseco
Valladolid
Duero
Ayllón

PORTUGAL
Toro
Tordesillas
Cuéllar
Cerezo
de Abajo

Fermoselle
Zamora
Medina
del Campo
Coca
Guadalajara
Henares

Ledesma
Arévalo
Segovia
San
Sebastián
de los Reyes
**Alcalá de
Henares**

Vitigudino
Tormes
Salamanca
Peñaranda de
Bracamonte
Colmenar Viejo
Collado
Villalba
MADRID
Arganda

Ávila

S P A I N
Fuenlabrada
Tajo

Ciudad Rodrigo
Nuñomoral
Béjar
Arenas de
San Pedro
Aranjuez
Ocaña

Sierra de Gredos
Candeleda
Valle de Tiétar
Alberche
Torrijos
Toledo
Villacañas

Plasencia
Navalmoral
de la Mata
Tiétar
Tajo
Talavera
de la Reina
Mora
Madridejos

Coria
Navahermosa
Montes de Toledo

Tajo
Guadalupe
Trujillo

Cáceres
Sierra de Guadalupe
Daimiel
Manzanares

Sierra de San Pedro
Navalvillar
de Pela
Herrera
del Duque
Guadiana
Ciudad Real

Miajadas

© Bartholomew Ltd 2003

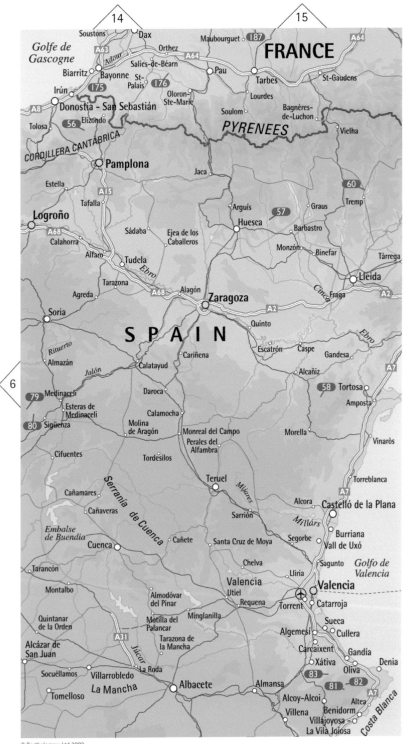

Map 7

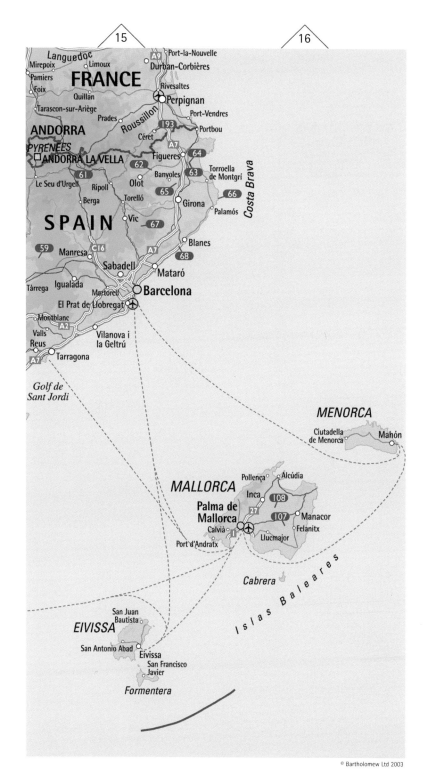

Map 8

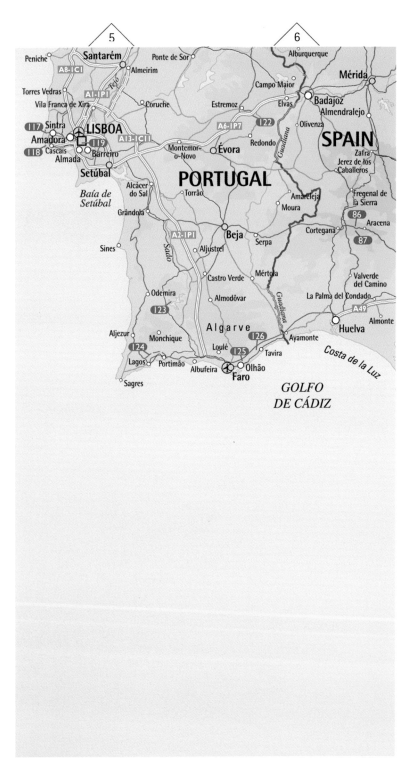

Map 9

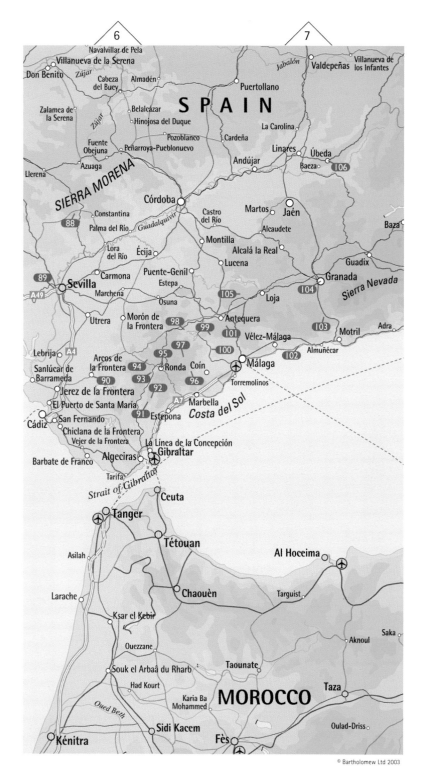

Navalvillar de Pela
Villanueva de la Serena
Don Benito
Zújar
Cabeza del Buey
Almadén
Puertollano
Jabalón
Valdepeñas
Villanueva de los Infantes

SPAIN

Zalamea de la Serena
Belalcázar
Hinojosa del Duque
La Carolina
Fuente Obejuna
Pozoblanco
Cardeña
Peñarroya-Pueblonuevo
Llerena
Azuaga
Linares
Úbeda
SIERRA MORENA
Baeza
106

Córdoba
Martos
Jaén
Constantina
88
Castro del Río
Baza
Palma del Río
Guadalquivir
Alcaudete
Lora del Río
Écija
Montilla
Alcalá la Real
Guadix
89
Carmona
Puente-Genil
Lucena
Granada
Sevilla
Estepa
104
Sierra Nevada
A49
Marchena
105
Loja
Osuna
Utrera
Morón de la Frontera
98
Antequera
103
Adra
99
101
Vélez-Málaga
Motril
Lebrija
97
100
Almuñécar
A4
95
102
Arcos de la Frontera
94
Ronda
Coín
Sanlúcar de Barrameda
93
Málaga
90
96
Jerez de la Frontera
92
Torremolinos
El Puerto de Santa María
A7
Marbella
Costa del Sol
Cádiz
San Fernando
91
Estepona
Chiclana de la Frontera
Vejer de la Frontera
La Línea de la Concepción
Barbate de Franco
Algeciras
Gibraltar
Tarifa
Strait of Gibraltar
Ceuta

Tanger

Tétouan
Al Hoceima
Asilah
Targuist
Larache
Chaouèn
Ksar el Kebir
Saka
Ouezzane
Aknoul
Souk el Arbaâ du Rharb
Taounate
Taza
Had Kourt
Karia Ba Mohammed
MOROCCO
Oulad-Driss
Kénitra
Sidi Kacem
Fès

Map 10

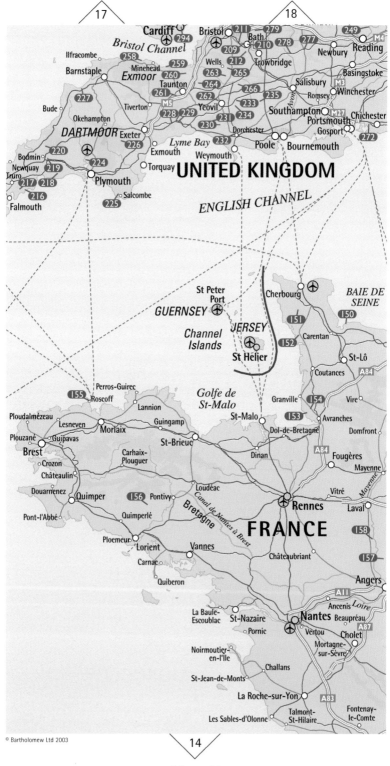

Cardiff 294 Bristol 211 279 249 M4
Bath 210 278 277 Reading
Bristol Channel 209 Newbury
Ilfracombe Wells 212 Trowbridge Basingstoke
258 Minehead 259 263 265 M3
Barnstaple *Exmoor* 260 Salisbury Winchester
261 Taunton 264 235 Romsey M27
227 262 266 Chichester
Bude Tiverton M5 Yeovil 233 Southampton Portsmouth
Okehampton 228 229 231 234 Gosport 272
DARTMOOR 230 Exeter Dorchester Poole Bournemouth
Bodmin 226 232
220 *Lyme Bay* Weymouth
Newquay 219 224 Exmouth
Truro Torquay **UNITED KINGDOM**
217 218 Plymouth
216 225 Salcombe
Falmouth

ENGLISH CHANNEL

St Peter Port Cherbourg *BAIE DE SEINE*
GUERNSEY 150
Channel Islands **JERSEY** 151 Carentan
152 St-Lô
St Helier Coutances A84

Perros-Guirec 155 Roscoff *Golfe de St-Malo* Granville 154 Vire
Lannion St-Malo 153 Avranches Domfront
Ploudalmézeau Guingamp Dol-de-Bretagne
Lesneven Morlaix St-Brieuc A84 Fougères
Plouzané Guipavas Dinan Mayenne
Brest Carhaix-Plouguer Vitré
Crozon Loudéac Rennes Laval
Châteaulin *Canal de Nantes à Brest* *Bretagne*
Douarnenez Quimper 156 Pontivy **FRANCE** 158
Pont-l'Abbé Quimperlé 157
Ploemeur Lorient Vannes Châteaubriant Angers
Carnac A11
Quiberon Ancenis *Loire*
La Baule-Escoublac St-Nazaire **Nantes** Beaupréau A87
Pornic Vertou Cholet
Noirmoutier-en-l'Ile Mortagne-sur-Sèvre
Challans
St-Jean-de-Monts
La Roche-sur-Yon A83
Les Sables-d'Olonne Talmont-St-Hilaire Fontenay-le-Comte

Map 11

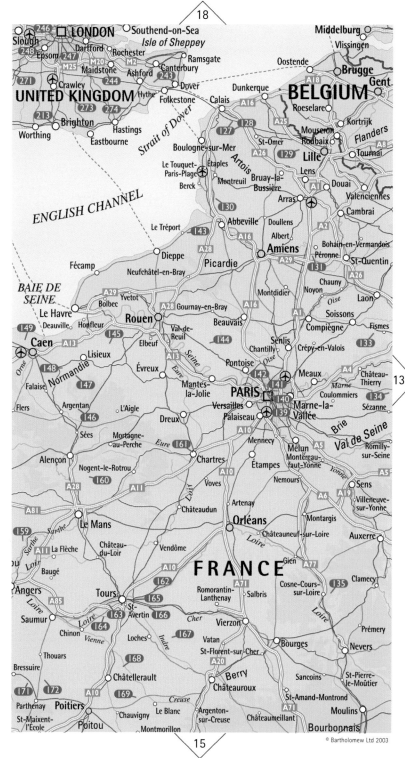

13

© Bartholomew Ltd 2003

Map 12

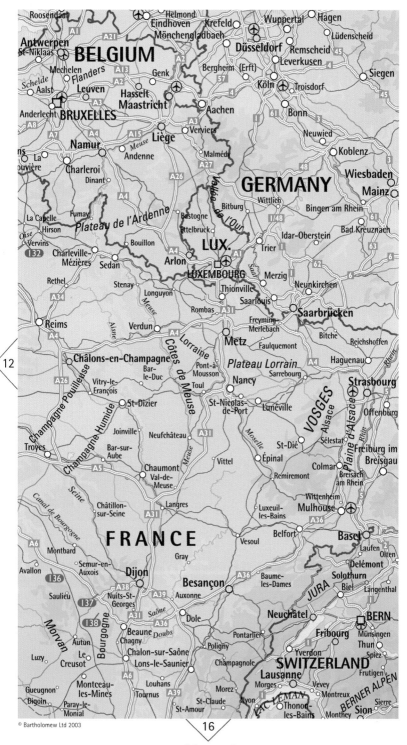

© Bartholomew Ltd 2003

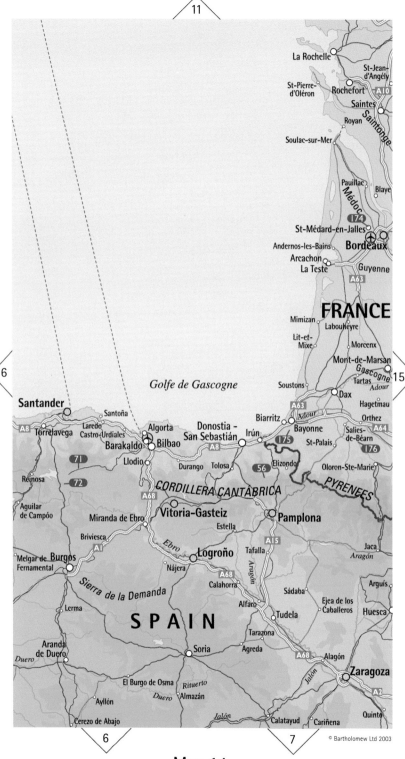

La Rochelle

St-Jean-
d'Angély

St-Pierre-
d'Oléron   Rochefort   A10

Saintes

Saintonge

Royan

Soulac-sur-Mer

Pauillac   Blaye

Médoc

174

St-Médard-en-Jalles
Andernos-les-Bains   Bordeaux
Arcachon   Guyenne
La Teste   A63

FRANCE

Mimizan   Labouheyre

Lit-et-   Morcenx
Mixe

Mont-de-Marsan
Gascogne

Golfe de Gascogne   Soustons   Tartas   Adour
Dax   Hagetmau

Santander   Santoña   Biarritz   Adour   Orthez
A8   Laredo   Algorta   Donostia -   Bayonne   Salies-   A64
Torrelavega   Castro-Urdiales   San Sebastián   Irún   de-Béarn   176
Barakaldo **Bilbao**   A8   175   St-Palais
Reinosa   Llodio   Tolosa   Elizondo   Oloron-Ste-Marie
71   Durango   56
Aguilar   72   **CORDILLERA CANTÁBRICA**   **PYRENEES**
de Campóo   A68
Miranda de Ebro   **Vitoria-Gasteiz**   **Pamplona**
Briviesca   Estella   Jaca
A1   *Ebro*   A15   *Aragón*
Melgar de **Burgos**   **Logroño**   Tafalla
Fernamental   Nájera   A68   *Aragón*   Arguís
Calahorra   Sádaba   Ejea de los   **Huesca**
Sierra de la Demanda   Alfaro   Caballeros
Lerma   **S P A I N**   Tudela
Tarazona
Aranda   Agreda   A68   Alagón
de Duero   **Soria**   **Zaragoza**
Duero   El Burgo de Osma   A2
Rituerto   *Jalón*
Ayllón   *Duero*   Almazán   Quinto
Cerezo de Abajo   *Jalón*   Calatayud   Cariñena

© Bartholomew Ltd 2003

Map 14

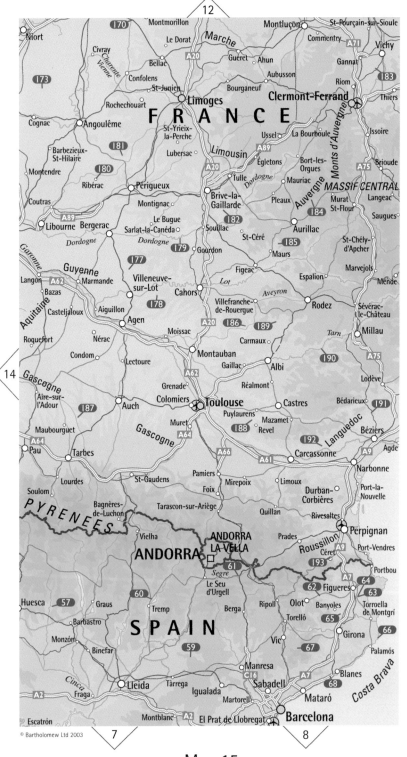

© Bartholomew Ltd 2003

Map 15

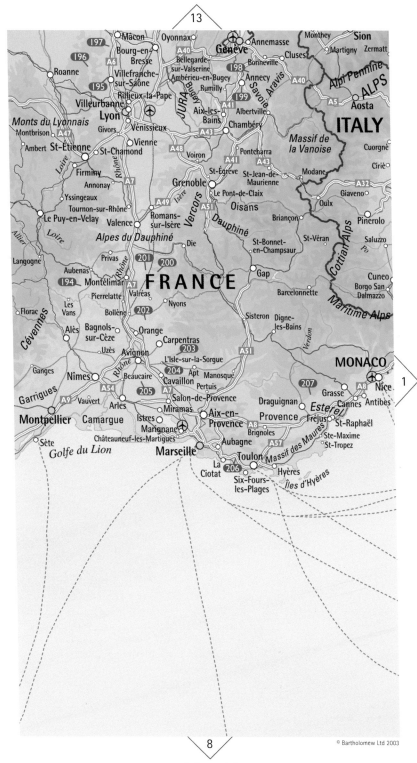

© Bartholomew Ltd 2003

Map 16

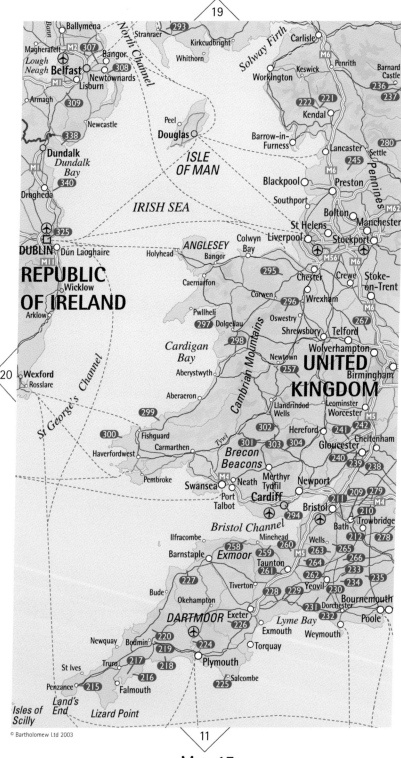

© Bartholomew Ltd 2003

Map 17

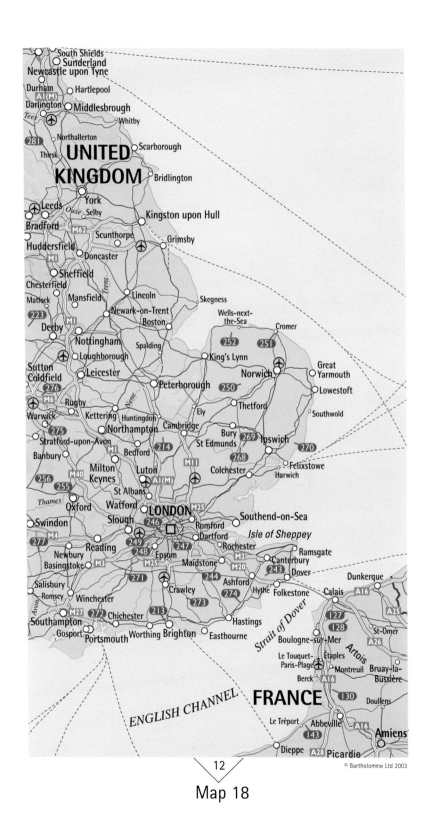

© Bartholomew Ltd 2003

Map 18

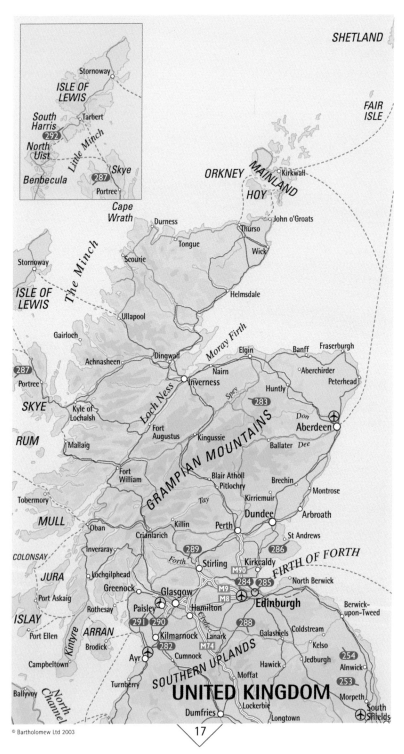

Map 19

© Bartholomew Ltd 2003

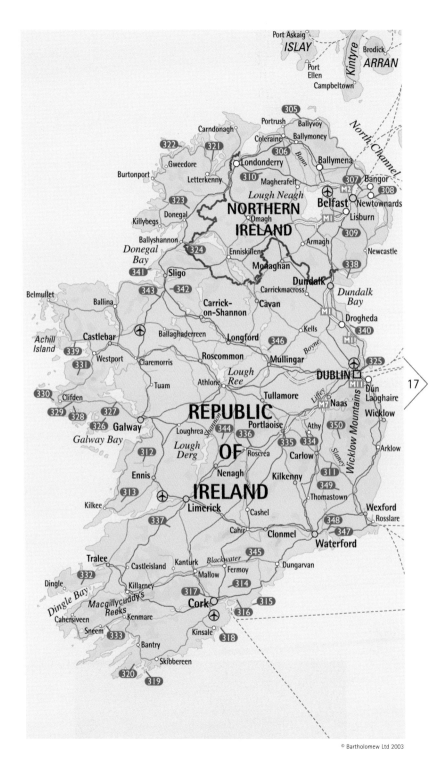

Map 20

italy

Photography by Michael Busselle

italy

Cascina Cesarina

Via dei Cesari 32, Frazione Gagnago, 28040 Borgo Ticino, NO, Italy

Drying bunches of maize and gourds hang from the balconies: palpable clues that this is a working farm. And in the big kitchen Lorraine uses home-grown organic produce – have lunch and dinner *en famille* or set off with a packed lunch. There is lots to do and Lorraine knows the area thoroughly. The bathroom is shared; bedrooms look over the farmyard or out across the wild garden, which has a play area for children, a pool and a barbecue. Only the occasional bark of a deer from the neighbouring nature reserve disturbs the peace.

- Italian Healthy Cooking: in English & Italian.
- Carnival with floats in Oleggio (Sundays in Feb).
- Ancient music festival, Lake Orta (June).
- Wildlife park with nesting storks.
- Local markets (Mondays, Wednesdays, Fridays).
- Designer factory outlets.

rooms	2: 1 double, 1 family.
price	€ 72–€ 82.
meals	Half board € 51–€ 61 p.p.
closed	Christmas & New Year.
directions	Exit A26 at Castelletto Ticino, follow SS32 for Novara until Borgo Ticino. From village follow signs to Gagnago. At top of hill, 2nd right down Via dei Cesari. Follow road down, left under arch at no. 25 & on 100m to house.

Lorraine Buckley

tel	+39 0321 90491
fax	+39 0321 90491
e-mail	cascinacesarinamail@yahoo.com

Restaurant with rooms

Il Torchio

Via Ghislanzoni 24, Loc. Vescogna, 23885 Calco, LC, Italy

If you enjoy the bohemian life you will love it here. Marcella and Franco, lively and intelligent, are artists; he also has an antiquarian bookshop in Milan. Enter through a stone archway into a secluded courtyard full of life and character. Upstairs: a double with a big old iron bed and a more contemporary children's room. Or stay in the next door converted hay barn: a large and open plan 'suite' with huge windows that look out through the trees to the village below and a glorious bathroom with hand-painted tiles. Chic Milan is a 30-minute drive.

- Lakes in Lombardy - Lecco & Como.
- Ski slopes, 1-hour drive.
- Canoeing on River Adda.
- Organic produce for sale.
- Folk festivals (May-September).
- Close to Milan & Verona.

rooms	3: 1 double, 1 twin, sharing bathroom; 1 suite (for 2).
price	From € 52-€ 67.
meals	Dinner from € 17.
closed	Rarely.
directions	At Calco right at lights after petrol station. Follow Corso Italia & right into Via Ghislanzoni, for Calco Superiore & Vescogna. At top drive on right of right-hand turn. After 100m turn into 2nd street on left (for Vescogna). On left.

Signora Marcella Pisacane

tel	+ 39 039 508724
fax	+ 39 0286 453229
e-mail	il_torchio@hotmail.com

B&B

map 1   entry 2

Villa San Pietro

Via San Pietro 25, 25018 Montichiari, BS, Italy

Vivacious Annamaria's US-style energy and Jacques' relaxed mood (he is a keen cycling fan) make for a pair of immensely hospitable hosts. Guests have a sitting room with a frescoed ceiling and good Italian antique furniture; bedrooms are immaculate, with a mix of new and antique. The most exceptional thing about the house is the large garden and terrace; there is also a pretty ground-floor *loggia* for some memorable meals (sophisticated 'regional' affairs, we are told). Montichiari lies on the shores of Lake Garda and has a historic centre.

- Italian, English & French language courses.
- Wine courses & tasting: in English, French, Italian & Spanish.
- Facials with Villa San Pietro's Botanical Skincare.
- Daily Excursions – Verona, Lake Garda, Mantova, Cremona, Brescia, Venice.
- Flea market in town (last Sunday of month).
- Castle, theatre, abbey & museum in town.

rooms	3 doubles.
price	From €85. Singles from €52.
meals	Dinner with drinks, from €25.
closed	Rarely.
directions	From Milan motorway A4 exit Brescia east. Follow signs for Montichiari, city centre & Duomo. Via S. Pietro leads off corner of central piazza.

Signori Jacques & Annamaria Ducroz

tel	+39 030 961232
fax	+39 030 9981098
e-mail	annajacques@rocketmail.com
web	www.art-with-attitude.com/villa/san_pietro.html

B&B

Hotel Cavallino D'Oro

Piazza Kraus 1, 39040 Castelrotto, BZ, Italy

The Cavallino d'Oro, or Little Gold Horse, is first mentioned in 1393 as an inn on the busy market square of this village at the foot of the Dolomites. This was Austria not so long ago, and local dress and customs are still very much alive. Rooms, often with wonderful views, have a fascinating mix of beds: some painted, some four-poster, some both. The doors to some are also painted, as are the beams in the quiet, muted sitting room. Breakfast is in a wood-panelled dining room with geraniums at the window. *All courses in English, Dutch and Italian.*

- Italian: in hotel & in village.
- Skiing.
- Alpine Flora: Dolomites.
- Photography: in village.
- Horse-riding: in village.
- Hiking in Dolomite Mountains.

rooms	15: 4 singles, 2 twins, 5 doubles, 4 suites.
price	From € 80. Suite from € 100. Singles from € 50. Half-board € 50–€ 75 p.p.
meals	Half/full-board available.
closed	November.
directions	A22 m'way, exit Bolzano Nord. Castelrotto signposted at exit. Hotel in market square in town centre.

Signori Susanna & Stefan Urthaler

tel	+39 0471 706337
fax	+39 0471 707172
e-mail	cavallino@cavallino.it
web	www.cavallino.it

Hotel

map 2   entry 4

Casa Belmonte

Via Belmonte 2, 36030 Sarcedo, VI, Italy

The house in seven hectares of vines and olive groves overlooks the small town. Mariarosa has turned her full attention to creating six luxurious rooms now that her children have flown the nest. Monogrammed sheets and towels, slippers and bathrobes, rich drapes, prints and antiques. Delicious breakfasts – fruits, cheeses, hams – are served in the garden room, and Roberto is proud of his small wine cellar. Elegance and simplicity, perfect taste and seduction – a uniquely Italian gift. Casa Belmonte is an easy launch pad for Venice, Padua, Verona and Piacenza.

- Swimming pool.
- Vineyards with wine for sale.
- Vicenza, 15km – Palladian architecture.
- Vicenza – open-air café-restaurants & bars.
- Venice.
- Opera at Verona.

rooms	6: 2 doubles, 1 twin, 1 single, 2 suites.
price	€ 129-€ 181. Singles € 103-€ 129. Suites € 181-€ 258.
meals	Breakfast € 15-€ 23. Light lunch available in summer.
closed	Rarely.
directions	Dueville exit from A31. Turn left & left again for Bassano. After approx 2km left for Sarcedo. Entrance 600m after lights to right of junction. Ring bell at gate.

Signora Mariarosa Arcaro

tel	+ 39 0445 884833
fax	+ 39 0445 884134
e-mail	info@casabelmonte.com
web	www.casabelmonte.com

Hotel

Pensione La Calcina

Fondamenta Zattere ai Gesuati, Dorsoduro 780, 30123 Venice, VE, Italy

Watch people from the terrace strolling along the Zattere and enjoy the sea breezes. Ruskin stayed here in 1876, and for many, this corner of Venice, facing the Guidecca and with old Venice just behind you, beats the crowds of San Marco any day. The hotel has been discreetly modernised by its charming young owners, and bedrooms are nicely furnished with antiques and parquet floors. Those at the front, with views, are more expensive – but worth it. A small roof terrace can be booked for romantic evenings and you breakfast on the floating terrace.

- La Piscina - hotel restaurant with real Italian cooking.
- Garden & roof terrace with canal views.
- Accademia Galleries – Venetian painting.
- Palazzo Grassi.
- Guggenheim Museum – 20th-century art.
- Gesuati Church - roof paintings by Tiepolo.

rooms	32: 20 doubles, 9 singles, 3 suites. 2 self-catering apartments for 2.
price	€99–€180. Single €75–€106. Suites & apartments €181–€239.
meals	Lunch €20–€30. Dinner €20–€30.
closed	Rarely.
directions	Water bus line 51 or 61 from Piazzale Roma or Railway Station. Line 82 from Tronchetto.

Signor Alessandro Szemere

tel	+ 39 0415 206466
fax	+ 39 0415 227045
e-mail	la.calcina@libero.it
web	www.lacalcina.com

Hotel & self-catering

map 2   entry 6

Castello di Roncade

Via Roma 14, 31056 Roncade, TV, Italy

Don't be mislead: the grandeur of the imposing entrance, splendid gardens and lovely 16th-century villa don't indicate sky-high prices. Two beautiful double rooms, furnished with antiques, are available in the villa itself; a third, on the ground floor, is converted for disabled use. Alternatively, and ideal for families, there are three very roomy and simply furnished apartments in the corner towers. Buy a few cases of the excellent estate wine. Dinner here is occasional, but the Baron and Baroness are extremely hospitable hosts.

- Ancient gardens.
- Venice, 15km.
- Own vineyard with wine for sale.
- Treviso, 10km – a miniature Venice.
- Monday market, 0.5km.
- Asolo Fortress.

rooms	3 doubles. Also 4 self-catering apartments.
price	€83-€93. Apartments €62-€72 per night.
meals	Self-catering in apartments.
closed	Rarely.
directions	Exit m'way to Trieste at Quarto d'Altino, follow Roncade. You can't miss the castle's imposing entrance.

Barone Vincenzo Ciani Bassetti

tel	+ 39 0422 708736
fax	+ 39 0422 840964
e-mail	vcianib@tin.it
web	www.castellodironcade.com

B&B & self-catering

Agriturismo La Faula

Via Faula 5, Ravosa di Povoletto, 33040 Udine, UD, Italy

An exuberant miscellany of dogs, donkeys and peacocks in a modern, working vineyard; a traditional Friuli farmhouse with the latest communication facilities. Luca and Paul give the same patience, energy and thoughtfulness to your comfort as to the demands of the wine business and farm. The house stands in gentle countryside at the base of the Julian Alps. Each beamed bedroom has its own modern bathroom, there is a bistro-style restaurant (closed during harvest) and on some nights there's a barbecue on the ancient pergola.

- The Italian Kitchen: in English & Italian, € 100–€ 200.
- Friuli Wine Tour: in English & Italian, € 175–€ 200.
- Painting: in English & Italian, € 100–€ 200.
- Psychotherapy: in English, German & Italian.
- Medieval castle museum, 5km.
- Palio of Udine - medieval festival & horse racing, 12km.

rooms	9 twins/doubles. 4 mini-apartments for 2-4.
price	€ 40–€ 49. Singles from € 40. Apartments from € 52.
meals	Breakfast € 5.70. Dinner from € 15.
closed	Rarely.
directions	SS54 from Udine towards Cividale; 3km on, left for Salt, then Magredis & Ravosa. From Ravosa, towards Attimis, then right, by shrine. La Faula on other side of bridge.

Paul Mackay & Luca Colautti

tel	+39 0432 666394
fax	+39 0432 666032
e-mail	info@faula.com
web	www.faula.com

B&B

map 2　entry 8

La Fenice

Via S. Lucia 29, Ca' de Gatti, 40040 Rocca di Roffeno, BO, Italy

Remo and Paolo, born at La Fenice, did much of the renovation themselves and you are likely to find them in overalls working on their latest project. Most of the bedrooms here have their own outside door; they are rather like spare rooms in a big house with an assortment of furniture that hangs together well, but a bit dark, as the windows are small. Breakfast is plenty of coffee, tea, chocolate, with bread or brioche; this region is admired for having the best cooking in the country. Take out one of the Anglo-Arab horses; a qualified instructor is on hand in the summer.

- Local Wine Tastings.
- Cookery, Local Dishes.
- Horse-riding.
- Paragliding.
- Maps of ancient paths, windmills & medieval fortresses.
- Bologna, Ferrara & Ravenna.

rooms	10: 6 doubles, 3 triples, 1 suite/family room.
price	From € 72. Half-board € 108 for two.
meals	Half-board available. Dinner € 20–€ 35.
closed	7 January–6 February.
directions	After 30km on the SS64 south from Bologna, right to Tole. Then, follow signs for Cereglio, after approx. 1.5km turn right. La Fenice is approx. 5km from Tole on right.

Signori Remo & Paolo Giarandoni

tel	+39 051 919272
fax	+39 051 919024
e-mail	lafenice@lafeniceagritur.it
web	www.lafeniceagritur.it

B&B

La Piana dei Castagni & La Civetta

Via Civetta 11, 40040 Rocca di Roffeno, BO, Italy

It's a scene of bucolic bliss, almost alpine in its serenity. You sit at what feels like the wooded head of the valley, on a rough grassy space near this little cottage, and are folded into the silence and the beauty of it all. This is why you are here, though there is much to be said for the bubbly and easy Valeria with whom you will quickly strike up a friendship. The setting compensates amply for the lack of luxury: you will be richly rewarded by the peace, the views and the novelty of a little-known area – not to mention the low price. *Self-catering in La Civetta for 2 or 6 available.*

- Local produce tasting.
- Making Fresh Pasta.
- Cookery, Local Dishes.
- Wild Herbs.
- Bologna & Florence.
- Medieval areas of interest.

rooms	4 doubles.
price	€ 60–€ 70.
meals	Half-board € 36–€ 40 p.p.
closed	December-March.
directions	From Florence, exit Sasso Marconi & at Piandivenola on right follow signs Vedegheto & Tole. From Tole follow signs S.Lucia & Castel d'Aiano & after crossroad Bocca Ravari, signed.

Signora Valeria Vitali

tel	+39 051 912717/051 912985
e-mail	info@pianadeicastagni.it
web	www.pianadeicastagni.it

B&B & self-catering

map 2   entry 10

Villa Elisa

Via Romana 70, 18012 Bordighera, IM, Italy

Maurizio and Rita take enormous pleasure in showing you the natural beauty and artistic heritage of the area. The hotel was built in the 20s, when pretty Bordighera was a quiet spot in which to spend the winter months. Maurizio's father was a keen painter and liked having artists to stay; walls are hung with the pictures they left him. Children are in their element with a pool and large airy playroom full of toys and games – in midsummer, activities are organised for them, too. The pebbled beach is a 10-minute walk down the hill and across the railway.

- Trekking in the Ligurian Riviera: in English, German, Italian.
- Guided Tours of Region: in English, German, Italian.
- Horse-riding, 10km.
- Vineyard with wine for sale.
- Oranges & Lemons Festival, 15km.
- Antique markets.

rooms	35: 5 singles, 30 doubles. Also 1 apartment for 4.
price	€ 105–€ 150. Singles € 75–€ 98. Half & full-board available for weekly stays.
meals	Lunch/dinner from € 40.
closed	5 November–20 December.
directions	Via Romana runs parallel to the main road through town (Via Aurelia). Villa Elisa at western end of Via Romana.

Signor Maurizio Oggero
tel	+39 0184 261313
fax	+39 0184 261942
e-mail	villaelisa@masterweb.it
web	www.villaelisa.com

Hotel

Ca' dei Duxi

Via C. Colombo 36, 19017 Riomaggiore, SP, Italy

The 18th-century house stands on the quiet main street of one of the *Cinque Terre* villages. Rooms are mostly big and plain; some have ancient ceiling beams like ships' masts. The views get better the higher up you are – there are a *lot* of stairs. Odd, charming quirks are kept: one bathroom is built into the rock, visible through a perspex screen. Giorgio is active on the council and wants tourists to get the best possible impression of Italy. Parking can be difficult – come by train if you can, and enjoy getting around by bus and boat. Best out of season.

- Diving: 100m, in English & Italian.
- Building a Dry-stone Wall: 200m, in Italian.
- Tasting local produce in bar.
- Visits to own vineyard.
- Excursions with canoes.
- Excursions with horses & bicycles.

rooms	6: 3 doubles, 3 family. Also 3 self-catering apartments.
price	€ 70–€ 120. Family € 90–€ 140. Apartments € 400–€ 700 per week.
meals	Dinner € 25–€ 50. Self-catering in apartments.
closed	Rarely.
directions	In La Spezia follow signs for Portovenere & Cinqueterre then Riomaggiore. There, main road to car park; park down main street, Hotel on right.

Signori Giorgio & Samuele Germano

tel	+39 0187 920036
fax	+39 018 7920036
e-mail	info@duxi.it
web	www.duxi.it

B&B & self-catering

map 1   entry 12

Villa Mimosa

Corlaga Bagnone, 54021 Bagnone, MS, Italy

Bagnone is a little medieval village of huge charm and the Villa Mimosa a warm and open-hearted oasis, run by people for whom hospitality is second nature. Their revamping of the old flour-mill has produced an individual house, full of colour and light. There's an attractive sitting room with a small grand piano, views over the richly-wooded hills, a small reading room stuffed with good books, bedrooms that are wickedly comfortable and food that is worth climbing the hills for. Jennie and Alan will be hugely helpful. *Children over 10 welcome.*

- Italian Cooking: in English & Italian, from € 80.
- Drawing & Painting: 35km, in English, from April.
- Sculpture: 35km, in English & Italian.
- Pony-trekking in mountains.
- 11th-century castle, 16km.
- Puccini Opera Festival (July/August), Torre del Lago.

rooms	4 twins/doubles.
price	€ 77–€ 98. Singles from € 46.
meals	Dinner with wine, from € 31.
closed	November-mid-February.
directions	Exit A15 Aulla & Pontremoli, for Bagnone. Through archway into town centre. In narrow part of main street, left into Via Niccolo Quatiere (signed Carabinieri). Left at 1st fork. At r'bout on to Corlaga for 1.7km. Park opp. church, walk back 50m to 1st house on left.

Jennie & Alan Pratt

tel	+39 0187 427022
fax	+39 0187 427022
e-mail	mimosa@col.it

B&B

Villa Anna Maria

Strada Statale dell'Abetone 146, 56010 Molina di Quosa, PI, Italy

A shady tropical paradise of a garden and a swimming pool among the bamboo. It is an intriguing place, very laid back and easy – even bizarre – but with the confidence of a villa that has bedrooms untouched since the 17th century. Billiards too, chess, a library and over 3,000 videos! – all very much in tune with the house and its slightly eccentric, hugely hospitable owners, who really do care more about people than they do about money. The B&B rooms can also be let as self-catering. Come with the same open minds as your hosts' and you will have a wonderful time.

- Cookery.
- Gardening.
- Horse-riding.
- Puccini Opera Festival (July/August).
- Thermal baths, San Giuliano.
- Antique markets, Pisa & Lucca.

rooms	6 doubles (can make up apartments for 2-8). Also 1 cottage for 3.
price	From € 100. Singles from € 70. Apartments € 700–€ 1,400; please ring for price of cottage.
meals	Dinner from € 40.
closed	Rarely.
directions	SS12 Pisa-Lucca. At S.Giuliano Terme, left down hill on SS12. After Rigoli on to Molina di Quosa. On right opposite pharmacy.

Signor Claudio Zeppi

tel	+39 0508 50139 or 0328 2334450
fax	+39 0508 50139
e-mail	zeppi@villaannamaria.com
web	www.villaannamaria.com

B&B & self-catering

map 1   entry 14

Locanda Senio

Via Borgo dell'Ore, 1, 50035 Palazzuolo sul Senio, FI, Italy

Instead of taking the A1 from Bologna to Florence, why not detour onto a calmer route? Then stay overnight here, in a pretty Apennine town at the bottom of the valley beside the Senio. This small inn, in the old part of town, provides something a little out of the ordinary: guided walks through the woods, gastronomic meanders through the Mugello valley, and a bit of cookery thrown in. Ercole and Roberta cook dinners using herbs and fruits of the forest. *All courses in English, French, German or Italian.*

- Cookery, Medieval & Local Dishes.
- Painting: spring-autumn.
- Italian.
- Wine & Local Cookery.
- Museum of medieval animals, 2km.
- Health centre nearby - Turkish bath, sauna, spa, pool.

rooms	6 twins/doubles. Also 2 apartments for 2-3.
price	€145–€215. Apartments €165–€245.
meals	Dinner from €35.
closed	Tuesdays & Wednesdays in winter.
directions	From Bologna motorway, A14 exit Imola, direction Rimini, then follow Riolo Terme & Palazzuolo sul Senio (45 mins from Imola). House in village centre.

Signori Ercole & Roberta Lega

tel	+39 055 8046019
fax	+39 055 8043949
e-mail	info@locandasenio.it
web	www.locandasenio.it

Inn

Villa La Sosta

Via Bolognese 83, 50139 Florence, FI, Italy

Just a 10-minute walk from the start of Florence's historic centre, this attractive turn-of-the-century house, once part of a large estate, stands in tranquil gardens off the Via Bolognese, the old post road. There are five large, elegant bedrooms, a tower room giving views of the surrounding country and a billiard room. It's a super house and Antonio and Giusy, a brother-and-sister-team, are charming. If ever the city's treasures start to pall, they organise a day in the vineyards, taking in lunch in a friend's farmhouse, or a trip to famous potteries.

- Wine Tour - Fiesole, San Gimignano, Greve, Rignana & Antinori estates.
- Ceramics Tours, Montelupo.
- Art exhibited in house.
- Accademy Gallery.
- Uffizi Gallery.
- Giardini di Orticultura.

rooms	5 doubles.
price	€ 100–€ 120. Single € 75–€ 95. Triple € 130–€ 150. Quadruple € 160–€ 180.
meals	Available locally.
closed	Rarely.
directions	Follow signs for Centre & Piazza della Libertà, then Via Bolognese. House on left. just before Total petrol station. Or no. 25 bus from railway station.

Antonio & Giuseppina Fantoni

tel	+39 055 495073
fax	+39 055 495073
e-mail	info@villalasosta.com
web	www.villalasosta.com

B&B

map 2   entry 16

Palazzo Magnani Feroni

Borgo San Frediano 5, 50124 Florence, FI, Italy

A palace built to impress. It was one of Europe's great antiques galleries. You step off a busy street into a cool entrance flanked by long wooden pews leading to marble busts, seated lions and great iron gates. A magnificent corridor runs along one side of the courtyard. It is lush, elegant – a brilliant, sparkling new conversion – and the rooms are vast with *cotto* tiles, rugs and antique furniture. Sweetest of all is the rooftop terrace, whence you may gaze in a superior manner over the famous rooftop jumble of Florence. You pay for it, and you will be lavishly spoiled.

- Italian.
- Wine-tasting.
- Specialised Cookery.
- Tour of Chianti Region with Wine-tasting.
- Cultural Tour of Florence.
- Fiesole - Etruscan & Roman village.

rooms	11 suites: 1 junior, 2 executives, 8 deluxes.
price	€ 260-€ 750.
meals	Room service à la carte available.
closed	Rarely.
directions	On Borgo San Frediano, 10m from corner of the Via de'Serragli (one block from the Arno). Check where to park when booking.

Dottore Alberto & Claudia Giannotti

tel	+39 055 2399544
fax	+39 055 2608908
e-mail	info@florencepalace.it
web	www.florencepalace.com

Hotel

Relais Villa l'Olmo

Via Impruneta 21, 50023 Impruneta, FI, Italy

The Relais is a clutch of beautifully converted apartments, all looking down over the valley and all shamelessly comfortable (definitely *di lusso*). You will find chunky Tuscan beamed ceilings, flowers, brilliantly designed kitchenettes, blue-and-white checked sofas – even your own swimming pool if you can't face splashing about with others in the big one. Claudia, your hostess, rents mountain bikes and mobile phones so you are never at a loss. Florence is only 15 minutes away by car, and can be reached by public bus. So you can have your cake, and eat it, too.

- Visits to Terracotta Artisans.
- Italian Cookery.
- Wine-tasting & Chianti Tours.
- Tours of little-known villages & farms.
- Florence Walking Tour.
- Golf, 8km.

rooms	7 self-catering apartments for 2-5; 3 villas for 2-6.
price	Apartments €90-€200 per day, villas €185-€344.
meals	Breakfast from €10. Dinner €20-€40.
closed	Rarely.
directions	Exit A1 at Firenze Certosa. At r'bout, take Tavarnuzze; in village, left to Impruneta. 100m past sign for Impruneta & after Shell station is track, right. Signed.

Signora Claudia Jerger

tel	+39 055 211311
fax	+39 055 2311313
e-mail	florence.chianti@dada.it
web	www.relaisfarmholiday.it

Self-catering

map 2   entry 18

Torre di Bellosguardo

Via Roti Michelozzi 2, 50124 Florence, Fl, Italy

Sheer old-aged dignity: the entrance hall has a beautiful painted ceiling and an ocean of floor. Imposing, mellow buildings, glorious gardens, inspirational views of Florence, and an indoor swimming pool and gym in the old orangery; another pool settles into a perfect lawn. Most bedrooms can be reached by lift but the tower suite demands a climb. Furniture is richly authentic, and there are surprises, such as a glass-walled bathroom looking over the garden. Signor Franchetti is often here; his manners and his English are impeccable. Florence is a 30-minute walk downhill.

- Garden with secret corners & swimming pool.
- San Miniato al Monte Church, 0.5km.
- 30-minute walk to centre of Florence.
- Walks through olive groves & vineyards.
- Medieval towns of Lucca, San Gimignano, Siena, Arezzo.
- Sports centre nearby.

rooms	16: 8 doubles, 1 single, 7 suites.
price	From € 280. Suites € 330–€ 430. Singles from € 160.
meals	Breakfast € 20–€ 25. Light lunches by pool, available in summer.
closed	Rarely.
directions	Exit A1 at Firenze Certosa, follow signs to Porta Romana or Centre. Left at Porta Romana on Via Ugo Foscolo; keep right & take Via Piana to end, then right into Via Roti Michelozzi.

Signor Amerigo Franchetti

tel	+ 39 055 2298145
fax	+ 39 055 229008
e-mail	torredibellosguardo@dada.it
web	www.torrebellosguardo.com

Hotel

Podere Torre

Via di San Cresci 29, 50022 Greve in Chianti, FI, Italy

This place exudes mellow contentment, thanks to the delightful Cecilia. Next to the house is Stalla, cool and shady with its own en suite shower room; Concimaia is reached across a mini *terazza* with flowers and table and chairs for two. This can be combined with the studio Fienile, with kitchenette. There are fluffy towels, cotton bed linen, blocks of Marsiglia soap, lavender bags and even candles and matches. Swallows nest in the laundry room, the roses thrive, and Cecilia provides the basics for you to rustle up a picnic supper and dine *al fresco*.

- Own rose gardens.
- Local wine & olive oil for sale.
- Grape harvests.
- Walking trails.
- Horse-riding, 30-minute drive.
- Golf, 30-minute drive.

rooms	2 doubles. Also 1 self-catering apartment for 2.
price	From € 77; from € 439 per week. Apartment from € 77 per day; from € 490 per week.
meals	Breakfast from € 8.
closed	Rarely.
directions	From Greve in Chianti take road to Pieve di San Cresci & follow signs for Agriturismo Poderre Torre for 3km on minor road.

Signora Cecilia Torrigiani

tel	+ 39 055 8544714
fax	+ 39 0558 544714
e-mail	poderetorre@greve-in-chianti.com
web	www.greve-in-chianti.com/poderetorre.htm

B&B & self-catering

map 2   entry 20

Casa Palmira

Via Faentina 4/1, Loc. Feriolo-Polcanto, 50032 Borgo S. Lorenzo, FI, Italy

A medieval farm expertly restored; your hosts have a flair for this sort of thing. The bedrooms open off an unusual landing with a brick walled 'garden' in the centre – all Stefano's work. They look out onto the gardens, where Assunta grows herbs and vegetables, or onto vines and olive trees. Stefano will take you round neighbouring villages in his van, or you can hire a mountain bike, tucking one of Assunta's packed picnic baskets on the back. Florence is only 10 miles away and the Etruscan-Roman town of Fiesole only five. *Please check in before 7pm.*

- Fresco Painting: 10km, in English & French.
- Truffle-hunting: 10-15km, in English & French, October-November.
- Olive-collecting & Pressing: 5km, in English & French, October-December.
- Cookery, Tuscan Dishes & Pasta Fresca: in English & French, €60-€100.
- Fiesole 9km - opera, ballet, theatre & music (June-September).
- Chestnut (marroni) festival, 10km (Oct/Nov).

rooms	7: 1 single, 4 twins/doubles, 1 triple, 1 family. Apartment for 2-3.
price	€65-€85. Single from €55; triple from €105; family from €125. Apartment from €500 per week.
meals	Dinner with drinks, from €25.
closed	10 January-10 March.
directions	A1 exit Barberino del Mugello, then Borgo S. Lorenzo, then SS302 via Faentina, towards Firenze. After Polcanta & Hulinaccio, sign for Ristorante Feriolo; on left.

Assunta & Stefano Fiorini

tel	+39 055 8409749
fax	+39 055 8409749
e-mail	palmira@cosmos.it
web	www.casapalmira.it

B&B

Fattoria Casa Sola

Via Cortine 88, 50021 Barberino Val d'Elsa, FI, Italy

Your apartments, 700m from the main house, are each on two floors with whitewashed walls, tiled floors, old wooden furniture and country cotton bedspreads. Your hosts, aristocratic but down-to-earth, take guests once a week round the vineyards, rounding off the visit with a glass of *Vin Santo* and biscuits. Tennis and riding are nearby and the pool is a surprise! You suddenly come across it in the olive groves. Barberino and San Donato have several restaurants, and you are only 30 minutes from Florence and Siena. *Minimum stay one week high season.*

- Cookery & Pasta Making: on site & 8km: in English.
- Tuscan-style Embroidery: in English, French, German.
- Tasting Wine & Oil: in English, French & German.
- Painting: in English, French & German.
- Guitar & Singing: in English, French & German.
- Theatre festival & concerts, 5km.

rooms	6 apartments: 1 for 2-3, 2 for 4, 2 for 4-6, 1 for 8.
price	€ 500–€ 800 per week.
meals	Self-catering.
closed	Rarely.
directions	From Firenze-Siena superstrada exit at San Donato in Poggio. Follow SS101 past church of San Donato. Right after about 1.5km to Cortine & Casa Sola.

Conte Giuseppe Gambaro

tel	+39 055 8075028
fax	+39 0558 059194
e-mail	casasola@chianticlassico.com
web	www.fattoriacasasola.com

Self-catering

map 2   entry 22

Sovigliano

Strada Magliano 9, 50028 Tavarnelle Val di Pesa, FI, Italy

This ancient beamed Chianti farmhouse is in a secluded and rural setting, though the towers of San Gimignano are within sight (on a clear day, at least). Guests stay either in self-catering apartments, one palatial with antiques and good, firm beds, or in one of the charming double rooms. A large communal kitchen with a fireplace makes a sociable place for guests to meet, but you can have your own space, too. What makes a stay here so special is the warm hospitality of the Bicego family, whose visitors, by all accounts, can scarcely tear themselves away.

- Regional Cookery: in English.
- Museums Tours: in English.
- Churches & Castles Tours.
- Clay Sculpting: in English.
- Guided Tour of Artist's Workshop: in English.
- Tasting of home-made produce.

rooms	4: 2 doubles, 2 twins. Also 4 apartments for 2-4.
price	€93–€110. Apartments €110–€235 per night.
meals	Dinner from €31.
closed	Rarely.
directions	Exit SS2 Firenze-Siena at Tavarnelle. On entering town right & follow Marcialla. Sovigliano just out of town; at the 4th r'bout veer left down lane signed Magliano; follow signs for house.

Signora Patrizia Bicego

tel	+39 055 8076217
fax	+39 055 8050770
e-mail	info@sovigliano.com
web	www.sovigliano.com

B&B & self-catering

Odina Agriturismo

Loc. Odina, 52024 Loro Ciuffenna, AR, Italy

The view over the Arno Valley is fantastic. Antonella takes considerable pride in Odina. The reception is in a beautifully restored, deconsecrated chapel, with a wonderful old bread-making chest. The apartments are all individual and each has its own sitting area outside, with proper garden furniture. Every bush and tree in the garden has been chosen with care, most being local species. The pool is large, as are the lovely bedrooms – all with oak beams and rustic antique furniture. If you don't want to cook, Antonella will point you in the right direction.

- Cookery: in English & Italian, October-November.
- Tuscan Gardening & Garden Visits: in English & Italian, Sat-Sat, May (min 8).
- Casa di Masaccio, 8km.
- Horse-riding, 5km.
- Tennis, 4km.
- 'Noleggio' mountain bikes.

rooms	4 apartments for 2, 5, 6, 7; villa for 8-10.
price	Apts €400-€1,350 per week; villa €1,600-€2,700.
meals	Self-catering.
closed	Rarely.
directions	From Florence A1 for Rome. Exit Valdarno. In Terranuova, follow Loro Ciuffenna. Before town, left for Querceto & Odina.

Signor Paolo Trenti

tel	+39 055 969304
fax	+39 0559 69305
e-mail	info@odina.it
web	www.odina.it

Self-catering

map 2   entry 24

Relais San Pietro in Polvano

Loc. Polvano 3, 52043 Castiglion Fiorentino, AR, Italy

Perched high in the hills and lavished with care this little hotel is a dream, its atmosphere one of calm and understated luxury. Beautiful bedrooms have terracotta tiled floors and kilims, plain white walls and beamed ceilings, and wide beds with wrought-iron bedheads dressed in crisp linen. The pool, on a terrace just below the hotel, has one of the best views going, as does the terrace restaurant. Food is home-made and delicious – even the bread is made in their own bread oven. Note that gates close at midnight!

- Antiques Market, Arezzo (1st weekend of month), 30-minute drive.
- Lake Trasimeno & boat trips to Isola Bella – baroque palace & gardens.
- Etruscan Museum, Cortona, 30-minute drive.
- Basilica of San Francis in Assisi, 60-minute drive.
- Ceramic town of Deruta, 45-minute drive.
- The Legend of the True Cross fresco in S. Francesco, Arezzo, 30-minute drive.

rooms	11: 3 doubles, 1 single, 7 suites.
price	€ 170–€ 300. Singles € 140.
meals	Dinner € 28–€ 45. Half-board available.
closed	November-March.
directions	At Castiglion Fiorentino follow signs for Cortona-Perugia. Left at third traffic lights towards Polvano. After 7km, left for Relais San Pietro.

Signor Luigi Protti

tel	+ 39 0575 650100
fax	+ 39 0575 650255
e-mail	polvano@technet.it
web	www.polvano.com

Hotel

La Locanda

Loc. Montanino, 53017 Radda in Chianti, SI, Italy

La Locanda appears to be just another Tuscan farmhouse, but pass through the two buildings and you enter a magical place. A soft green lawn edged with Mediterranean shrubs slopes gently down to a beautiful pool with decking; a covered terrace off to one side overlooks Volpaia. The house throbs with bold colours and lively fabrics: inside are a sunny living room with open fireplace and inviting sofas. Bedrooms are generous in every way, with large beds and beautiful bathrooms. Martina cooks while Guido acts as host – you'll find it hard to stir.

- Cookery: 4km, in English.
- Wine-tasting: 4km, in English, € 18.
- Library of Italian art books.
- Golf, 30km.
- Antiques market in Arezzo (1st Sunday of month).
- Terraces with beautiful views.

rooms	7: 4 doubles, 2 twins, 1 suite.
price	€ 180–€ 235. Suite from € 250. Singles € 165–€ 215.
meals	Dinner from € 30.
closed	Mid-November-end March.
directions	From Volpaia village square take narrow road to right which becomes a track. Follow for approx. 2km past a small sign marked La Locanda to left, on for 1km to group of houses.

Signori Guido & Martina Bevilacqua

tel	+39 0577 738833
fax	+39 0577 738833
e-mail	info@lalocanda.it
web	www.lalocanda.it

Inn

map 2   entry 26

Borgo Casa Al Vento

Loc. Casa al Vento, 53013 Gaiole in Chianti, SI, Italy

A mild air of untidiness rare in Tuscany – but proceed to your airy rooms and unwind in this marvellously peaceful rural retreat. There's a rustic mood here with beams and terracotta; dralon, nylon and velour are in evidence too... the views, however, are undeniably lovely, and you can breathe the wonderful pure air and sleep like a baby. The owners are seldom in evidence but the obliging Sri Lankan custodians will make sure you feel comfortable. Sun terrace, garden, pool, tennis court (extra charge) and mountain bikes (ditto) are all on the spot.

- Cookery: in English.
- Wine-tasting: in English.
- Art: in English.
- Vineyard with wines for sale.
- Medieval villages.
- Castles in surrounding area, 10km.

rooms	3 apartments for 4.
price	€450–€1,100 per week.
meals	Breakfast €8. Dinner from €25.
closed	Rarely.
directions	Exit A1 at Valdarno. Follow signs for Siena & Gaiole in Chianti, about 20km. At Gaiole in Chianti, follow signs to Casa al Vento, about 3km.

Signor Giuseppe Gioffreda

tel	+39 0577 749068
fax	+39 0226 40754
e-mail	info@borgocasaalvento.com
web	www.borgocasaalvento.com

Self-catering & B&B

Fattoria Guicciardini

Viale Garibaldi 2/A, Piazza S. Agostino 2, 53037 San Gimignano, SI, Italy

These simple but immaculately run and comfortable self-catering apartments are cunningly converted from a 15th-century building. There are entrances from both outside the city walls and from Piazza S. Agostino (in the church are frescoes by Benozzo Gozzoli). Get up early and watch the mists drop away from the surrounding countryside to expose the vineyards of the famous Vernaccia wine to the Tuscan sun. Listen to the street musicians, then stroll around when the hoards have gone and the fairytale towers are floodlit. Magical.

- Cusona Farm.
- San Gimignano.
- Summer festival (July & August).
- Winter festival (October-March).
- Fiera delle Messi – medieval spring fiesta (June).
- Local museums.

rooms	8 apartments: 5 for 2-4, 3 for 4-6.
price	€ 114–€ 140 per day; € 684–€ 840 per week.
meals	Self-catering.
closed	Rarely.
directions	Exit Florence-Siena motorway at S. Gimignano & Poggibonsi Nord. Fattoria in centre of S. Gimignano.

Signor Tuccio Guicciardini

tel	+ 39 0577 907185
fax	+ 39 0577 907185
e-mail	info@guicciardini.com
web	www.guicciardini.com

Self-catering

map 2   entry 28

Il Colombaio

Podere Il Colombaio, No 12 , Torri, 53010 Sovicille, SI, Italy

Arty, dramatic, vibrant – as soon as you walk in you see that creative minds have been at work. Strong reds, a mosaic-topped table and a Scandinavian stove built by Daniele. It's a bit like a live-in art gallery, and the old knotted timbers, pitted stone steps and well-trodden tile floors take a tolerant view. Bedrooms are named after the pictures which adorn them and have all the essentials (nothing cosy or frilly) and leafy views through ancient glass. The land around is forested, terraced and olive-groved to the hilt, and belonged once to the monastery at Torri.

- Pottery: in English & Italian, € 15 per hour.
- Own art gallery.
- Hot spring, 15km.
- Siena, 15km.
- Florence, 60km.
- San Gimignano, 35km.

rooms	6 doubles/triples, all with private bath.
price	From € 87. Triples from € 107. Singles from € 77.
meals	Lunch & dinner available nearby.
closed	Rarely.
directions	From Siena SS223 for Grosseto. After 12km, right for Rosia. Left for Torri at junction by 2 tall cypresses. Follow avenue & just before it ends 1st left, an unpaved road. House signed after 20m.

Daniele Buraggi & Barbara Viale

tel	+39 0577 344027
fax	+39 0577 344027
e-mail	ilcolombaio@tin.it
web	www.toscanaholiday.com

B&B

Castello di Ripa d'Orcia

Via della Contea 1/16, 53027 S. Quirico d'Orcia, SI, Italy

One can only stand in awe. The castle is the family's home and heritage, of which they are hugely proud, and guests feel privileged to share it. All the rooms and apartments are big and simple but warm and welcoming, too, many with breathtaking views. There is a day room for guests, filled with lovely furniture and with stacks of books to pour over. Breakfast is served in a small annexe off the main restaurant (it serves good regional dishes). This is a paradise for those looking for complete escape, and will keep lovers of history and architecture happy for days.

- Vineyard with wine for sale.
- Thermal baths.
- Hiking in Val d'Orca Park.
- Friday market, 10km.
- Bike hire, 5km.
- Siena, 45km.

rooms	6 twins/doubles. Also 8 self-catering apartments: 5 for 2, 3 for 4.
price	€98-€130. Singles €90. Apartments €490-€575 per week (for 2), €649-€750 (for 4).
meals	À la carte dinner available.
closed	November-15 March.
directions	From SS2 follow San Quirico d'Orcia. Right over bridge & follow road round town walls for 700m. Right again (signed); on for 5.3km.

Famiglia Aluffi Pentini Rossi

tel	+ 39 0577 897376
fax	+ 39 0577 898038
e-mail	info@castelloripadorcia.com
web	www.castelloripadorcia.com

B&B & self-catering

map 2   entry 30

Villa Iris

Strada Palazzo di Piero 1, 53047 Sarteano, SI, Italy

Fabio is Italian and Hashimoto is Japanese; her influence has given the house an unusual blend of eastern and western design. The bedrooms, big and light, have been designed out with the greatest attention to detail. Local apricot marble in the bathrooms, where soft towels add a touch of luxury. A leisurely breakfast of Tuscan delicacies – local meats, honey and bread – is served in the conservatory; even in the cooler months you feel you are dining *al fresco*. Doze in the garden, cool off in the pool, explore the archaeological treasures of ancient Etruria.

- Decorating Porcelain: in English & Italian.
- Wine-tastings & Gourmet Food Tours.
- Medieval villages.
- Etruscan towns of Sarteano & Chiusi.
- Thermal baths, 3-5km.
- Pienza, Montepulciano & Cortona - art & architecture.

rooms	5: 4 doubles, 1 suite.
price	€155-€165. Suite €230.
meals	Dinner €35.
closed	Rarely.
directions	Exit A1 at Chuisi-Chianciano Terme. Follow signs to Sarteano & on for Chianciano. After approx 4km, right at blue signpost marked Villa Iris.

Signor Fabio Moretto

tel	+39 0578 265993
fax	+39 0578 265993
e-mail	villairis@ftbcc.it
web	www.villairis.it

B&B

Hotel Villa Ciconia

Via dei Tigli 69, Loc. Ciconia, 05019 Orvieto, TR, Italy

This elegant 16th-century villa is shielded from noise by its large, shady gardens. Cavernous rooms ramble throughout, some rather austere, but all impressive. Two large dining rooms decked with tapestries and frescoes occupy the ground floor, their chilly proportions offset by huge fireplaces; the breakfast room is more intimate, with ancient tiled floors. The regional food is delicious. Bedrooms are mostly large and uncluttered; some have iron bedsteads with the VC insignia. Signor Petrangeli runs the hotel almost single-handedly but always finds time for you.

- Italian Language.
- Guided tours - historical, artistic, gastronomic.
- Mountain Bike Trips.
- Horse-riding.
- Umbria Jazz Festival, Orvieto (27 December-1 January).
- Corpus Domini Festival, Orvieto (June).

rooms	12 doubles.
price	€ 124–€ 155. Singles € 108–€ 134.
meals	Lunch/dinner from € 18.
closed	Rarely.
directions	Exit A1 at Orvieto. From roundabout SS71 for Arezzo. Villa approximately 1km on left.

Signor Valentino Petrangeli

tel	+39 0763 305582
fax	+39 0763 302077
e-mail	villaciconia@libero.it
web	www.bellaumbria.net/hotel-villaciconia

Hotel

map 2   entry 32

Locanda Rosati

Loc. Buonviaggio 22, 05018 Orvieto, TR, Italy

From the moment you turn off the road (whose proximity is quickly forgotton) the atmosphere is comfortable and friendly. The house has been gently modernised but remains firmly a farmhouse. Flowers, books and magazines are scattered; tables are simply laid. Giampiero and Paolo are natural hosts and dinner is informal and unbelievably good value. Bedrooms are uncluttered, with white linen and a splash of colour in the curtains. The house is surrounded by gardens, from the highest point of which you can see the spiky skyline of Orvieto.

- Italian.
- Cookery: in English & Italian.
- Horse-riding: 5km, in Italian.
- Orvieto Cathedral.
- Umbria Jazz Festival, Orvieto (27 December–1 January).
- Local markets (Tuesdays, Thursdays, Saturdays).

rooms	10: 4 doubles, 1 single, 5 family.
price	€103–€120. Singles €85–€100. Half-board available.
meals	Dinner from €27.50.
closed	7 January–February.
directions	Exit A1 at Orvieto, take road to Viterbo, Bolsena & Montefiascone. After 10km Locanda on right.

Signor Giampiero Rosati

tel	+39 0763 217314
fax	+39 0763 217314
e-mail	info@locandarosati.orvieto.tr.it
web	www.locandarosati.orvieto.tr.it

Inn

Abbazia San Pietro in Valle

Via Case Sparse di Macenano 4, 05034 Ferentillo, TR, Italy

Ancient, venerable, spectacular, the abbey sits tranquilly on the side of a wooded valley. Most of the plainly furnished rooms have views over the valley and nearly all open off a courtyard – if it's raining you'll need an umbrella for the dash from room to reception! The cloisters are lovely, the setting beautiful, and there are plenty of places to sit and watch the light changing round the towers and cypresses. Below is the Nera where in summer you can go rafting from Scheggino, and, across the valley, a deserted village said to be the first human settlement in Umbria.

- Truffle Hunting & Cooking: in Italian (interpreter on request).
- Cookery: in Italian (interpreter on request).
- Wine-tasting: in Italian (interpreter on request).
- Italian Language: in English & Italian.
- Church with pre-Giottesque frescoes.
- Festival of The Two Worlds, Spoleto (July), 17km.

rooms	22: 19 twins/doubles, 3 suites.
price	€ 110–€ 125. Suites € 130–€ 145.
meals	Dinner from € 26. Restaurant à la carte.
closed	November-March.
directions	A1 from Rome exit at Orte then SS206 to Terni; exit for Terni East & take SS209 (Visso, Norcia & Cascia); after 20km follow signs.

Signorine Letizia & Chiara Costanzi

tel	+39 0744 780129
fax	+39 0744 435522
e-mail	abbazia@sanpietroinvalle.com
web	www.sanpietroinvalle.com

Hotel

map 3　entry 34

Relais Il Canalicchio

Via della Piazza 13, 06050 Canalicchio di Collazzone, PG, Italy

This old *castello* in the lush green Umbrian countryside is almost a principality in itself: 51 rooms, two pools, gardens, gym and, of course, a tower, all within the fortress walls. Some rooms are tucked under the beamed eaves; many open onto little balconies. Perhaps those in the tower are the nicest: the views from the eight windows sweep in all directions over an endless valley of olive groves, vineyards and woods. Downstairs enjoy a game of billiards and a glass of *grappa*, having dined in the splendid restaurant. Others may prefer to retreat to the quiet of the library.

- Cookery: 4km, €55.
- Pottery: 10km, in English.
- Wine-tasting.
- Horse-riding: 4km.
- Ceramics museum, 10km.
- Own sauna & gym.

rooms	51: 32 doubles, 19 suites.
price	€149–€179. Singles €120–€143. Suites €209–€253.
meals	Lunch/dinner: set menu from €34, or à la carte.
closed	Rarely.
directions	From Rome A1 towards Firenze, exit Orte. E45 Perugia-Cesena, come off at Ripabianca & follow sign towards Canalicchio.

Signora Dorine Kunst

tel	+39 075 8707325
fax	+39 075 8707296
e-mail	relais@relaisilcanalicchio.it
web	www.relaisilcanalicchio.it

Hotel

Locanda del Gallo

Loc. Santa Cristina, 06020 Gubbio, PG, Italy

A wash with history, and the unmistakable feel of a colonial home. Rooms have limewash walls which accentuate perfectly the hardwood furniture and oriental artefacts; bedrooms have carved four-posters and an air of tranquillity. Doze in wicker armchairs, enjoy drinks at dusk. The *gallo* (cockerel) is almost everywhere you look; according to Balinese tradition, he wards off evil sprits. Other traditions are upheld: healthy food, genuine flavours, veg from the garden, home-baked bread and cakes. And the pool, like a mirage, clings to the side of the hill.

- Breathing techniques: in English & Italian.
- Yoga: in English.
- Voice & Song: in English, 6-18 July.
- Trekking on bridlepaths.
- Cipriani cooking course: in English & Italian.
- Swimming pool with panoramic view.

rooms	9: 6 doubles, 3 family suites.
price	From € 102. Suites for 4 from € 184. Half-board from € 70 p.p.
meals	Dinner € 19.
closed	January-February.
directions	Exit E45 at Ponte Pattoli for Casa del Diavolo; towards S Cristina 8km; 1st left 100m after La Dolce Vita restaurant, on to Locanda.

Marchesa Paola Moro

tel	+39 075 9229912
fax	+39 075 9229912
e-mail	info@locandadelgallo.it
web	www.locandadelgallo.it

Inn

map 2   entry 36

Hotel Palazzo Bocci

Via Cavour 17, 06038 Spello, PG, Italy

A beautiful townhouse right in the centre of medieval Spello. The soothing trickle from a fountain greets you as you enter the small courtyard; then, a series of gloriously fine reception rooms with painted friezes. Bedrooms are simpler, with white walls and chestnut beamed ceilings. Breakfast is served in one of the special sitting rooms or on the tiled terrace which overlooks the town's ancient rooftops – a perfect place for sundowners. Cross the street to the restaurant – once the village oil mill – where you dine under a delightful rick-vaulted ceiling.

- Cookery: in English & Italian, all year, except bank holidays, May & September, € 620.
- Wine with Cellar Visits: in English & Italian, € 280.
- Art & Pottery: 20km, in English & Italian, € 375.
- Walking Tours: € 280.
- Festival of olives & oil (February & December).
- Vineyard with wine for sale, 3km.

rooms	23: 15 doubles, 2 singles, 6 suites.
price	€ 130–€ 150. Singles € 70–€ 90. Suites € 180–€ 250.
meals	Lunch & dinner at Il Molino restaurant, from € 30.
closed	Rarely.
directions	From Assisi follow signs for Foligno; after 10km, leave main road for Spello. Hotel opposite Church of Sant'Andrea in town centre.

Signor Fabrizio Buono

tel	+39 0742 301021
fax	+39 0742 301464
e-mail	bocci@bcsnet.it
web	www.palazzobocci.com

Hotel

Villa Rosa

Voc. Docciolano 9, Montemelino, 06060 Magione, PG, Italy

A beautifully restored farmhouse looking out over an agricultural plain, with Perugia in the distance. Distant church bells, the hum of a tractor... yet you are 5km from the superstrada – a great base for touring Umbria and Tuscany. Megan, who is Australian, and Lino, with the enthusiasm of youth, are keen to help people enjoy every aspect of the area. There are antiques and paintings throughout the house, and the bedrooms are quite separate. Breakfast is good, with freshly squeezed orange juice and home-made jam. Wonderful views and a pool, too.

- Cookery with Perugian Chef: Sundays & Mondays.
- Mushroom & Truffle Hunting.
- Asparagus Picking: spring.
- Euro Chocolate Festival, Perugia, 15km (October) & Jazz Festival (July).
- Saltwater pool on site, riding & golf nearby.
- Knitwear & cashmere factory outlets.

rooms	2: 1 double, 1 twin. Also 1 cottage for 5, 1 flat for 2.
price	€ 80. Half-board from € 60 p.p. Cottage & flat € 400–€ 900 p.w.
meals	Dinner with wine, from € 20.
closed	Rarely.
directions	Exit Perugia-Bettolle at Corciano, for Castelvieto through village (via underpass & bridge) to roadside shrine. Left & on to second shrine; right uphill. House after a couple of bends.

Megan & Lino Rialti

tel	+39 075 841814
fax	+39 0758 41814
e-mail	meglino@libero.it

B&B & self-catering

map 2   entry 38

Azienda Agrituristica Il Quadrifoglio

Strada Licini 22, Colle Marconi, 66100 Chieti, CH, Italy

Those in the know travel many miles to be looked after by Anna, who always makes her guests feel comfortable and at ease. The house is modern, undistinguished but very pleasant, in the middle of farmland just beyond Chieti. Bedrooms are decorated using simple print fabrics, terracotta and cane; the self-contained apartment has kitchen and log fire. Enjoy the large sitting-dining area, balcony and garden – perfect for children, with wooden summer house, swing and climbing frame. Anna will cook a sumptuous dinner if you ask her.

- Cookery: in English.
- Dough Modelling: in Italian.
- Local historical museum, 3km.
- Old earthern houses of Casalincontrada.
- Bikes available.
- Walking country on doorstep.

rooms	5: 3 doubles, 1 family, 1 suite. Also 1 apartment.
price	€ 45–€ 55. Family from € 57. Suite from € 70.
meals	Lunch/dinner from € 13.
closed	Rarely.
directions	From A25 for Chieti. Right onto SS5 for Popoli-Manoppello. After 1.7km left to Chieti after 5km turn right for Colle Marconi. Right onto Strada Licini & right again. 1st driveway on right.

Signora Anna Maria D'Orazio

tel	+39 0871 63400
fax	+39 0871 63400
e-mail	anndora@tin.it

B&B & self-catering

Casa in Trastevere

Vicolo della Penitenza 19, 00165 Rome, RM, Italy

Deep in the fascinating old quarter of Trastevere, the area has a lively atmosphere with shops, restaurants and bars. Signora Nicolini has furnished the sunny first-floor apartment as if it were her own home: there is plenty of room, with an open-plan living room and screened kitchen, white sofas, a good collection of prints, kilims and antique pieces. The big double bedroom has a beautiful hand-quilted and embroidered bedspread. Great to come back here and put your feet up after a long day, before going out again to explore this magical city. *Minimum stay four nights.*

- Santa Maria, Trastevere.
- Botanical Vegetable Garden.
- Palazzo Farnesina.
- Palazzo Corsini.
- Bramante's Tempietto.
- Ponte Sisto.

rooms	Apartment for 2-4.
price	From € 103 per night (for 2-3), from € 155 (for 4).
meals	Self-catering.
closed	Rarely.
directions	From Ponte Sisto cross Piazza Trilussa, right into Via della Lungara, right into Via dei Riari & right again into Vicolo della Penitenza.

Signora Marta Nicolini

tel	+ 39 0669 924722
fax	+ 39 0669 787084
e-mail	info@casaintrastevere.it/info@insiemesalute.it
web	www.casaintrastevere.it

Self-catering

map 3   entry 40

Casa Trevi

Via in Arcione 98, 00187 Rome, RM, Italy

A hop, skip and a jump from Rome's most famous fountain (illustrated), the Casa Trevi. Follow a passage and find yourself in a courtyard, with olive and orange trees. On three sides are 17th-century buildings – on the fourth, a modern monstrosity! The apartments are minimalist, functional and clean, with terracotta-tiled floors, plain white walls, comfortable beds. There are no windows but the double glass-paned doors let in plenty of light. Hobs and fridges are provided in the kitchen areas but serious cooking is not catered for. *Minimum stay four nights.*

- Trevi Fountain.
- Pantheon.
- Palazzo del Quirinale.
- Piazza di Spagna.
- Spanish Steps.
- Via Margutta - lined with artists' studios.

rooms	2 apartments: 1 for 2-3, 1 for 4.
price	Apartment for 2-3 from € 103 per day, apartment for 4 from € 155.
meals	Self-catering.
closed	Rarely.
directions	Details on booking but no parking provided & surrounding streets are pedestrianised. 10 minutes by taxi from central railway station; nearest metro stop: Piazza di Spagna.

Signora Marta Nicolini

tel	+ 39 0669 787084
fax	+ 39 06 69787084
e-mail	info@casaintrastevere.it

Self-catering

Ⓔ

La Tana dell'Istrice

Piazza Unita 12, 01020 Civitella D'Agliano, VT, Italy

Tuscia is less famous than Tuscany and Umbria, yet rich in natural beauty and culture. La Tana dell'Istrice is in a palace in the central square, opposite a castle in a state of photogenic decay. The house has been beautifully converted without sacrificing the original character. A big drawing room with comfortable sofas, antiques and books provides the keynote. Bedrooms, like all the best country-house guest rooms, have desks and comfortable armchairs. Food (organic) and wine is taken seriously here – this is part of a big wine-producing estate.

- Cookery: in English & Italian, Monday-Friday, four hours, € 160 p.p. with meal (min. 4).
- Yoga: in English.
- Vineyard Visits, Tastings & Dinner: in English & Italian, Mon-Sat, € 75 p.p. (min.4).
- Private functions - max. 60.
- Terme dei Papi - thermal baths.
- Vineyards & cellars with wine for sale.

rooms	12: 9 doubles, 3 suites.
price	From € 135. Suites from € 226. Half-board € 226-€ 318 for two.
meals	Dinner from € 47.
closed	10-26 December; 7 January-21 March; 1-15 August.
directions	Perugia, for Orvieto direction. 100m after Baschi station, left to Castiglione in Teverina. There, towards Civitella. 5km on, right at x-roads. 6km further on. Hotel under watch tower up steep road.

Signora Alessandra Falsetti

tel	+39 0761 914501
fax	+39 0761 914815
e-mail	mottura@isa.it
web	www.motturasergio.it

Hotel

map 3   entry 42

Il Cortile

Via Roma 43, 80033 Cicciano, NA, Italy

The black door in the suburban street opens onto a beautiful courtyard rich in bougainvillaea, jasmine and lemon trees. Originally a summer residence for the Nucci family, Arturo's forebears, the villa now has accommodation in two self-contained units – perfect for families with children. Meals, which are delicious, are served in the main part of the house or in the courtyard, and there is an inviting sitting room/library. Bedrooms are cool, with pale washed walls, tiled floors and antique furniture. Sijtsken is a charming, thoughtful hostess and a fantastic cook.

- Cookery: in English, Dutch & Italian.
- Floral Decorations: in English, Dutch & Italian.
- Guided Tours of Region: in English, Dutch & Italian.
- Early-Christian basilicas at Cimitile, 3km.
- Festivale dei Gigli (lilies), Nola, 5km.
- Historic Nola & Avella, 5-10km.

rooms	2 apartments: 1 for 2-3, 1 for 4-5.
price	€58-€64.
meals	Dinner with wine, from €21.
closed	Rarely.
directions	From Rome or Naples: highway to Bari; exit Nola. Follow signs to Cimitile & Cicciano. A 10-minute drive from the highway.

Signori Arturo & Sijtsken Nucci

tel	+39 081 8248897
fax	+39 081 8264851
e-mail	dupon@libero.it

B&B

Villa en Rose

Via Torretta a Marmorata, 22, 84010 Ravello, SA, Italy

The position is superb for walkers, halfway between Minori and ravishing Ravello, on a marked footpath which was originally a mule trail. Actually, the *only* way to get here is on foot, with about 15 minutes' worth of steps down from the closest road. The house, with pool, is set amid lemon groves – the locals are squeezing a living out of Limoncello. The position is special, the apartment functional. If you don't fancy self-catering, the walk up to the main square in Ravello would at least earn you a cappuccino and a brioche. *Minimum three nights.*

- Villa Rufolo & Gardens, Ravello (recitals March-November).
- Villa Cimbrone & Gardens, Ravello.
- Museum of Amalfi's hand-made paper.
- Pompeii.
- Fiordo di Furore – eco-museum.
- Boat trips, Sorrento to Capri.

rooms	1 self-catering apartment for 2.
price	From € 104 per night.
meals	Breakfast on request, from € 6.
closed	Rarely.
directions	Directions given at time of booking.

Signora Valeria Civale
tel   +39 0898 57661
e-mail   valeria.civale@tiscali.it

Self-catering

map 4   entry 44

Azienda Agrituristica Seliano

84063 Paestum, SA, Italy

Shelley described the ancient site of Paestum as "inexpressibly grand". You are just a stone's throw away at the Seliano, run by Baroness Cecilia Baratta and her sons. Cecilia cooks delicious meals for guests and family, who eat together round a big table in the vaulted dining room, or outside on the terrace next to the rose garden. The bedrooms, in beautiful rustic style, are in the stone barn or circular pigeon loft. If you ask nicely, Ettore might take you to see their 560-strong buffalo herd, sitting regally up to their necks in black mud. *Minimum stay two nights.*

- Cookery: in English, French & Italian.
- The Antique Trade: in English, French & Italian.
- Archaeological area, 2km.
- Monastery of Padula, 50km.
- Amalfi Coast, 50km.
- National Park of Cilenio, 30km.

rooms	14: 2 twins/doubles, 12 family.
price	€70–€115. Half-board €50–€70 p.p.
meals	Lunch/dinner with wine, €15–€26.
closed	Mid-January–mid-February; November.
directions	From A3 motorway at Eboei to Paestrum. Right onto SS18 to Paestrum. After 1km, into driveway marked Seliano.

Baroness Cecilia Baratta Bellelli

tel	+39 0828 724544
fax	+39 0828 723634
e-mail	seliano@agriturismoseliano.it
web	www.agriturismoseliano.it

B&B

La Mola

Via Adolfo Cilento 2, 84048 Castellabate, SA, Italy

A grand old 17th-century palace incorporating a 12th-century tower. The huge olive oil press found in the cellars during restoration – which now forms the base of a vast glass-topped drinks table – gives the hotel its name. The sea, from a spectacular vantage point, is the main component of the surroundings: your room will look out onto it, as do all the communal sitting areas and the terrace. Rooms are pristinely furnished. La Mola is the ancestral home of Signor Favilla, who spends summer here with his wife, running the hotel with amiable efficiency.

- Neapolitan Cookery.
- Diving: 2km.
- Ruins of Paestum, 18km.
- Vineyard with wine shop, 2km.
- Cilento National Park.
- Castellabate (World Heritage Site).

rooms	5 doubles.
price	€104–€114. Singles from €77.
meals	Dinner with wine, €31–€39.
closed	November–March.
directions	From Naples A30 south to Battipaglia, then Agropoli & Castellabate. House in historic centre.

Signori Francesco & Loredana Favilla

tel	+39 0974 967053
fax	+39 0974 967714
e-mail	lamola@lamola-it.com
web	www.lamola-it.com

Hotel

map 4   entry 46

Villa Cheta Elite

Via Nazionale, 85941 Acquafredda di Maratea, PZ, Italy

A godsend in these parts, where there are few really nice hotels. The view of the coastline below will keep you rooted to the spot – most probably on one of the terraces in the scented, tropical garden. Or cross the road and plunge down 165 steps to a pebble beach to swim. Bedrooms have good, slightly maiden-auntish furniture and plenty of light; the public rooms are more elaborately furnished. Guests dine at their own tables but once dinner is over Lamberto and Stefania are good at encouraging conversation. There is a small sitting room and library.

- Yoga - on terrace or in garden: in English, German & Italian, € 15 per hour.
- Sailing Trips: 4km, in English & Italian, June-September, € 60 per day p.p.
- Guided walks into the Maquis.
- Flower & folkloric market (Fridays), 8km.
- National Park of Pollino.
- Seasonal Mediterranean cooking.

rooms	20 doubles.
price	€ 120–€ 220. Half-board € 72–€ 119 p.p.
meals	Breakfast € 10. Lunch/dinner € 30.
closed	Rarely.
directions	From A3, Lagonegro-Maratea exit. After 10km right onto SS104 to Sapri. There, left-hand turn onto coast road for Maratea. Villa 9km along coast, above road on left in Acquafredda.

Signora Stefania Aquadro

tel	+39 0973 878134
fax	+39 0973 878135
e-mail	villacheta@tin.it
web	www.villacheta.it

Hotel

Il Giardino di Iti

Contrada Amica, 87068 Rossano, CS, Italy

The farm has been in the same family for three centuries and has been renovated by its owner, Baroness Francesca Cherubini. A huge, arched doorway leads to a courtyard and vast enclosed garden, where meals are often served. At night the citrus and olive trees glow with lights hidden among the branches. Some rooms open directly off the courtyard and retain the character of the original – wooden furniture, fireplaces, terracotta floor tiles. Each is named after one of the crops; you may sleep in the Lemon or Peach room – or Aubergine, or Cucumber.

- Cookery: in English & Italian, March, June, Sept, Dec, €30 per day.
- Jam & Marmalade Making: in English & Italian, March, June, Sept, Dec, €30 per day.
- Weaving on Old-fashioned Loom: English & Italian, Mar, June, Sept, Dec, €400 (2 days).
- Découpage: in English & Italian, March, June, Sept, Dec, €10 per day.
- 11th-century archaeological site, 11km.
- Byzantine finds & exhibits, 6km.

rooms	12 large rooms for 4-6, 10 with shower, 2 with kitchen.
price	Half-board €31–€49 p.p. Full-board €41–€59 p.p.
meals	Self-catering also possible.
closed	Rarely.
directions	Leave A3 Salerno-Reggio Calabria at Sibari exit; Rossano road (SS106) to Contrada Amica; on for Paludi. Shuttle service from Rossano coach & train station on request.

Baroness Francesca Cherubini

tel	+ 39 0983 64508
fax	+ 39 0983 64508
e-mail	info@giardinoiti.it
web	www.giardinoiti.it

B&B & self-catering

map 4   entry 48

spain

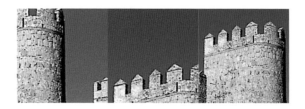

Photography by Michael Busselle

spain

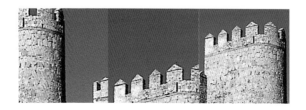

Casa Grande de Trives

Calle Marqués de Trives 17, 32780 Poboa de Trives, Orense, Spain

This noble village house was one of the first in Galicia to open to guests; like good claret it has got better and better. The rooms are in a separate wing, big and elegantly uncluttered with wooden floors, the best mattresses and wonderful cotton sheets. There's a sitting room where you can have a quiet drink, and an enchanting garden. Breakfast is taken in a dining room where the rich furnishings and classical music vie with the sumptuousness of the buffet. A marvellous place, and a most gracious welcome from mother and son. *Grand Cru* Galicia!

- Canoeing Trips: 4km, in Spanish & English, €60.
- Catamaran Trips: 25km, in Spanish, €15.
- Knitting: in Spanish & English, €30.
- Mountain bikes for hire.
- Riberia Sacra monasteries.
- Indoor/outdoor pools & reservoir for watersports.

rooms	9 twins/doubles.
price	From €49–€60. Singles €40–€48.
meals	Dinner from €18.
closed	Rarely.
directions	From Madrid, A-6 for La Coruña. Exit 400 for N-120 for Monforte de Lemos. At km468, exit for A Rua & Trives, then right at lights onto C-536 for Trives. On left in centre of village.

Adelaida Alvarez Martínez

tel	+34 988 332066
fax	+34 988 332066
e-mail	informacion@casagrandetrives.com
web	www.casagrandetrives.com

B&B

Pazo Bentraces

Bentraces, 32890 Barbadás, Orense, Spain

The delectable *palacio* was built for a bishop. Angeles will unravel the web of its history and of the three-year restoration project, which resulted in one of the most elegant manor-house hostelries in Spain. The plushness within is hinted at by a Florentine-style façade and the ornate gardens that lap up to the walls. Push aside the heavy doors to discover a world of books, rugs, engravings, marble staircases and warm colours. No-one could fail to enjoy the choice of sitting rooms, the enormous breakfast room in the vibrant kitchen and the sumptuous bedrooms.

- Tour of Ribeira Sacra monasteries: 25km, in Spanish, €9.
- Visit to Ribeiro bodegas: 28km, in Spanish, €12.
- Catamaran sailing.
- Jewish quarter of Ribadavia, 22km.
- Allariz, 12km.
- Romanesque Orense.

rooms	7: 5 doubles, 2 suites.
price	€94-€130. Singles from €80.
meals	Breakfast from €9. Dinner from €30.
closed	22 December-2 January.
directions	From Orense for Madrid N-525; just past 'km7' marker, N-540 for Celanova to Bentraces. Here at 'Bar Bentraces', right; house beside church. Ring bell at main gate.

Angeles Peñamaría Cajoto

tel	+34 988 383381
fax	+34 988 383035
e-mail	info@pazodebentraces.com
web	www.pazodebentraces.com

Hotel

map 5   entry 50

Finca Río Miño

Carril 6, Las Eiras, 36760 O Rosal, Pontevedra, Spain

Tony and Shirley know the people, villages, food and wines of Galicia like few others. Their 350-year-old farm with terraced vineyards and *bodega* carved in solid rock is located on the bank of the Miño with views to Portugal. In the vast garden are two pine-clad lodges built by Tony: simply furnished, with a small kitchen (though breakfast can be provided), sitting room and two bedrooms. In the main house is a guest room with sitting room and an unforgettable terrace. All this, a pool-with-a-view and river beaches at the end of the track.

- Port Wine Appreciation: on estate & 20km, in English, Sunday eve/Monday am, €35.
- Albarino Wine Appreciation: on site & 5km, in English, Wednesday morning, €25.
- La Guardia – lobster capital of Galicia, 8km.
- Albarino wine routes, 1km.
- Monte Tecla – Celtic settlement & museum, 8km.
- One-day spa & beauty treatments, 35km.

rooms	1 double. Also 2 self-catering lodges for 4.
price	From €66.
meals	Breakfast from €8. Gourmet dinner from €30 inc. port tastings (Sun).
closed	November-March.
directions	Vigo N-550 to Tuy. La Guardia exit, then C-550 for 15km. Just after km190 marker, left at 'Restaurante Eiras' sign, over next crossroads; signed to left after 1.5km.

Tony Taylor-Dawes

tel	+34 986 621107
fax	+34 986 621107
e-mail	finca_dawes@email.com
web	www.fincariomino.com

B&B & self-catering

Hotel Quinta Duro

Camino de las Quintas 384, 33394 Cabueñes, Asturias, Spain

The estate of the Velázquez-Duro family is a haven of greenery and 100-year-old trees, girdled by a high stone wall. You are just to the east of Gijón and overlook the city; the house, though 800m from the main road, is quiet and secluded. Hospitable Carlos has recently redecorated the guest rooms as well as the rest of the interior; it is stylish yet homely. Panelled walls and period Portuguese and English furniture show the family's love of quality and detail. The bronze statue in the garden is of Carlos's grandfather, casting a wistful eye on all who visit.

- Contemporary Ceramics, Beginners & Advanced: in Spanish & English, €300 (1 week).
- Scuba-diving: 3km, in Spanish, July-September, €250.
- Golf courses: 4km.
- Botanical garden.
- Beach & swimming pools, 5km.
- Sports centre, 5km.

rooms	11 twins/doubles.
price	€65–€94. Singles from €60.
meals	Restaurants close by.
closed	Mid-January–mid-February.
directions	From Gijón towards Santander on motorway, then N-632. Then right for Santurio & Cefontes. After 500m, left, then 400m further to large entrance gates on right.

Carlos Velázquez-Duro

tel	+34 985 330443
fax	+34 985 371890
e-mail	quintaduro@terra.es
web	www.hotelquintaduro.com

Hotel

Hotel Casona de Bustiello

Ctra. Infiesto - Villaviciosa s/n, 33535 Infiesto, Asturias, Spain

The mix of traditional Asturian and modern architecture gives this house an eccentric look. The shallow roof is dominated by a large, obtrusive dormer window, but enter that room in the attic space and you'll find it delightful, with rosy walls, sloping ceilings and an entertaining mass of beams. All the rooms are painted in warm colours and furnished with confidence and restraint, keeping a cosy, rural feel. From the sitting room with its big bookcases, a door leads to a long, windowed gallery – a wonderful place to take in the views of the Sierra de Ques.

- Canyoning (adventure sport): 20km, in English.
- Introduction to Horse-riding: in English.
- Personal Development: in Spanish.
- Golf: 15km.
- Cider Museum, 6km.
- Covadouga Basilica, 15km.

rooms	10 twins/doubles.
price	€ 60–€ 100.
meals	Lunch/dinner € 13–€ 20.
closed	Rarely.
directions	From Oviedo, N-634 for Santander. 2km before Infiesto, left on AS-255 for Villaviciosa. On right after 4km.

Aurora Huergo

tel	+34 985 710445
fax	+34 985 710760
e-mail	info.hcb@hotelcasonadebustiello.com
web	www.hotelcasonadebustiello.com

Hotel

Hotel Posada del Valle

Collia, 33549 Arriondas, Asturias, Spain

After two years of searching the hills and valleys of Asturias, Nigel and Joann found the home of their dreams – a century-old farmhouse just inland from the rugged north coast. They are nurturing new life from the soil (they are a fully registered organic farm) while running a small guesthouse. The apple orchard has been planted, the flock graze the hillside and the menu celebrates all things local. Rooms are seductive affairs with wooden floors below and beams above. Most memorable of all: the glass-fronted dining room with views of the soaring Picos.

- Guided Walks: in English.
- Rural Heritage in Asturias: in English, €25-€30.
- Picos de Europa National Park, 20km.
- Unspoilt beaches, 12km.
- Pre-Roman architecture, 15km.
- Paleolithic art, Tito Bustillo & El Buxu.

rooms	12 doubles.
price	€49-€77. Singles €42-€45.
meals	Breakfast from €6. Dinner €15-€18.
closed	15 October-31 March.
directions	N-634 Arriondas, then AS-260 for Mirador del Fito. After 1km, right for Collia. Through village (don't turn to Ribadesella). Hotel 300m on left after village.

Nigel Burch

tel	+34 985 841157
fax	+34 985 841559
e-mail	hotel@posadadelvalle.com
web	www.posadadelvalle.com

Hotel

map 6   entry 54

Hotel Torrecerredo

Barrio Vega s/n, 33554 Arenas de Cabrales, Asturias, Spain

The views from Torrecerredo are stunning – "a double glory for hearts and eyes". The hotel itself is a modern building, with a somewhat stark frontage, on a hillside just outside the busy town of Arenas de Cabrales. Bedrooms are simple affairs with no great charm; the best are those on the first floor at the front. What lifts the hotel into the 'special' league for us is its dining/sitting room in which guests are treated to simple home cooking. Few know the area as intimately as Jim and Pilar and they are generous with time and advice. Ask about low season offers.

- Multi-activity Guided Tours: in English, April-December, € 399.
- Mountain Bike Tours: in English, April-October, from € 170 (2-7 days).
- Natural History: in English, April-December, € 120.
- Self-guided walking weeks.
- Beaches, 20km.
- Fiestas (summer).

rooms	19: 15 doubles, 4 singles.
price	€ 29-€ 65. Singles € 17-€ 39.
meals	Lunch/dinner from € 10.
closed	January-February.
directions	From Santander N-634 for Oviedo then left on N-612 for Potes. In Panes C-6312 (A-S114) to Arenas de Cabrales. Through town & right after Hotel Naranjo de Bulnes. Signed.

Pilar Saíz Lobeto

tel	+34 985 846640
fax	+34 985 846640
e-mail	torretours@fade.es
web	www.picosadventure.com

Hotel

Venta de Donamaría

Barrio Ventas 4, 31750 Donamaría, Navarra, Spain

Donamaría has a long tradition of receiving travellers and your present-day hosts are sophisticated, welcoming, amusing folk who love the finer things in life. These two old village houses (guest rooms in one, restaurant in the other) are packed full of antiques, old toys and a few surprises to boot; it all creates an intimate, relaxed atmosphere, some of it tongue-in-cheek. This is a place to linger over lunch or dinner; connoisseurs rave about the traditional Navarre dishes. The rooms are all that you'd hope for – big, timbered, intimate.

- Señorío de Bertiz Nature Reserve, 4km.
- Local granary & mill.
- Local craft shops.
- Leurtza Lakes, 6km.
- Gulf of Viscay beaches, 40km.
- San Fermîn fiestas, Pamplona (July), 40km.

rooms	5 twins/doubles.
price	From € 60.
meals	Lunch/dinner from € 12 set menu, € 27–€ 30 à la carte. No meals Sunday evening or Monday.
closed	Rarely.
directions	From San Sebastián, N-121A for Pamplona. Then right into San Esteban & Doneztebe for Saldías. Donamaría 2km from San Esteban.

Imanol Luzuriaga

tel	+34 948 450708
fax	+34 948 450708
e-mail	donamariako@jet.es

Restaurant with rooms

map 7   entry 56

Hostería Sierra de Guara

Oriente 2, 22144 Bierge, Huesca, Spain

Rosa and her sisters run this *hosteria* with unaffected charm. Birds are a theme here: note the painted wooden panels on the reception desk. Bedrooms are uncluttered, with cool modern tiled floors, beds with slender metal bedheads and drapes, and an armchair or two. The large terrace has views of the village and its hilltop church. The dining room is huge, with frescoes of medieval viticulture – a sort of latter-day *Book of Hours*. At the back of the house is an almond orchard, which comes into its own in February when the blossom begins.

- Wine-tasting: in Spanish, spring & autumn, approx. € 150.
- Geology & Flora of Guarda: 15km, in Spanish & French, spring & autumn, approx. € 30.
- Birdwatching: 15km, in Spanish & English, spring & autumn, approx. € 42.
- Olive Oil Factory Visits & Tasting: in Spanish, spring & winter, approx. € 100.
- Natural Park of Guara on doorstep.
- Own pool & botanical garden.

rooms	14: 11 doubles, 3 junior suites.
price	€ 60–€ 75. Singles from € 44.
meals	Lunch/dinner from € 18.
closed	January; 24 & 25 December.
directions	From Huesca, N-240 for Lleida. 5km after Angües, left to Abiego, then left to Bierge. Hostería on left at village entrance.

Rosa Viñuales Ferrando

tel	+34 974 318107
fax	+34 974 318107
e-mail	info@hosteriadeguara.com
web	www.hosteriadeguara.com

Hotel

La Torre del Visco
Apartado 15, 44580 Valderrobres, Teruel, Spain

Renew body and spirit in this superbly renovated medieval estate house. Standards of comfort, decoration and food are high, yet it is a deeply relaxing place. Peace is total inside and out, with neither phone nor TV to disturb you in your room. After a day of discovery in the beautiful Bajo Aragón, settle with one of a thousand books in front of a great log fire. Food is their passion and you will eat superbly on a feast of own-farm produce and a fine selection of wines. Breakfast is served around the big, polished kitchen table; dinner, if it's fine, on the terrace.

- Cookery: in English & Spanish (2-3 days).
- Spanish Wine: in English & Spanish.
- Local History & Culture: in English & Spanish.
- Aragonese Architecture: in English & Spanish.
- Walking Tours: in English & Spanish.
- Horse-riding Tours: in English & Spanish.

rooms	14: 11 doubles, 3 suites.
price	€ 130-€ 170. Singles € 110 (full-rate at weekends).
meals	€ 35.
closed	7-22 January.
directions	Barcelona A-7 south for Valencia. Exit junction 34 Reus. N420 Reus, Falset, Mora & Gandesa. There right for Alcañiz, but left in Calaceite to Valderrobres. There, left for Fuentespalda; after 6.2km, right. Track to hotel.

Jemma Markham

tel	+34 978 769015
fax	+34 978 769016
e-mail	torredelvisco@torredelvisco.com
web	www.torredelvisco.com

Hotel

map 7   entry 58

Can Cuadros

Major 3, 25211 Palouet-Massoteres, Lérida, Spain

To describe this 1,000-year-old castle as a mere hotel is to do it an injustice: each room is a step back in time. Josep and Àngels are seeking to relive the traditions of this corner of Catalonia. Bedrooms are full of fascinating artefacts and nothing escapes the hand of history – not even the bathrooms, wittily named Can Felip after the infamous oppressor of the Catalans. The dining room is magical, with an old wine press for a fireplace. You dine on ancient recipes, organic and expertly cooked… all washed down with organic wines and home-made laurel brandy.

- Medieval Cookery: in English & Spanish.
- Furniture Restoration: in English & Spanish.
- Medieval History: in Spanish.
- Enology (wine-making): 45km, in English & Spanish.
- Skiing; trekking; mountaineering: 40km.
- Cava vinyards & bodegas, 45-minute drive.

rooms	8 twins/doubles.
price	€ 50–€ 70. Singles from € 36.
meals	Breakfast from € 5. Lunch/dinner from € 12.
closed	Rarely.
directions	From Barcelona N-II to Cervera. Here, right to Guissona, then right to Massoteres, then follow signs to Palouet.

Josep Arasa

tel	+34 973 294106
e-mail	can_cuadros@airtel.net
web	www.cancuadros.com

Hotel

Casa Guilla

Santa Engracia, Apartado 83, 25620 Tremp, Lérida, Spain

Richard and Sandra Loder have a head for heights and, after returning from Africa, quietly set about restoring the buildings that make up Casa Guilla, perched high on a rocky crag. A fortified Catalan farmhouse, parts of which are 1,000 years old, the house is an amazing labyrinth. There is a large sitting room with an open hearth and a library on the mezzanine floor. The bedrooms are simply but cosily furnished, with heavy old beams and low ceilings. Tuck into big breakfasts and generous dinners – accompanied by that incomparable view.

- Birds, Butterflies & Plants: in Catalan, Spanish & English.
- Geology: in Catalan, Spanish & English.
- Romanesque Architecture: in Catalan, Spanish & English.
- Whitewater rafting & kayaking.
- Winter & summer skiing.
- Rock-climbing & hang-gliding.

rooms	4: 2 doubles, 1 twin, 1 family.
price	Half-board for two €93–€110. Half-board singles from €46.50. VAT included.
meals	Picnic from €4.50. Dinner included.
closed	November-February.
directions	After 1.5km on C-13 from Tremp to Pobla de Segur, left on road signed 'Santa Engracia 10km'. Next to church, reached by own road; parking at house.

Richard & Sandra Loder

tel	+34 973 252080
fax	+34 973 252080
e-mail	info@casaguilla.com
web	www.casaguilla.com

B&B

map 7   entry 60

Fonda Bíayna

Sant Roc 11, 25720 Bellver de Cerdanya, Lérida, Spain

The heart of the village for many generations, this *fonda* proudly upholds its tradition of hospitality. In the restaurant, hearty and delicious regional food and an impressive array of Spanish wines are enjoyed by a fast turnover of visitors and locals alike. Bedrooms have polished wooden floors and are solidly furnished; some on the upper floor open onto a wooden balcony edged with geraniums. The bathrooms are unremarkable but have decent-sized baths. A place for adventurers who like to return to the communal warmth of a village inn.

- Horse-riding: 2km, in English, French & Spanish, € 60 per day.
- 4x4 Routes: in English, French & Spanish, € 60.
- Skiing; caving; canoeing; rafting.
- Cathar castles.
- Thermal spa.
- Romanesque architecture.

rooms	17: 10 doubles, 7 twins.
price	From € 64. Singles from € 46. VAT included.
meals	Lunch/dinner from € 14. VAT included.
closed	Christmas day.
directions	From Barcelona, C-1411. After Cadi tunnel, follow signs for El Seu de Urgell & Bellver. In Bellver, park in Sant Roc square. C/Sant Roc leads to Fonda from the square.

Jordi Solé

tel	+34 973 510475
fax	+34 973 510853
e-mail	fondabiayna@ctv.es
web	www.fondabiayna.com

Inn

Can Jou

La Miana, 17854 Sant Jaume de Llierca, Gerona, Spain

Leave the rest of the world behind. The farm is high on a hill, overlooking miles of forest of oak and beech – wonderful. No wonder Mick and Rosa were inspired to revive this old farmstead in search of the good life: by working the land and restoring the old barn to share it with guests. Bedrooms are simply and attractively furnished with a mix of old and new and lively colour schemes. Rosa's cooking is excellent and many ingredients come from the farm; dinners are friendly affairs around one huge table. For nature without the hotelly extras, head here.

- Horse-trekking: in English, € 12 per hour.
- Six-day Treks from Mountain to Sea: in English, € 800 full-board.
- Hiking routes information.
- Nature reserves, 5km.
- Beaches, 1-hour drive.
- Forest & mountain landscape.

rooms	14 twins/doubles.
price	€ 70–€ 80. VAT included.
meals	Lunch/dinner from € 15.
closed	Rarely.
directions	From Figueres, N-260 to Besalú & Sant Jaume de Llierca. Left into village, then 2nd left into c/Industria. On for 6km along track to house, marked at all junctions.

Mick Peters

tel	+34 972 190263
fax	+34 972 190444
web	www.canjou.com

B&B

map 8   entry 62

El Molí

Mas Molí, 17469 Siurana d'Emporda, Gerona, Spain

El Molí is a modern building, but it more than earns a place in the 'special' category alongside its older Catalan neighbours. The house is modelled on the traditional *mas*, with tiled floors, wooden furniture and big rooms with views to the fields and woods beyond. Maria's food is exceptionally good value; vegetables, chicken and beef come straight from the farm and are accompanied by a good local red wine with an infusion of *hierbas* to finish. At breakfast, try the home-made yogurt and jams. Maria, who speaks excellent English, helps you plan your day.

- Antique Furniture Restoration: 8km, in Spanish.
- Drawing & Painting: 8km, in Spanish.
- Ceramics: 30km, in Spanish.
- Monasterio de San Pere de Rhodas.
- Salvador Dali Museum, Figuere.
- Sunday antiques market.

rooms	6: 1 double, 1 suite, 2 triples, 2 quadruples.
price	€ 55–€ 67. Singles from € 50. VAT included.
meals	Dinner from € 11. VAT included.
closed	Rarely.
directions	A7 exit 4; for Figueres on N-II. After 3 km, right to Vilamalla. There, follow signs to Siurana. Signed in village.

Maria Sanchís Pages

tel	+34 972 525139
fax	+34 972 525139
e-mail	casaelmoli@teleline.es
web	www.girsoft.com/elmoli

B&B

Can Navata

Baseia, 17469 Siurana d'Empordà, Gerona, Spain

Amparo has lived in Siurana all her life and renamed this 19th-century farmhouse after her father's native village. You enter through an invitingly shady porch into the living areas, decorated in the colourful regional style. The bedrooms are furnished with family heirlooms and four have a seasonal theme – we loved the light and airy 'summer' room. Another room has been converted for wheelchair access. This is an excellent place for children: there is a playroom, a big garden and farm animals to meet. You'll find *amistat* here – the Catalan for friendship.

- Golf.
- Costa Brava, 8km.
- Salvador Dalí Museum, 8km.
- Cadaqués - Dalí's house, 30km.
- Romanesque architecture, 5km.
- Ampurias Roman ruins, 10km.

rooms	6 twins/doubles. Also 1 self-catering apartment for 6.
price	From € 60. Apartment from € 120 per day (min. 3 nights).
meals	Dinner from € 12.
closed	Rarely.
directions	From Figueres N-II then GI-31 (C-252) for L'Escala. After 4km right for Siurana. Can Navata on left as you enter Baseia.

Amparo Pagés

tel	+34 972 525174
fax	+34 972 525756
e-mail	apages@teleline.es
web	www.cannavata.com

B&B & self-catering

map 8   entry 64

Can Fabrica

17845 Santa Llogaia del Terri, Gerona, Spain

This characterful 17th-century *masía*, surrounded by fields, woods and Pyrenean views, is your holiday home. Bedrooms are smallish and nicely furnished with old pieces and soft materials that set off the stone walls. The kitchen/dining room is beautifully equipped, the sitting room cosy and there's a pool in the garden. Ramón and Marta have environmentalist leanings, and by planting trees and farming their land have created a blissful corner of peace. A lovely place with a kind, vivacious hostess; one of our favourite places to stay in Spain. *Minimum stay two nights.*

- Horse-riding: 7km.
- Golf: 7km.
- Watersports, 7km.
- Wednesday market, Banyoles.
- Mountain bike hire, 7km.
- Walking trails from door (with maps).

rooms	4: 3 doubles, 1 single.
price	From € 200 per day, € 1,000 per week.
meals	Self-catering.
closed	4 weeks January-February.
directions	Leave A-7 at exit 6 onto C-66 for Banyoles. After 8km bear right for Cornellà del Terri then at r'bout towards Medinya. After 2.5km left to Santa Llogaia; through village, 400m of track to house on left.

Marta Casanovas

tel	+34 972 594629
fax	+34 972 594629
e-mail	canfabrica@terra.es

Self-catering

Hotel Llevant

Francesc de Blanes 5, 17211 Llafranc, Gerona, Spain

This is one of the Costa's most popular independent hotels. Everything sparkles, from bathroom to crockery to the turquoise sea that (almost) laps its way to the door. The bedrooms are all-white, straightforward affairs, large and airy, with every mod con. What makes the hotel special is the restaurant/terrace on the promenade – ever animated, especially come evening *paseo* (stroll) time. What better place to watch the world go by, with the hotel's prize-winning cooking an accompaniment? In high season you are required to have lunch or dinner here.

- Golf.
- Tennis Club: 1km.
- Salvador Dalí Museum, Figueres.
- Botanical Gardens, 2km.
- Route of medieval villages.
- Fish market, 9km.

rooms	24 twins/doubles.
price	Half-board for two €150–€203. VAT included.
meals	Breakfast from €8. Lunch/dinner from €22 set menu, from €36 à la carte. VAT included.
closed	10-30 November.
directions	Barcelona A-7 to exit 9 (San Feliu); past Palamos to Palafrugell. Signs to Llafranc; hotel in centre on sea front. Park in street.

María Carmen Farrarons-Turró

tel	+34 972 300366
fax	+34 972 300345
e-mail	hllevant@arrakis.es

Hotel

map 8   entry 66

Xalet La Coromina

Carretera de Vic 4, 17406 Viladraú, Gerona, Spain

This building dates from the turn of the century when wealthy Catalans built summer retreats away from sticky Barcelona. It has kept its elegant exterior, but has been thoroughly modernised inside. Each bedroom has its own personality with antiques, good bathrooms and stupendous views. And the car rally memorabilia? Gloria's husband, Antonio Zanini, was one of Spain's most successful drivers. The Coromina also prides itself on its food and uses local produce in season. Expect delicious mushroom dishes made with local *setas* when they spring up after the rain.

- Walking Tours: 1km, in English, Spanish, French, first Sunday of month, € 4.
- Polo: 3km, in Spanish, € 20.
- Horse-riding: 3km.
- Medieval City of Vic, 18km.
- Flower Market (Tuesdays).
- Montseny Nature Reserve.

rooms	8 twins/doubles.
price	€ 84–€ 90. Single from € 70.
meals	Lunch/supper from € 25.
closed	26 January-20 February
directions	From Girona C-25. Exit km202, then follow GI-543 to Viladraú. In village towards Vic: hotel on right after 50m.

Gloria Rabat

tel	+34 93 884 9264
fax	+34 93 884 8160
e-mail	xaletcoromina@xaletcoromina.com
web	www.xaletcoromina.com

Hotel

Can Rosich

Apartado de Correos 275, 08398 Santa Susanna, Barcelona, Spain

This old *masía*, hidden away up a thickly wooded valley, is more than two centuries old, yet has been completely rebuilt. Cooking is wholesome, delicious and amazing value – the price includes good Catalan wine. Bedrooms, named after regional birds and animals, are large and comfy. Beds are antique but mattresses new and you'll find a be-ribboned bundle of towels on your duvet – an elegant touch from a gracious hostess. Nearby trains can whizz you to and from Barcelona in just one hour, and you are very close to the beach. A great favourite.

- Botanical Gardens at Blanes, 8km.
- Tordera market, 11km.
- Swimming pool, 1.5km.
- Golf course, 25km.
- Sta. Coloma thermal spa, 25km.
- Modernist architecture, 10km.

rooms	6: 5 doubles, 1 twin.
price	€42–€46.
meals	Breakfast from €6. Supper with wine, from €13.
closed	20-27 December.
directions	From A-7, exit 9 Maçanet; N–II for Barcelona to Santa Susanna; here, right at 1st r'bout for 'nucleo urbano'; signs for 2km to Can Rosich. From Barcelona, C-32 Mataró & Girona; exit 122 Pineda & S. Susanna, then as above.

Montserrat Boter Fors

tel	+34 937 678473
fax	+34 937 678473
e-mail	canrosich@canrosich.com
web	www.canrosich.com

B&B

map 8   entry 68

La Posada del Marqués

Plaza Mayor 4, 24270 Carrizo de la Ribera, León, Spain

There are few places to stay in Spain as special as this old pilgrim's hospital. Carlos Velázquez and his wife graciously greet their guests before showing them to their rooms; set round a first floor gallery, they are filled with family heirlooms. One has a terrace over the cloisters; all are enchanting. The sitting and games rooms downstairs are similarly furnished with comfy armchairs and sofa in front of the hearth. At dinner there's good regional food and wine; afterwards, a post-prandial game of snooker. Kind and erudite hosts in a beguiling setting.

- Nuns Choir, Monastery of Carrizo (daily 9pm).
- Hop harvest – late summer.
- Monday market.
- Local swimming pool.
- Golf course.
- Exhibition of cathedral models.

rooms	11 twins/doubles.
price	€70–€80. Singles from €60. VAT included.
meals	Dinner from €14.
closed	10 January-end-February.
directions	From León, N-120 for Astorga. After 18km, right on LE-442 to Villanueva de Carrizo. Cross river into Carrizo de la Ribera. Ask for Plaza Mayor.

Carlos Velázquez–Duro

tel	+34 987 357171
fax	+34 987 358101
e-mail	marques@aletur.es
web	www.aletur.es/marques

Hotel

La Posada Regia
Calle Regidores 9-11, 24003 León, Spain

This is a bright star in the firmament of newly-opened hotels in Spain. The building first saw the light in 1370 and the dining room incorporates part of an old Roman wall. The warm ochre and beamed reception strikes a welcoming note as you arrive and the staff could not be more friendly. A fine old staircase leads up to the bedrooms which are some of the cosiest and most coquettish that you'll come across. (Avoid the attic rooms in summer.) Bathrooms have robes and embroidered towels. The restaurant is one of León's most renowned.

- Sports, multi-activity.
- Hot-air ballooning.
- Swimming pool & sports centre, 1km.
- Leon Cathedral & Botine's Palace by Gaudi.
- Local market (Wednesday, Saturday).
- Golf course, 15km.

rooms	20: 14 doubles, 6 singles.
price	From €90. Singles from €55. VAT included.
meals	Lunch/supper from €30.
closed	Rarely.
directions	Hotel in town centre 150m from Cathedral. Park in Parking San Marcelo on Plaza de Santo Domingo, then 100m walk to hotel.

Verónica Martínez Díez

tel	+34 987 213173
fax	+34 987 213031
e-mail	marquitos@regialeon.com
web	www.regialeon.com

Hotel

map 6   entry 70

El Prado Mayor

Quintanilla del Rebollar 53, 09568 Merindad de Sotoscueva, Burgos, Spain

The impressive façade of the 16th-century Prado Mayor hides behind a solid arched gateway. Via a small garden with a columned terrace — lovely for summer breakfasts — enter what feels like a warm family home. Here are antiques, marble tops and ornate framed mirrors. Breakfast is delicious; lunch and dinner are stout affairs with home-grown vegetables and good local meats. Your hosts are delightful people who are happy to tailor-make any itinerary for you, and the lush landscape is a well-kept secret that breathes culture and history.

- Walking routes from door.
- Rafting, sailing & canoeing.
- Horse-trekking.
- Personalised itineraries, spring–autumn.
- Villa de Espinosa de Los Monteros, 7km - Tuesday market.
- Ôjo Guarena Caves & Nature Reserve, 7km.

rooms	6 twins/doubles.
price	€48–€54. Singles €36–€42.
meals	Breakfast from €5. Dinner from €12.
closed	Rarely.
directions	From Burgos on N1 to Briviesca. Then towards Oña. There, N–629 for Espinosa de los Monteros. Village 7km after Espinosa de los M. on C-6328 to Reinosa.

Fernando Valenciano Velasco

tel	+34 947 138689
fax	+34 947 138689
e-mail	pradomayor@arrakis.es
web	www.pradomayor.com

B&B

Posada Molino del Canto

Molino del Canto s/n, 09146 Barrio La Cuesta, Burgos, Spain

This 13th-century mill, restored by the young owner Javier, is both authentic and exquisite. The stonework blends perfectly with its surroundings and the style of the simple façade is continued inside. The dark little entrance hall, cool in summer, warm in the colder months, takes you through to a cosy, low-beamed sitting room with a log fire and handmade furniture. Go up the old wooden staircase to discover the bedrooms, a splendid surprise: each has a homely sitting room down and a bedroom up. Breakfast and home-cooked regional food are excellent.

- Horse-riding: 4km, in Spanish, €24.
- Rafting & Canoeing: 9km, June–September.
- Birdwatching: in Spanish & English, no charge.
- Romanesque Art & Architecture: no charge.
- Archaeological palace, 30km.
- Markets, 30km.

rooms	6 twins/doubles.
price	From €75. Singles from €53. VAT included.
meals	Dinner from €19. VAT included.
closed	Rarely.
directions	From Burgos N-623 for Santander. North of Quintanilla de Escalada, at km66, exit for Gallejones. On for Villanueva Rampally. There, left for Arreba. Signed to right after 2.6km.

Javier Morala

tel	+34 947 571368
fax	+34 947 571368

B&B

map 6　entry 72

La Tejera de Fausto

Carretera la Salceda a Sepúlveda km7, 40173 Requijada, Segovia, Spain

The stone buildings of the Tejera de Fausto stand in glorious isolation. It's no coincidence that the roofs are terracotta; tiles (*tejas*) were made here, hence the building's name. Decoration is warm and appealing and bedrooms have no telephone or TV. The restaurant is wonderful, with interconnecting rooms where fires blaze in colder months; specialities are roast lamb, suckling pig and boar. Jaime is a gregarious host and regales you with information about the area. There are often wedding parties at weekends in the summer, so visit on a weekday.

- Horse-riding; quad-biking; hang-gliding; fishing: 10 minute-drive.
- Mediaeval walled village of Pedraza.
- La Granja de San Ildefonso - royal palace.
- Architecture of Segovia.
- Duraton Nature Reserve.
- Enebrajejo Caves.

rooms	9: 7 doubles, 2 suites.
price	€ 75-€ 150.
meals	Lunch/dinner from € 24.
closed	Rarely.
directions	From Segovia, N-110 for Soria to La Salceda. Then left for Pedraza. On left, after Torre Val de San Pedro.

Jaime Armero

tel	+34 921 127087
fax	+34 915 641520
e-mail	info@latejeradefausto.com
web	www.latejeradefausto.com

Hotel

El Zaguán
Plaza de España 16, 40370 Turégano, Segovia, Spain

El Zaguán is every inch the grand Castilian house: in dressed stone, with its own stables and *bodega*, and right on the beautiful town square. Downstairs is a lively bar and dining room: pine beams, wafer bricks and terracotta floors, with beautifully dressed tables and soft lighting. The sitting room has squashy sofas, a woodburner and a view of the castle and you sleep in style; no two bedrooms are the same and they are among the most handsome we've seen. A warm, quiet and cosy hostelry with hardworking, cheery and likeable Mario at the helm.

- Canoeing: 18km, in Spanish & English.
- Horse-riding: 18km, in Spanish & English.
- Speleology (study of caves): 18km, in Spanish & English.
- Turégano Castle.
- Museum of Angels.
- Forestry museum, 3km.

rooms	15: 12 doubles, 3 suites.
price	€ 60–€ 100. Singles € 42–€ 60.
meals	Breakfast from € 5. Lunch from € 21. Dinner from € 18.
closed	22 December-8 January.
directions	From Segovia, N-601 Valladolid. After 7km, right for Turégano & Cantalejo. In main village square.

Mario García
tel	+34 921 501165
fax	+34 921 500776
e-mail	zaguan@el-zaguan.com
web	www.el-zaguan.com

Hotel

map 6   entry 74

El Milano Real

Calle Toleo s/n, 05634 Hoyos del Espino, Ávila, Spain

Surrounded by the Gredos mountains, this unassuming hotel has a Swiss feel, heightened by the carved wood of the balconies and the warm atmosphere within. There is a beautiful ornamental garden and some superb 'themed' suites – Japanese, New York penthouse-style, and English with four-poster. The dining room here draws people like a magnet – not only delicious food, but Francisco has a selection of over 100 favourite wines to choose from, each given his own personal score out of ten. You are 90 minutes from Madrid: perfect for a day trip.

- Wine-tasting: in English & Spanish, €3.50.
- Stargazing & Astronomy: in hotel observatory, in English & Spanish, €15.
- Gredos Mountains National Park.
- Hotel wine cellar.
- Medieval Avila, 50-minute drive.
- Celtic & Roman ruins, 0.5km.

rooms	21: 13 doubles, 8 suites.
price	€70–€145. Singles €65–€135.
meals	Breakfast from €7. Lunch from €30. Dinner from €35.
closed	Rarely.
directions	From Avila N-110 for Bejar & Plasencia. After 6km, N-502 left for Arenas de San Pedro; after 40km, right on C-500 to Hoyos del Espino. Hotel to right.

Francisco Sánchez

tel	+34 920 349108
fax	+34 920 349156
e-mail	info@elmilanoreal.com
web	www.elmilanoreal.com

Hotel

La Posada del Pinar

Pozal de Gallinas s/n, 47450 Pozal de Gallinas, Valladolid, Spain

Exuding quality and charm, La Posada del Pinar captures the essence of Castilla-León. Dating back to the early 17th century, it is idyllically sheltered from any hubbub by 300 acres of pine forest. The sitting room is relaxed and intimate and leads through to an elegant arched dining room with woodburning oven, frequently used to cook mouthwatering roasts. Behind the hotel is the old chapel, whose airy grandeur is perfectly suited to receptions and banquets. Bedrooms, named after local towns famous for *mudéjar* monuments, are large and well furnished.

- Mycology (study of mushrooms): in English & Spanish, autumn, no charge.
- History of Mudéjar Art: in English & Spanish, monthly, no charge.
- Wine-tastings: 15km, in English & Spanish, €5.
- Trekking from house.
- Thermal spa: 7km.
- Mudéjar architecture in Olmedo, 12km.

rooms	19: 2 quadruple, 2 single, 15 twins.
price	€75–€85. Singles €65–€75.
meals	Breakfast from €5. Lunch/dinner from €20.
closed	7-27 January.
directions	From Valladolid, N-620 for Tordesillas, then N-VI for Madrid. Exit km157 for Olmedo to Pozal de Gallinas. Posada signed to right on entering village; 3.2km further.

Ignacio Escribano

tel	+34 983 481004
fax	+34 915 646191
e-mail	info@laposadadelpinar.com
web	www.laposadadelpinar.com

Hotel

map 6   entry 76

Casa Bermeja

Plaza del Piloncillo s/n, 45572 Valdeverdeja, Toledo, Spain

Angela happened upon this big old house in a village that the 20th century seemed to have passed by, and realised a long-held dream – to share it with friends. Luckily for us she later decided to share her home with paying guests too. Architect brother Luis took renovation in hand and Angela, an interior designer, took care of decoration. Beyond the exuberant façade is a coquettish home, with colours inspired by Castille. The sitting and dining rooms have beamed ceilings and terracotta floors, and the bedrooms are attractive, comfortable and quiet.

- Monastery of Guadalupe.
- Medieval town of Toledo.
- Moorish town remains.
- Scenic routes in Tietar & Jerte valleys.
- Walking, riding & fishing.
- Birdwatching region.

rooms	16: 7 doubles, 9 suites.
price	€93–€168. Singles from €73.
meals	Lunch/supper from €18.
closed	Rarely.
directions	From Madrid, N–V/E-90 for Badajoz. Exit at km148 marker for Oropesa. From here, signs to Puente del Arzobispo; then right to Valdeverdeja. In main square, opp. Town Hall (Ayuntamiento), left to house.

Angela González
tel	+34 925 454586
fax	+34 925 454595
e-mail	zabzab@arrakis.es

Hotel

Hostal Descalzos
Calle de los Descalzos 30, 45002 Toledo, Spain

Hostal Descalzos sits high up by the old city wall, yards from El Greco's house. Fittings are modern, furniture is pine, floors are white-tiled, bedspreads are spotless. But it is the view – especially at night when the bridge across the Tagus is illuminated – that you will remember: choose room 11, 12, 21 or 22. The family are quiet, unassuming folk, and serve you breakfast in a tiny downstairs room. At the foot of the hostal is a pretty walled garden with a fountain and flowers – a marvellous place to sit out and watch the sun set over the Meseta.

- Guided Visits of Toledo: 500m, weekly, € 12.
- Swimming pool & jacuzzi on site.
- Toledo Cathedral.
- Trasito Synagogue.
- Church of Santo Tome.
- El Greco Museum.

rooms	12 twins/doubles.
price	€ 45–€ 65. Singles from € 30.
meals	Available locally.
closed	Rarely.
directions	In Toledo, signs to old town. At town walls (Puerta de la Bisagra), right; on with wall on left until signs for hostel to left; signed to right in front of house 'El Greco'.

Julio Luis García

tel	+34 925 222888
fax	+34 925 222888
e-mail	h-descalzos@jet.es
web	www.hostaldescalzos.com

Hotel

map 6   entry 78

Hospedería Rural Salinas de Imón

Calle Real 49, 19269 Imón, Guadalajara, Spain

This elegant house began life as a convent in the 17th century, then became a lowly salt warehouse. The heavy studded door now opens onto a mosaic of different styles and atmospheres. A sitting room vibrates with bright sofas, antiques and huge repro paintings by Luis Gamo Alcalde. Each guest room is themed; one is decorated with signed photos of musicians, another has a Louis XVI-style cradle. A log-fired library leads to a peaceful garden where the towers of the original building rise and a secluded swimming pool blends in with its surroundings.

- Painting: in Spanish, Mondays–Saturdays, € 600, with B&B.
- Furniture Restoration: in English, French & Spanish, Monday–Saturdays, € 600, with B&B.
- Ballroom Dancing: in Spanish, Mondays–Saturdays, € 600, with B&B.
- Medieval town of Atienza.
- Spa (from October 2003).
- Valley of river Salado - with vultures.

rooms	12: 11 doubles, 1 suite.
price	€ 75–€ 150. Singles from € 66.
meals	Lunch from € 23. Dinner from € 23.
closed	Rarely.
directions	From Madrid N-II/E-90 towards Zaragoza. Left to Sigüenza; here take C-110 for Atienza to Imón. Hotel on main square of village.

Jaime Mesallés

tel	+34 949 397311
fax	+34 949 397311
e-mail	sadeimon@teleline.es
web	www.salinasdeimon.com

Hotel

Hotel Valdeoma

19266 Carabias, Guadalajara, Spain

This small hotel, overlooking the mountains of Guadalajara, is unmistakeably modern with fine features that blend beautifully with the older elements of wood and granite. The entrance, with its metal staircase and parquet floor, made by Gregorio himself, gives Valdeoma a lovely informal feel. Bedrooms have been finished in warm colours and have bathrooms of earth-coloured marble. Both dining room and sitting room glow with period furniture, fireplaces and big glass balcony doors. From here, Valdeoma's most precious jewel: the view.

- Spanish language course: €1,200 p.w. full-board.
- Furniture Restoration: in English, €900 p.w. full-board.
- Horse-trekking.
- Hot-air ballooning.
- Microlight flying lessons.
- Medieval towns of Sigüenza & Atienza.

rooms	10 twins/doubles.
price	From €95–€105. Singles from €90.
meals	Dinner from €21.
closed	Rarely.
directions	From Madrid N-II/E-90 for Zaragoza then left for Sigüenza; there CM-110 for Atienza. After 7km left for Carabias. There, left past church, up hill. House at end of narrow street on right.

Gregorio Marañón

tel	+34 600 464309
fax	+34 600 466921
e-mail	valdeoma@airtel.net
web	www.valdeoma.com

Hotel

map 7   entry 80

Hotel Els Frares

Avenida del País Valencià 20, 03811 Quatretondeta, Alicante, Spain

Brian and Pat transformed a 100-year-old ruin to create their village inn and restaurant. The constant flow of visitors adds life and colour to the village; just behind, jagged peaks rise to almost 5,000 feet. Good mattresses ensure deep sleeps, fabrics are bright, and some rooms have their original floor tiles. The cosy dining and sitting rooms are good to return to after a day's trekking (though not at the height of summer!). The menu celebrates local dishes and *tapas*, yet still finds a place for imaginative veggie alternatives; many ingredients are home-grown.

- Guided Walking: in English, September–June, from €440 p.w. half-board.
- Spanish Cookery & Culture: in English, July-August, from €545 p.w. full-board.
- Cuisine, Wine Culture & History: in English, July-August, from €545 p.w. full-board.
- Dramatic mountain scenery.
- Moorish hill forts, 2km.
- Caves, 20km.

rooms	9 doubles.
price	€48–€60. Singles €32.
meals	Breakfast from €5. Lunch/dinner from €18.
closed	8-25 January.
directions	From Alicante A-7, junc. 70, onto A-36 Alcoi; CV-70 Benilloba, left to Gorga; sharp right through village & 5km to hamlet of Quatretondeta.

Patricia Fagg

tel	+34 965 511234
fax	+34 965 511200
e-mail	elsfrares@terra.es
web	www.mountainwalks.com

Hotel

El Chato Chico

Plaza de la Iglesia 6, 03788 Beniaya - Vall d'Alcalá, Alicante, Spain

At the last count Beniaya had just 14 inhabitants! Yet in the Middle Ages it was important enough for the Imam of the Moorish King Al-Azraq to have built himself a residence next to the mosque. The Walmsleys have brought this building back to life – you can see one of the original Moorish arches in the sitting room. The guesthouse has a snug feel; bedrooms and public rooms are smallish but your well-being is guaranteed thanks to good beds and the most peaceful of settings. At dinner don't expect purely Spanish food but do expect something special.

- Cookery: 4km, in English, June, July, December, January, from € 600 (4 days).
- Painting: 4km, in English, from € 150 (2 days).
- Valencia.
- Guadalest mountain village.
- La Cova de Rull caves.
- Moorish towns & castles.

rooms	5 twins/doubles.
price	€ 44–€ 56. Singles € 28–€ 34. VAT included.
meals	Dinner with wine, € 18–€ 20. VAT included.
closed	Rarely.
directions	Alicante, for S. Vicente; A-36 Alcoy, then N-340. 3km before Alcoy, right to Benilloba & Gorga. At Gorga junc. for Facheca. Just before Tollos, sign to Beniaya (4km).

Paul Walmsley

tel	+34 96 551 4451
fax	+34 96 551 4161
e-mail	elchatochico@wanadoo.es

B&B

map 7   entry 82

La Casa Vieja

Calle Horno 4, 46842 Rugat, Valencia, Spain

This peaceful house combines 450 years of old stones with a contemporary feel for volumes and shapes. There are original arches, columns, twisty beams, ancient floor tiles, a well in the lounge and views to the orange-clad hillsides. A double-height sitting area faces an immense inglenook where deep sofas hug you as you sip your welcome sherry before dining, indoors or out. Bedrooms are full of character and country antiques, with kettles, tea and coffee to remind you of home. Cooking follows the seasons; market-fresh produce from the new restaurant.

- Painting: in English.
- Horse-riding: 2km, in English.
- Golf Tuition: 15km, in English.
- Hot-air ballooning.
- Mountain walking, 1km.
- Ice caves at Mariola National Park.

rooms	7: 6 doubles, 1 suite.
price	€76–€118. Singles from €60.
meals	Dinner from €28.
closed	Christmas & New Year.
directions	From Valencia A-7 south, then exit 60. From Alicante exit 61 on A-7 northbound. N-332 for Gandia; exit onto CV-60 for Albaida. Exit for Terrateig, Montechelvo, Ayelo de Rugat & Rugat. Through Montechelvo; Rugat 2nd village to left, signed.

Maris Andres Watson

tel	+34 962 814013
fax	+34 962 814013
e-mail	info@lacasavieja.com
web	www.lacasavieja.com

B&B

Casa Salto de Caballo

La Fontañera s/n, 10516 Valencia de Alcántara, Cáceres, Spain

Follow a narrow road across glorious, rolling hills to the furthest reach of the province of Cáceres. Eva was so taken with it all that she left Germany to restore this elegant village house. The old floor tiles and shutters remain, along with good solid comfort and a lack of gimmickry. And it is all beautifully clean. Eva prepares innovative vegetarian meals (she is a nutritionist) and simple, *tapas*-style suppers – or you might prefer to walk into Portugal for dinner! Generous hostess, generous prices and as far from the madding crowd as you could wish to be.

- Week-long Walking Tour: in English, July-September, €380.
- Horse-riding: 5km, in Spanish, €80 per day.
- Yoga: in English & Spanish, July-September, €80 per day.
- Pottery: in English, €90 per day (from 2004).
- Natural swimming pool, 5km.
- Golf, 5km.

rooms	5 doubles.
price	€45–€50. VAT included.
meals	Lunch/dinner from €12.
closed	Occasionally in winter.
directions	From Cáceres N-521 for Portugal; through Valencia de Alcántara, then right for San Pedro. After 2km, right for La Fontañera; last house on left in village, signed.

Eva Speth

tel	+34 927 580865
fax	+34 927 580865
e-mail	saltocaballo@gmx.net

B&B

map 5   entry 84

Casa Manadero

Calle Manadero 2, 10867 Robledillo de Gata, Cáceres, Spain

This is a welcoming hostelry where you can self-cater, with a warm and rustic style. It is in one of the region's prettiest towns, surrounded by forests of oaks, olive groves and vineyards. The tiny restaurant has heavy old beams, delicate lighting and excellent regional food – Caridad has pillaged the family recipe books for your benefit. Apartments vary in size and layout following the dictates of the original building; they all are centrally heated, with fully-equipped kitchens and good views. This is a place which is actively helping to preserve regional differences.

- Distillation, Making Local Spirits: in Spanish, autumn & winter, € 100.
- Jam-making: in Spanish, autumn, € 50.
- Nature reserve & waterfalls, 5km.
- Natural pond for swimming, 5-minute drive.
- Local wine cellars.
- Architecture of Robledillo de Gata.

rooms	5 apartments: 4 for 2-4, 1 for 4-6.
price	€ 40–€ 75 per apartment per night. Singles € 30.
meals	Breakfast from € 5. Lunch/dinner from € 10.50 set menu.
closed	Rarely.
directions	Navalmoral de la Mata to Plasencia C-551. Here, C-204 Pozuelo de Zarzón; 100m after village, turn for Robledillo. 30km to village.

Caridad Hernández

tel	+34 927 671118
fax	+34 927 671173
e-mail	info@casamanadero.com
web	www.casamanadero.com

Self-catering

Finca Buen Vino

Los Marines, 21293 Aracena, Huelva, Spain

Set in a divinely isolated spot amid thick woods, you'd never guess Buen Vino was less than 30 years old. Many of the materials Sam and Jeannie used were shipped in from far corners of Spain; the arched doors and the staircase have that seductive patina that only time can give. Jeannie is a Cordon Bleu cook and our candlelit dinner on the terrace was superb. The guest rooms are all different – one has a bathtub with a view – and share a drawing room and study. There are also three cottages to rent, each with its own pool, and the pretty village is a 20-minute walk.

- Cookery: March & October, €900 (6 nights full-board) p.p.
- Guided Walks (6+ people).
- Aracena Caves, 8km.
- In heart of Aracena nature reserve.
- Swimming pool with poolhouse (May-October).
- Seasonal organic veg from garden & home-produced Serrano ham.

rooms	4 doubles. Also 3 self-catering cottages.
price	From €160. Singles €80. Ring for self-catering prices.
meals	Dinner from €30.
closed	July-August; Christmas & New Year.
directions	From Sevilla N-630 north 37km, then N-433 for Portugal & Aracena. Los Marines 6km west of Aracena. Finca 1.5km west of Los Marines, to right at km95 marker.

Sam & Jeannie Chesterton

tel	+34 959 124034
fax	+34 959 501029
e-mail	buenvino@facilnet.es
web	www.buenvino.com

B&B & self-catering

map 9   entry 86

Molino Rio Alájar

Finca Cabezo del Molino s/n, 21340 Alájar, Huelva, Spain

Come for the peace, the delicious ham or, in November, for the mushrooms. The self-catering stone cottages are as much part of the natural scenery of this secret valley as the cork trees which surround it. Each has a terrace, and is finished to a high standard by the Dutch owners, Peter and Monica. The larger houses have underfloor heating and log fires and steep stairs to the upper sleeping area. The smaller house is open-plan and has no kitchen but you can cook in the reception building. There is a beautiful pool, and plenty of places to eat in Alájar.

- Spanish lessons.
- Guided Walks.
- Furniture Decoration: in Spanish, spring.
- Caves of Aracena, 13km.
- Mosque at Almonaster la Real, 13km.
- Donkey rides.

rooms	5 houses for up to 6.
price	€ 460–€ 770 per week.
meals	Self-catering.
closed	Rarely.
directions	From Sevilla, N-630 for Mérida. Then N-433 to Aracena. Left on A-470 to Alájar. After Alájar, at km13/14, left & follow signs.

Peter Jan Mulder

tel	+34 959 501282
fax	+34 959 125766
e-mail	rioalajar@wanadoo.es
web	www.molinorioalajar.com

Self-catering

Las Navezuelas

A-432 km 43.5, Apartado 14, 41370 Cazalla de la Sierra, Sevilla, Spain

A place of peace and great natural beauty, Las Navezuelas is a 16th-century olive mill on a farm set in 136 hectares of green meadows, oak forest and olive groves. The house is pure Andalucía with beams and tiles; the garden is a southern feast of palms and orange trees, rambling wisteria and jasmine. Rooms are fresh, light and simple and there is a welcoming dining room with log fires in winter. The menu includes delicious local dishes made almost exclusively with ingredients from the farm and the friendly young owners go out of their way to help and give advice.

- Birdwatching Tours: on farm & 15km, in English, French & Italian.
- Pottery: 3km.
- Flamenco Dance & Guitar.
- Spanish language.
- Unique eco-system of Dehesa & biosphere reserve.
- Old mines in Cerro del Hierro.

rooms	6: 4 doubles, 2 suites. Also 4 self-catering studios & 1 apartment.
price	From €55–€65. Singles from €48.
meals	Lunch/supper from €15.
closed	7 January-25 February.
directions	From Sevilla A-431 to Cantillana. Here take A-432 for El Pedroso & Cazalla. Pass km43 marker; after 500m, right at sign for Las Navezuelas.

Luca Cicorella

tel	+34 95 4884764
fax	+34 95 4884594
e-mail	navezuela@arrakis.es
web	www.lasnavezuelas.com

B&B & self-catering

map 10   entry 88

Casa el Marqués

c/ En medio 40-42, 41950 Castilleja de la Cuesta, Sevilla, Spain

There is a strong sense of being hidden away here: your holiday house is tucked behind the high wall of the Casa de Cultura, in the grounds of a former olive mill. Enter a simply furnished house, with cool tiled floors and period furniture, whose two bedrooms, one with a balcony, are clean and uncluttered. Downstairs are the bathroom and living room, with furniture outside should you wish to spill into the sun. Those who like to escape the noise and dust of the city will relish the prospect of taking a dip in the pool – an added bonus. *Private parking.*

- Guided Visits to Sevilla: 3km.
- Guided Visits to Torrequemada Olive Grove & Mill: 3km.
- Doñana National Park, 30-minute drive.
- Own pool.
- Golf course.
- Horse-riding.

rooms	Self-catering house for 4.
price	€ 109-€ 180 per day.
meals	Restaurant 5-minute walk.
closed	Rarely.
directions	Sevilla-Huelva A-49. At km3, exit for Castilleja. Over 1st r'bout, then left. Next r'bout, left onto main street. Right at *Telepizza*, for Casa de Cultura. Next to Casa de Cultura, behind high wall.

Macarena Fernandez-Palacio

tel	+34 629 791188
fax	+34 954 160419
e-mail	informacion@casaelmarques.com
web	www.casaelmarques.com

Self-catering

La Casa Grande

Maldonado 10, 11630 Arcos de la Frontera, Cádiz, Spain

Set on the edge of whitewashed Arcos, this is a spectacular site. At night, from its terrace, you look out to floodlit churches and the vast surrounding plain. The house is 300 years old and contains many original features. In true *Andaluz* style, a colonnaded patio is the axis around which the house turns; reception rooms lead off to all sides. The cosy lounge is also a library with thousands of books, some written by Elena. Decoration is stylish and homely, with gorgeous bedrooms. Take breakfast or a light *tapas* supper on the unforgettable terrace!

- Andalucian Art & Culture Tour: in English, for 2: €55/€80 half/full day.
- Intensive Spanish: in English & Spanish, €30 (3 hours), €50 (5 hours).
- Walking tours: in English.
- Mountain bikes for hire.
- Jerez bodegas, 30km.
- Grazalema National Park, 26km.

rooms	6: 4 doubles, 2 suites for 4.
price	€69–€121. Singles from €57.
meals	Breakfast from €7. Lunch/dinner €18–€20.
closed	13 January–13 February.
directions	In Arcos follow signs to Parador. Park in square in front of Parador & walk to end of c/Escribano (just to left of Parador). Right & Casa Grande is 2nd hotel in street. Number 10.

Elena Posa Farrás

tel	+34 956 703930
fax	+34 956 717095
e-mail	info@lacasagrande.net
web	www.lacasagrande.net

B&B

map 10   entry 90

El Nobo

Apartado 46, 29480 Gaucín, Málaga, Spain

Gaucín has long been popular among the ex-pat community and this is one of the area's most gorgeous homes. The position is amazing: from the shaded terrace you can see Gibraltar, the Straits and the mountains of Africa. The gardens are awash with colour... and stunning pool (pictured). The drawing room pays full homage to that view-of-views thanks to enormous French windows: an enchanting spot at breakfast and dinner. The bedrooms are flamboyant and Sally is a gregarious and entertaining hostess – her *tapas* are delicious. *Credit card payment incurs supplement.*

- Painting, Spirit of Andalucia: on site & in Morocco, in English, September, €1,095.
- Morocco Tours: Tangiers, 1-3 days.
- Cookery.
- Walking Tours.
- Natural History Tours.
- Tennis court & pool.

rooms	4: 1 double, 2 twins, 1 suite. Also 1 self-catering cottage for 2.
price	€108–€118. Singles from €60. VAT included.
meals	Full English breakfast, all drinks & tapas included.
closed	July-Aug; Christmas/New Year.
directions	Málaga-Cádiz N-340; right to Manilva & on to Gaucín. Right at T-junction for 500m. Where 'La Fructosa' sign points left, sharp right downhill. 1km on left.

Sally Von Meister

tel	+34 952 151303
fax	+34 952 117207
e-mail	info@elnobo.co.uk
web	www.elnobo.co.uk

B&B & self-catering

Banu Rabbah

Sierra Bermeja s/n, 29490 Benarrabá, Málaga, Spain

Benarrabá is named after the Berber tribesman who first settled here – the Banu Rabbah of the hotel's name. What makes this place special is its exhilarating position: 2,000 feet up with a magnificent sweep of mountain, white village and hillsides. The building has a cumbersome design but wins points for its bedrooms with generous terraces. Hand-painted wooden beds and bright bedspreads add a merry note and French windows bring in the light and the view. The restaurant features local produce: try the hot gazpacho and the local almond cakes for dessert.

- 4x4 Off-roading: 20km, in English & Spanish, € 27.
- Wildflower Walks: 5km, in English & Spanish, spring.
- Astrology & Holistic Health Consultations: 5-15km, in English & German, € 60.
- Painting courses planned - ask for details.
- Local caves, Roman ruins & nature reserve.
- Friday market.

rooms	12 twins/doubles.
price	€ 55-€ 60. Singles from € 47.
meals	Breakfast from € 3. Lunch from € 12. Supper from € 15.
closed	Rarely.
directions	From Málaga N-340 for Cádiz. Then A-377 via Manilva to Gaucín. Here towards Ronda on A-369; after 4.5km, right to Benarrabá. Signed.

Jesús García

tel	+34 952 150288
fax	+34 952 150005
e-mail	hotel@hbenarraba.es
web	www.hbenarraba.es

Hotel

 map 10   entry 92

Molino del Santo

Bda. Estación s/n, 29370 Benaoján, Málaga, Spain

Pauline and Andy moved south in search of the good life, and restored a century-old mill in a spectacular area. Rooms and restaurant wear local garb – terracotta tiles, beams, rustic chairs; the best rooms have private terraces. Their reputation for good Spanish food is established: most hotel guests are British but the Spanish flock in at weekends. Staff and owners are generous with advice on walks from the hotel. Fresh flowers everywhere and a delicious pool, perfect for families. The Molino gets the balance just right between friendliness and efficiency.

- Guided Walks: in English.
- English Language: 15km.
- Horse-riding: 20km, in Spanish.
- Paragliding & Adventure Sports: in Spanish, with a little English.
- Ronda.
- Grazalema Nature Park.

rooms	18: 15 doubles, 3 suites.
price	€ 80–€ 220. Singles € 62–€ 200. VAT included.
meals	Lunch from € 10. Dinner from € 20.
closed	Mid-November-mid-February.
directions	From Ronda, C-339/A-473 Sevilla; after km118 marker, left for Benaoján. After 10km, having crossed railway & river bridges, left to station & follow signs.

Andy Chapell

tel	+34 952 167151
fax	+34 952 167327
e-mail	molino@logiccontrol.es
web	www.andalucia.com/molino

Hotel

El Tejar

Calle Nacimiento 38, 29430 Montecorto, Málaga, Spain

El Tejar looks out from a hillside near Ronda to a panorama of almond groves and jagged peaks. The house is the highest in the village and is made up of a deliciously labyrinthine series of spaces on many levels; the decoration is intimate, colourful, southern, and there are masses of books and magazines too. Andalucian dinners are served at a candlelit table; wine and conversation flow easily. Guy has written books on walking and will take you to the most enchanting places. The views from the terrace are sublime. *English, French, German, Spanish spoken.*

- Guided Walking: spring, autumn, winter, from €30.
- Guided Historical Walking Tour of Ronda: from €30.
- Accompanied trips to Seville (+ walking tour of Santa Cruz & tapas lunch): from €50.
- Shiatsu & Massage: from €30.
- Day trips by jeep to 'white' villages & Grazalema Park: from €30.
- Horse-riding: from €35.

rooms	4: 1double, 2 twins, 1 suite.
price	From €70. Singles from €50. VAT included. May, June, Sept, house rented from €975 weekly.
meals	Breakfast from €4. Picnic from €7.50. Dinner with all drinks, from €25. No meals Saturday/Sunday.
closed	May-September (house rented).
directions	Round Ronda on A-376. After 20km, right into Montecorto. At top of village via track thru pines. Ask for 'la casa del inglés' if lost!

Guy Hunter-Watts

tel	+34 952 184053
fax	+34 952 184053
e-mail	eltejar@mercuryin.es
web	www.rusticblue.com/zc111.htm

B&B & self-catering

map 10　entry 94

Alavera de los Baños

San Miguel s/n, 29400 Ronda, Málaga, Spain

A charming hotel at the heart of the old Tanners Quarter – sheep-grazed pastures to one side, cobbled ascents to hilltop Ronda on the other. You are right next to what was the first public baths of the Moorish citadel. Christian and Inma have created a building that is Hispano-Spanish in feel, and are the nicest hosts. Smallish rooms have an oriental feel; terracotta shower rooms are delightful. Do book a terrace room which leads to a little verdant garden and delicious pool. Breakfasts are different each day and dinners have a Moorish slant. *Children under two welcome.*

- Advanced Spanish: € 15 per hour.
- Horse-riding: in town, in English & Spanish.
- Walking; climbing; kayaking; hot-air ballooning: in town, English, Spanish, German.
- 13th-century Moorish spa baths.
- Roman ruins at Acinipo.
- Oldest bullring in Spain, Ronda.

rooms	10 twins/doubles.
price	€ 70-€ 80. Singles from € 50. VAT included.
meals	Lunch/dinner from € 22.
closed	December & January.
directions	In Ronda, directly opposite Parador hotel, take calle Rosmario. Right at end & down hill to Fuente de los Ocho Caños. Here left, then 1st right to Arab Baths; hotel next door. Park here.

Christian Reichardt

tel	+34 952 879143
fax	+34 952 879143
e-mail	alavera@ctv.es
web	www.andalucia.com/alavera

Hotel

Hotel Cerro de Híjar

Cerro de Híjar s/n, 29109 Tolox, Málaga, Spain

This hotel is in a wonderful, remote position, on a bluff 2,000 feet above sea level. There is a terrific sense of light and space throughout, enhanced by creamy stucco walls and attractive furniture; modern paintings and prints, some by Andalucía's best artists, hang on every wall. Bedrooms are large, beautifully finished and dazzlingly clean. You'll eat and drink well here for the cooking is inspired – traditional Andalucían with a modern touch. Martin, Guillermo and Eugenio run the place in an eco-friendly manner. A memorably welcoming place.

- Spanish: in English & Spanish, € 200.
- Andalucian Cookery: in English & Spanish, € 180.
- Flamenco Dancing: in English & Spanish, € 180.
- Natural History & Outdoor Pursuits: in English & Spanish, € 300.
- Fuente Amargosa spa, 2.5km.
- Situated in biosphere reserve.

rooms	18: 5 doubles, 9 twins, 4 suites.
price	€ 67–€ 105. Singles from € 59.
meals	Lunch/supper from € 24.
closed	Rarely.
directions	From Málaga, Cártama road. Filter right to Coín, then onto A-366 for Ronda. Left to Tolox, through village to Balneario (spa), then right up hill for 2.5km to hotel.

Guillermo Gonzalez

tel	+34 952 112111
fax	+34 952 710395
e-mail	cerro@cerrodehijar.com
web	www.cerrodehijar.com

Hotel

map 10   entry 96

Hotel Posada del Canónigo

Calle Mesones 24, 29420 El Burgo, Málaga, Spain

Your arrival in the mountain village of El Burgo will be memorable – little visited, it will give you as real a taste of Andalucían mountain life as can be found anywhere. This grand old village house is another good reason for coming. Bedrooms are simple with tiled floors, old bedsteads and lots of family things. It is all spotless and your charming hosts are proud of every last corner. There is a small dining room leading to a little patio where you breakfast in the morning sun, and a newly opened *bodega*-style restaurant where local dishes are on offer.

- Horse-trekking in hills: 6km, in Spanish, € 12 per hour.
- 4x4 Off-roading: 1km, in Spanish & English, € 65 per day.
- Canyoning (adventure sport): 1km, in English & Spanish, € 53 for 3 hours.
- Caving: 1km, in English & Spanish, € 55 for 4 hours.
- Ronda, 24km.
- Sierra de las Nieves - biosphere reserve.

rooms	12 twins/doubles.
price	€ 54–€ 60. Singles from € 39. VAT included.
meals	Lunch/supper from € 11.
closed	24 December.
directions	From Torremolinos to Cártama then on to Calea, Alozaina, Yunquera & El Burgo. Right into village & ask; hotel next to San Agustín church.

Álvaro Pérez

tel	+34 952 160185
fax	+34 952 160185
e-mail	reservascanonigo@telefonica.net
web	www.laposadadelcanonigo.com

Hotel

Molino de las Pilas

Ctra. Vieja de Ronda s/n, 29327 Teba, Málaga, Spain

Built in 1882, the mill was in ruins when Pablo decided to restore; it took him three years. Extremely comfortably furnished in an attractive rustic style, it has good beds and fine bathrooms. What makes it unforgettable is the remarkable restaurant in the mill itself. All the old workings are still in place: great grindstones for mashing the olives, massive beamed press and huge *tintajas* set in the floor to store the oil. Paco's cooking is remarkable: delightful salads, superb fish, fabulous marinaded partridge – at amazingly reasonable prices. Very special.

- The World of Olive Oil: in English, €60 per day.
- Andalucian Cookery: in English, €60 per day.
- Massage: in English, €60 per day.
- Introduction to Aromatherapy: in English, €70.
- Moorish castle & history museum, 2km.
- Cave paintings & carvings, 10km.

rooms	6 doubles.
price	€60-€70. Singles from €55. VAT included.
meals	Lunch/dinner from €20.
closed	10-31 January.
directions	From Málaga, A-357 for Campillos. After Ardales, cross bridge at lake, left at km11 to Teba (ignore 1st road to Ronda & Teba, signed at km19). After 6km, right at petrol station, up hill. Signed to left after 1km.

Pablo Moreno Aragón

tel	+34 952 748622
fax	+34 952 748647
e-mail	info@molinodelaspilas.com
web	www.molinodelaspilas.com

Inn

map 10   entry 98

Cortijo Valverde

Ctra. Alora-Antequera km 35.5, 29500 Álora, Málaga, Spain

This is rural Spain at its best. The 40 acres of land around Valverde are still farmed (fields of sunflowers, olive groves and citrus trees surround you) and the farmhouse has a traditional, rustic feel. In one direction the house looks up at the Torcal; in the other, to whitewashed Álora. Rod's excellent cooking makes full use of fresh produce. After aperitifs on the terrace, try the grilled goat's cheese or flambéd prawns and relax in the pleasant atmosphere: Rod and Moyra are the warmest of hosts. Bedrooms are in their own *casitas* and are comfortable and stylish.

- Horse-riding, all levels: 15-minute drive, €150 (5 days).
- Spanish: in Spanish, November-March, €170 (5.5 days).
- El Chorro gorge & lakes.
- El Torcal mountains.
- Own large pool.
- Moorish hill village of Álora.

rooms	7: 3 doubles, 4 twins.
price	From €96. Singles €66.
meals	Lunch from €8; dinner €28.
closed	12 January-7 February.
directions	From Málaga, A-357 for Campillos, then A-343 to Álora. Don't go into village. Cross river up to T-junc. by Bar Los Caballos, then left for Valle de Abdalajis. Pass km35.5 & follow sign to right for Tierra Nueva. After 300m, sharp left up to Cortijo.

Moyra & Rod Cridland

tel	+34 952 112979
fax	+34 952 112979
e-mail	cortijovalverde@mercuryin.es
web	www.cortijovalverde.com

B&B

Casa Rural Domingo

Arroyo Cansino 4, 29500 Álora, Málaga, Spain

Domin and Cynthia are friendly folk with an infectious *joie de vivre*. They were inspired when they chose this plot: high above Álora, with marvellous views of the Ronda Sierra. Guests can choose between B&B or self-catering apartments; our choice would be one of the B&B rooms: large, with comfortable beds, bright rugs and terracotta floors. Life in the warmer months centres on the poolside terrace and the atmosphere is relaxed; guests mingle easily, perhaps for a game of boules or a barbecue. Children are positively liked here, rather than tolerated.

- Canyoning (adventure sport): 50km, Spanish, English, Flemish, French, Apr–Oct, €50.
- Rafting: 40km, in Spanish, Flemish, English, French, mid-May–mid-September, €40.
- Walking & Painting Tours with Artist: 5km, in English, Spanish, Swedish, €55 half day.
- Body & Mind Workout: 2km, in English, Flemish, Oct/Nov, €220 p.p. (for 4); €150 (6).
- Horse-trekking – for adults & children.
- Flamenco shows (Friday/Saturday), 3km.

rooms	5 twins/doubles. Also self-catering apartments.
price	€60–€75. Singles €39. VAT included.
meals	Restaurant 1km.
closed	December–January
directions	Málaga airport, N-340 Algeciras. After 500m, right for Churriana & Coín. 2nd roundabout, right to Cártama; A-357 for Campillos. 16km on, right for Álora. T-junc., right; after 200m, left. At next T-junction track to farm.

Cynthia Doms

tel	+34 952 119744
fax	+34 952 119744
e-mail	casadomingo@airtel.net
web	www.casaruraldomingo.com

B&B & self-catering

map 10   entry 100

La Posada del Torcal

Carretera La Hoya-La Higuera, 29230 Villanueva de la Concepción, Málaga, Spain

A fetching small hotel a short drive from the Torcal National Park, whose base elements – tile, beam and woodwork – are true to local rustic tradition: inside and out feels thoroughly *Andaluz*. Open-plan bedrooms, dedicated to different Spanish artists, allow you to sip your drink from a corner bath yet not miss a second of the amazing views beyond. Underfloor heating warms in winter, Casablanca fans cool in summer. Many of the dishes on the menu are local/Spanish but there are a number of more familiar-sounding ones, too.

- Painting: in English.
- Guided walks: in English.
- Tennis & all-year heated pool on site.
- Horse-riding from hotel.
- El Chorro gorges, 25km.
- Ancient town of Antequera, 25km.

rooms	10: 9 twins/doubles, 1 suite.
price	€ 160–€ 180. Singles from € 110.
meals	Lunch/dinner from € 30 à la carte. VAT included.
closed	Rarely.
directions	Málaga N-331 Antequera, exit 148 for Casabermeja. There, right for Almogía; next left to Villanueva. At top of village, left at junction; after 1.5km right for La Joya & La Higuera. Hotel 3km on left.

Michael Soffe

tel	+34 952 031177
fax	+34 952 031006
e-mail	posadatorcal@codesat.net
web	www.eltorcal.com/PosadaTorcal

Hotel

Hotel Paraíso del Mar

Prolongación de Carabeo 22, 29780 Nerja, Málaga, Spain

This resort town of the Costa del Sol is hardly an auspicious beginning when searching for that 'special' hotel, but the Paraíso is just that. In a quieter corner of town, it stands at the edge of a cliff looking out to sea. The remarkable terraced gardens drop down towards the beach: jasmine, palms and bananas give it a southern air. Many rooms have a view and some a terrace; ask for one of the quietest. Beneath are a sauna and a hot-tub dug out of rock. It is all run on solar energy and is just the place to recharge your batteries and still survive the *costa*.

- Spanish: from 5 May, €288 (intensive 2 weeks); from €34 per lesson (for 2).
- Spanish, One-to-one: Mondays, €28 per lesson.
- Caves of Nerja, 4km.
- Village of Frigiliana, 6km.
- Large sports centre, 1km.
- Marina, 12km.

rooms	17: 10 twins/doubles, 7 suites.
price	€58–€132. Singles €49–€132.
meals	Restaurants nearby.
closed	Mid-November–mid-December.
directions	From Málaga N-340 for Motril. Arriving in Nerja follow signs to Parador; Paraíso next door.

Enrique Caro Bernal

tel	+34 952 521621
fax	+34 952 522309
e-mail	info@hispanica-colint.es
web	www.hotelparaisodelmar.com

Hotel

map 10   entry 102

El Cortijo del Pino

Fernán Núñez 2, La Loma, 18659 Albuñuelas, Granada , Spain

Albuñuelas is a fetching little place surrounded by citrus groves. El Cortijo del Pino sits high on a bluff above and takes its name from the 200-year-old Aleppo pine that stands sentinel over the house and valley. The sober lines of the building have an Italian feel and the sandy tones which soften the façade change with each passing hour. James is a painter and his artist's eye, combined with Antonia's flair for interior decoration, has helped create a gorgeous home. Bedrooms are big, beamed and terracotta-tiled with comfortable beds and excellent bathrooms.

- Painting: in English & Spanish, May & September, € 720 p.w.
- Swimming pool in gardens.
- Horse-riding.
- Walking trails.
- Alhambra Palace, 1-hour drive.
- Sierra Nevada - skiing.

rooms	5: 4 twins, 1 single.
price	From € 75. Singles from € 40.
meals	Restaurants close by.
closed	Rarely.
directions	From Málaga towards Granada. Before Granada motorway to Motril, exit 153 for Albuñuelas. Opposite bus stop, right & follow steep road to house.

James Connel

tel	+34 958 776257
fax	+34 958 776350
e-mail	cortijodelpino@eresmas.com
web	www.elcortijodelpino.official.ws

B&B

Hotel Reina Cristina

Calle Tablas 4, 18002 Granada, Spain

A big, 19th-century townhouse, close to the cathedral and the bustling, pedestrianised Bib-Rambla square. The larger rooms are set round a cool courtyard with a neo-*mudéjar* ceiling, a fountain, geometric tiles, aspidistras and marble columns – all of it in sympathy with tradition and climate. The dining room has the original Art Deco fittings and a series of photos from the period when Spain's most revered poet, Garcia Lorca, lived. Eat in at least once – the Rincón de Lorca restaurant was recently voted the top hotel eatery in town.

- Scenic & Cultural Tours.
- Granada's old quarter.
- La Alhambra Palace & Cathedral.
- Alpujarra region, 1-hour drive.
- Walking & mountain sports in Sierra Nevada, 35-minute drive.
- 'Costa Tropical' beaches, 1-hour drive.

rooms	43 twins/doubles.
price	€ 88–€ 100. Singles from € 70.
meals	Breakfast from € 7. Lunch/supper from € 21.
closed	Rarely.
directions	From A-92 exit 128 onto Mendez Nuñez (becomes Avenida Fuentenueva). Just before Hotel Granada Center, right into Melchor Almagro (becomes Carril del Picón). Left at end into c/Tablas. On left. Private parking.

Federico Jiménez González

tel	+34 958 253211
fax	+34 958 255728
e-mail	clientes@hotelreinacristina.com
web	www.hotelreinacristina.com

Hotel

map 10   entry 104

Cortijo La Haza

Adelantado 119, 14970 Iznajar, Córdoba, Spain

An old farmhouse in the olive belt that stretches from here across nearly half of Andalucía. Tim and Keith, quiet and friendly, left teaching and catering to set up in this remote spot. The 'rustic' feel of a traditional *cortijo* has been beautifully preserved: walls have a rough render, bedsteads are wrought iron and older country pieces have been restored. Bedrooms have Egyptian cotton sheets, fluffy towels and their own bath or shower rooms. The dining room is cosy, but in good weather you will spill out into the courtyard. Vegetarians are well catered for.

- Iznajar Lake.
- Park Natural 'Sierra Subbética'.
- La Alhambra, Granada, 1-hour drive.
- Pottery at La Rambla.
- Costa del Sol beaches, 1-hour drive.
- Washington Irving route.

rooms	5: 3 doubles, 2 twins.
price	From €67. Singles from €57.
meals	Dinner from €17.
closed	Rarely.
directions	From Málaga airport, N-340 for Málaga (Antequera). Then N-331 & A-359 for Granada. After 24km, exit 1 onto A-333 for Iznajar. After km55 marker, left on CV-174 for 100m, left by small school for 2.6km. Signed to right.

Tim Holt & Keith Tennyson

tel	+34 957 334051
e-mail	info@cortijolahaza.com
web	www.cortijolahaza.com

B&B

Maria de Molina

Plaza del Ayuntamiento s/n, 23400 Úbeda, Jaén, Spain

In the heart of Úbeda is an imposing Renaissance square – its finest *palacete* has been converted into a small, coquettish and very comfortable hotel. The building surrounds a courtyard, to one side of which is an enormous dining room that seats up to 600; you, however, dine in a more intimate one, or on the fountain-graced patio in summer. The restaurant serves very good fish and roast meats. Bedrooms are excellent and each individually decorated, and staff are attentive and charming. This hotel is making waves and we recommend it wholeheartedly.

- Medieval town of Úbeda.
- Renaissance architecture.
- Renaissance dinners.
- Cazorla National Park.
- Historic re-enactments in town.
- Renaissance village of Baeza.

rooms	20: 18 twins/doubles, 2 suites. Also 3 apartments.
price	€71-€127. Singles €45-€65.
meals	Lunch/supper from €17.
closed	Rarely.
directions	In Úbeda, follow signs for 'Centro Histórico'. Hotel next to Town Hall (Ayuntamiento) & Plaza Vázquez de Molina. Signed.

Juan Navarro López
tel	+34 953 795356
fax	+34 953 793694
e-mail	hotelmm@hotel-maria-de-molina.com
web	www.hotel-maria-de-molina.com

Hotel

map 10   entry 106

Es Passarell

2a Vuelta No. 117, 07200 Felanitx, Mallorca , Spain

Es Passarell is testimony to the boundless energy of María Dolores ('Lola') who saw in these old stones a vision of better things. You approach this isolated farm through a swathe of colour made up of palm and vine, honeysuckle and geranium. No two bedrooms are alike and size and configuration follow the dictates of the old farm buildings. The mix of antique furnishing and modern art feels good and you can see why glossy magazines have featured the place. Breakfast is buffet and big; twice-weekly there are gourmet dinners with delicious wines.

- Cookery: € 12 per day.
- Spanish: November-March, € 12 per day.
- Horse-riding: 10km.
- Monasteries route, 8km.
- Golf course & beach, 16km.
- Tennis court & swimming pool.

rooms	4 doubles. Also 6 self-catering apartments.
price	€ 85–€ 145. Singles € 63–€ 105.
meals	Lunch/supper € 12–€ 40.
closed	Rarely.
directions	From Llucmajor to Porreres; here, towards Felanitx. Between km2 & km3 markers, at sharp bend, right; after 2.5km, house on right, signed.

María Dolores Suberviola

tel	+34 971 183091
fax	+34 971 183091

B&B & self-catering

Leon de Sineu

Carrer dels Bous 129, 07510 Sineu, Mallorca, Spain

Sineu, mellow in the sunlight, is one of Mallorca's oldest towns. The Leon has a lovely façade and is fresh, clean and welcoming. An arch spans the entrance hall, beyond which is a large covered terrace where one can sit and admire the garden. The bedrooms, opening off a staircase of almost Parisian splendour, are a mix of antique dark wooden beds, the odd Moroccan ornament or rug and simple white walls. Senora Gálmez Arbona recreates the atmosphere of a Mallorcan home. The Leon also has one of the best restaurants in town.

- Golf course: 20km.
- Wednesday market.
- Old quarter on doorstep.
- Own swimming pool.
- Palma, 27km.
- Venue for wedding parties.

rooms	8: 3 doubles, 3 twins, 1 single, 1 suite.
price	€ 115-€ 140. Singles from € 90. VAT included.
meals	Lunch/supper from € 20. VAT included.
closed	20 November-20 December.
directions	Head for town centre. Hotel signed.

Francisca Gálmez Arbona

tel	+34 971 520211
fax	+34 971 855058
e-mail	reservas@hotel-leondesineu.com
web	www.hotel-leondesineu.com

Hotel

map 8　entry 108

portugal

Photography by Michael Busselle

portugal

Quinta do Convento da Franqueira

Carvalhal CC 301, 4755-104 Barcelos, Portugal

This wonderful 16th-century monastery is hidden away among pine trees, cork oaks, eucalyptus and cypress. Five centuries on, the granite buildings have been restored to their former grace by the Gallie family and the results are delightful. Rooms, one with sitting room, are lovely and generously proportioned. There's a four-poster in one, old prints, pretty bedside lamps and tables and stuccoed ceilings. All are individual and the bathrooms have hand-painted tiles. Children have swings in the gardens and a rocking horse. A huge terrace overlooks lush gardens.

- Wine-tasting with owner: in English, May–October.
- Painting with Artist Paul Waplington: 40km, in English, May–October.
- Estela golf course: 12km.
- Spring-fed 16th-century pool, vineyard & winery.
- Thursday market in Barcelos, 5km.
- Faria Castle & Celtic village, 1km.

rooms	5: 4 twins/doubles, 1 family flat with kitchenette.
price	€ 100–€ 110. Singles € 60–€ 70.
meals	Available locally, 3km.
closed	November–May.
directions	From Braga, N103 to Barcelos; at end of N103 right round ring road. Then 3rd right for Póvoa de Varzim. Under bridge, then left to Franqueira. Through village; middle road of 3 up hill into woods to bar. Right, then left after church.

Piers & Kate Gallie

tel	+351 253 831606
fax	+351 253 832231
web	www.quintadafranqueira.com

B&B & self-catering

Casa de Casal de Loivos

Casal de Loivos, 5085-010 Pinhão, Portugal

One of the best views anywhere! The house is in the village, yet you see no other dwelling – only the river Douro far below, winding its way through steep hills terraced with vineyards. Tradition, comfort and gentility are the hallmarks here. Manuel is a truly old-fashioned, charming gentleman; he speaks perfect English and usually sports a cravat – this is a place where you dress for dinner. Excellent meat and fish dishes are created from old family recipes. The view-filled bedrooms are gorgeous and elegantly furnished. You'll feel halfway between earth and heaven.

- Port Wine: English, € 100.
- Fishing: 7km.
- Swimming pool.
- Traditional Portuguese cooking.
- Artisans' work on display.
- Wine museum, 10km.

rooms	6 twins/doubles.
price	€ 89–€ 95. Singles from € 70.
meals	Dinner from € 25.
closed	Christmas & January.
directions	From Pinhão to Alijó; 1st right & up through vineyards until Casal de Loivos. On right at end of village.

Manuel Bernardo de Sampayo

tel	+351 254 732149
fax	+351 254 732149
e-mail	casadecasaldeloivos@ip.pt
web	www.casadecasaldeloivos.com

B&B

map 5   entry 110

Casa de Vilarinho de São Romão

Lugar da Capela, Vilarinho de São Romão, 5060-630 Sabrosa, Portugal

An excellent refurbishment of a 17th-century house overlooking the Pinhão valley – in Portugal's celebrated port wine region. Cristina gave up teaching art to concentrate on the house, then a ruin; later she turned her attention to the vineyards around. The mood is light and airy, with pale wooden floors strewn with kilims and rugs, white walls, enormous rooms, grand paintings. The lounge is huge with large yellow sofas and lots of wood. Breakfasts are generous, with fruit from the farm. Outside are a shaded terrace, a pool and gravelled courtyard with pond.

- Cookery, Traditional Portuguese: 3km, in English, French & Portuguese, €70 per day.
- Wine-tasting, 1km.
- Tennis, 3km.
- Boat trips on river Douro, 12km.
- Train journeys along the Douro & Tua valleys.
- Outdoor circuit training centre.

rooms	6 twins/doubles.
price	€79. Singles €64.
meals	Dinner from €20.
closed	Christmas.
directions	From Vila Real to Pinhão through Sabrosa; in Vilarinho de São Romão, you will see granite gateway & chapel on left. Through gate.

Cristina van Zeller

tel	+351 259 930754
fax	+351 259 930754
e-mail	vilarinho@pax.jazznet.pt
web	www.casadevilarinho.com

B&B

Casa Campo das Bizarras

Rua da Capela 76, Fareja, 3600-271 Castro Daire, Portugal

The garden and orchard – with pool and tennis – are a delight, the joint passions of Marina, a retired science teacher. Her grandfather's house has bags of rustic character, with walls of great blocks of stones. Some bedrooms are in the main house, but most are in outbuildings. Some have kitchenettes hidden behind wooden doors, so the country character is maintained. Public rooms are small and full of old domestic and rural-abilia; the reading room has a bar and pool table. It's all very cosy and there are plenty of places in which to sit and relax, outside and in.

- Horse-riding: 5km, in English & Portuguese.
- Canoeing & Rafting: 2km, in English & Portuguese.
- Guided Mountain Walks: 1km, in English & Portuguese.
- Paintball: 3km, in English & Portuguese.
- Bikes for hire on site.
- River beach, 2km.

rooms	5 twins/doubles. Also 4 self-catering apartments.
price	€60–€70. Singles €45–€55.
meals	Lunch/dinner from €16. Restaurants 2km.
closed	November–29 December.
directions	From Castro Daire to Fareginha. In Fareja left at sign for 'Turismo Rural'. Past church, up narrow cobbled lane, Bizarras on right.

Marina Rodrigues Moutinho
tel	+351 232 386107
fax	+351 232 382044
e-mail	casa.das.bizarras@mail.telepac.pt
web	www.casa-das-bizarras.web.pt

B&B & self-catering

map 5   entry 112

Casa O Nascer Do Sol

Vale da Carvalha, Carvalho, 3360-034 Penacova, Portugal

Lucy and Hans are delightful hosts and cannot do enough for you. A modern house in a peaceful village; the beamed lounge/dining room is cosy with Flemish paintings and leather sofas, bedrooms are simple. Breakfasts are generous and you can make yourself sandwiches for lunch – locals pop in daily to drop off the freshest produce. The garden has a small pool and there are pines, olive trees and eucalyptus all around. Hans, who is something of a wine expert, will take you to a typical, local restaurant on your first evening if you choose. *Minimum stay 3 days.*

- Windmill Tour with Itinerary: 150km, English, no charge.
- Mountain Tour with Itinerary: English, no charge.
- Guided Tastings of Portuguese Bubbly: 25km, English, no charge.
- Penacova & river Mondego - swimming, kayaking & water sports.
- Walks in Europe's oldest forest, Buçaco, 15km.
- Luso & Curia hot springs, 15-25km.

rooms	6 doubles.
price	€36–€46.
meals	Restaurants nearby.
closed	Rarely.
directions	Exit A1 Lisbon-Porto at Coimbra-Norte; IP3 for Viseu & Guarda; take exit 10 for Penacova N235 Luso & Bussaco. Hans will meet you to guide you the 15km to Vale de Carvalha.

Hans & Lucy Ghijs de Voghel

tel	+351 239 476871
fax	+351 239 476872
e-mail	npp72198@mail.telepac.pt
web	www.casaonascerdosol.com

B&B

Casa de Sol Nascente

Rua de Alagoa, Taipa, Requeixo, 3800-881 Aveiro, Portugal

East meets west in 'the house of the rising sun'. The architecture is the work of Ian's Japanese wife Chizu, an artist. You enter to a column of glass around which curves a flight of stairs; light floods in through large windows. The bedrooms contain pieces from around the world; the suites are particularly well furnished. Chizu and Ian are excellent hosts and create a gentle mood and a family atmosphere – this is a great place to come with children. Meals from Chizu are superb and span a range of Portuguese and Japanese cooking. A welcoming and tranquil place.

- Meditation: in English & Portuguese.
- Horse-riding: 10km, in English & Portuguese.
- Off-road trekking & rustic farm visit.
- Bara, 20km - beach resort.
- Nature trails & birdwatching.
- Monastery cities of Porto, Coimbra, Aveiro.

rooms	4: 2 twins/doubles, 2 suites. Also 1 apartment for 6-8.
price	€ 78–€ 90. Singles from € 45. Apartment € 930 per week.
meals	Lunch/dinner € 10–€ 25.
closed	Rarely.
directions	A1; EN235 for Aveiro; immediately right to Mamodeiro; at 1st café, 1st junc. right to Requeixo. On to Taipa. Road bends down to right; at bend take smaller road going up on right; last house, 800m.

Ian M Arbuckle

tel	+351 234 933597
fax	+351 234 933598
e-mail	arbuckle@mail.telepac.pt
web	www.solnascente.aveiro.co.pt

B&B & self-catering

map 5   entry 114

Quinta da Geía

Aldeia das Dez, 3400-214 Oliveira do Hospital, Portugal

Life at Quinta da Geía centres on the lively bar and restaurant – it is well frequented by the local folk who obviously approve of the modern-Portuguese cooking. Bedrooms are large, light and functional; they have pine floors, interesting angles and are beautifully finished. A suite or apartment would be perfect for families. Your hosts have mapped out the best walks in the area – follow ancient (Roman) pathways through forests of oak and chestnut. An exceptional place. *Minimum stay in apartments one week in summer, three nights rest of year.*

- Painting: in English.
- Horse-riding: 15km, in English.
- Management Training: in English.
- Mountain Climbing: 10km, in English.
- Canoeing: 10km.
- Historic village of Piódaó.

rooms	16: 15 doubles, 1 family room. Also 3 self-catering apartments for 4-6.
price	€62-€120. Singles from €55.
meals	Lunch from €15. Dinner from €22.
closed	2-22 January.
directions	From Coimbra, IP3 to intersection with IC6. 10km before Oliveira, at Vendas de Galizes, right signed 'Hotel Rural' for 14km.

Fir Tiebout

tel	+351 238 670010
fax	+351 238 670019
e-mail	quintadageia@mail.telepac.pt
web	www.quintadageia.com

Hotel & self-catering

Casa Lido

Monte da Portelinha, Silveira, 6030-021 Fratel, Portugal

A pretty cluster of Beira cottages high above the Tejo, on the edge of a village frozen in time. The cottages are gorgeous, thanks to the talents of Lise and Udo. The house for four has wooden ceilings, white walls, carved beds, beautiful lighting; the cottage for two has a spiral stair and a woodburning stove; the barn, also for two, has a mezzanine, huge window and terrace. You share a delicious walled pool, and Lise tells you all you need to know, like when the bread and fish men come, and the best local *festas*. If you don't feel like cooking, Udo is a fabulous chef.

- Open-air Painting; Sketching; Wood Sculpture: February, June-July & November.
- Gourmet Weeks: in English.
- Hill-top Villages & Castles Tour: within 1-hour drive, in English, May & October.
- Olive Harvesting & Oil Production: within 6km, in English & Portuguese, early Dec.
- River beaches & cascades.
- Artist's studio for living/working available.

rooms	3 self-catering houses.
price	€ 192-€ 560 per week.
meals	Dinner with wine, € 20-€ 30. Restaurant 3km.
closed	Rarely.
directions	A1 Lisbon-Porto, exit 7 onto IP6. IP2-A23, exit 16 Silveira. Right Riscada-Juncal; under dual c'way; left at T-junction for Riscada & Silveira. Pass Riscada exit; on until sign for Silveira. In village, follow road round to right; at end.

Lise & Udo Reppin

tel	+351 272 566393
mobile	+ 351 914 111469

Self-catering

map 5   entry 116

Quinta Verde Sintra

Estrada de Magoito,84, Varzea de Sintra, 2710-252 Sintra, Portugal

This is a family home with an easy, friendly atmosphere. Nature is bountiful here and the house, set well back from the road, is wrapped around by honeysuckle, palms, bay trees, cedar and succulents. The apartments have large sitting rooms and well-equipped kitchens, and the bedrooms matching fabrics and tiled floors softened by small rugs. Bathrooms sparkle. Breakfast, a generous spread, is taken in the breakfast room or, on summer mornings, out on the terrace, with views of the lush Sintra hills.

- Ceramic Painting: in English, Portuguese & French.
- Cookery: in English, Portuguese & French.
- Guided Trips to Sintra & Lisbon: in English & Portuguese.
- Walking & Climbing: 5km, in English & Portuguese.
- Horse-riding: 5km, in English & Portuguese.
- Beaches, 5km.

rooms	5 twins/doubles. Self-catering apartments for 2-4.
price	€65–€95. Singles from €55.
meals	Dinner €10–€12.
closed	Rarely.
directions	From Sintra, signs to Ribeira de Sintra; to x-roads, pass tram lines to Café Miranda. After 1km, right for Magoito. After r'bout, left, then right. At Varzea de Sintra, after 1.5km, on right.

Cesaltina de Sena

tel	+351 219 616069
fax	+351 219 608776
e-mail	mail@quintaverdesintra.com
web	www.quintaverdesintra.com

B&B & self-catering

Fortaleza do Guincho

Relais & Châteaux, Estrada do Guincho, 2750-642 Cascais, Portugal

The crest at this 17th-century cliff fortress reads 'Where the earth ends the sea begins'. As you are almost surrounded by the crashing Atlantic waves you tend to agree. There's an enormous, balconied, courtyard entrance with a high glass ceiling, suits of armour and modern chandeliers. Bedrooms have watery views, the heaviest curtains, bathrobes and every luxury imaginable. The contrast between the luxury inside and the wild windy turbulance outside is part of the fun. Play at being rugged on that dramatic headland, then retreat for a slap-up dinner.

- Winter garden in ancient cloister.
- Restaurant with Michelin star.
- Guincho beach – white sands & surfing.
- Sintra – walled hillside city of palaces & castles.
- Sintra-Cascais Natural Park.
- Estoril & Sintra golf course coast.

rooms	27: 24 twins/doubles, 3 suites.
price	€ 165-€ 330. Singles € 155-€ 320. Suite € 285-€ 385.
meals	Lunch/dinner from € 38.
closed	Rarely.
directions	From Lisbon, A5 to Cascais, then EN91. At 1st r'bout for Birre; over 2nd r'bout signs to Torre until reach sea. Right, on for 6km till you see hotel on left. Signed.

Isabel Ferreira Froufe

tel	+351 214 870491
fax	+351 214 870431
e-mail	reservations@guinchotel.pt
web	www.guinchotel.pt

Hotel

map 9   entry 118

Pálacio Belmonte

Páteo Dom Fradique 14, 1100-624 Lisbon, Portugal

Frederic is a specialist in sustainable development and won an award for his use of traditional materials in this 15th-century palace. Bedrooms in warm colours have soft sheets, heated tiles, antique furniture; some have original frescoes and all have gorgeous bathrooms and phenomenal views. Suites are elegant, private and peaceful; the Bartolomeu de Gusmão suite is in the top of one of the Moorish towers and has an octagonal sitting room with a roof terrace. The pool is black marble, surrounded by orange and lemon trees. Sensational.

- Special pool & gardens.
- Tennis, 15-minute drive.
- Flower market, 10-minute drive.
- Castles & museums.
- Fishing ports.
- Flea market, 1km.

rooms	9 suites.
price	€350–€1,900.
meals	From €250 with wine, in suite only.
closed	Rarely.
directions	At foot of Lisbon Castle, just outside walls. Call first to arrange parking card.

Frederic Coustols

tel	+351 218 816600
fax	+351 218 816609
e-mail	office@palaciobelmonte.com
web	www.palaciobelmonte.com

Hotel

Solar de Alvega

EN 118-km149, Alvega, 2205-104 Abrantes, Portugal

The Marquês de Pombal built the house in the 18th century and it is as imposing as ever, with views to the stream, a waterfall and countryside beyond. Maria Luiza and her husband Paul have restored it to its former grandeur. Sumptuous bedrooms have polished parquet floors and antique beds with elaborate wooden headboards; all are different – one room in the tower has five windows and access to the *mirante*, the roofed balcony; another opens onto a beautiful little chapel. And do try the *jardineira* stew: meat and vegetables with potatoes and peas – delicious.

- Cheese & Wine-tasting: 20km, in English & Portuguese.
- Canoeing: 20km, in English & Portuguese, summer.
- Horse-riding: 10km, in English & Portuguese.
- Golf: 10km, in English & Portuguese.
- Karting: 10km, in Portuguese.
- Boat trip on river Tagus, 5km.

rooms	6 family.
price	€ 70–€ 90. Singles from € 70.
meals	Lunch/dinner € 15–€ 20.
closed	February.
directions	A1 Lisbon-Oporto. Exit Torres Novas; east on A23; exit Mouriscas. Signs for Portalegre. House 5km after exit from A23.

Paul Mallett

tel	+351 917 610579
fax	+351 213 161114
e-mail	solaralvega@yahoo.co.uk
web	www.solardealvega.com

Hotel

map 5   entry 120

Quinta do Troviscal

Alverangel - Castelo de Bode, 2300 Tomar, Portugal

The house, which looks out across the vast reservoir, is set at the edge of an inlet surrounded by tall pines, poplars and eucalyptus. Vera and João are an engaging couple and their home is a long-fronted villa that is a smooth blend of modern and traditional Portuguese: American oak ceilings, slate floors, hand-painted St Anna bathroom tiles. All rooms open onto a shaded terrace, where breakfast feasts are served. Stroll down terraces and through shaded pergolas to the Troviscal's floating pontoon, with boat to row. Wonderful. *Self-catering house for 4-8 also available.*

- History of Portugal: in English, French, German & Spanish.
- Canoeing: 15km.
- Horse-riding: 15km.
- Own diving/boating pontoon.
- Historic churches of Tomar, 15km.
- Donkey-riding, 30km.

rooms	3: 2 doubles, 1 suite.
price	€75–€85. Suites €90–€120. Self-catering €125–€140 per day.
meals	Available locally.
closed	Rarely.
directions	From Tomar or Lisbon for Castelo de Bode. On for 6km & follow signs for Quinta do Troviscal & Turismo Rural; after 2km sign points to track to right. Follow to Quinta.

Vera Sofia Sepulveda de Castel Branco

tel	+351 249 371318
fax	+351 249 371862
e-mail	vera@troviscal.com
web	www.troviscal.com

B&B & self-catering

Herdade do Monte Branco

Rio de Moinhos, 7150 BRB Borba, Portugal

Few places are more tranquil than this estate on a sunny hillside near Borba. The restored farmhouse and outbuildings have been converted into apartments, some small, some large. They are very well furnished in Alentejo style, with old furniture hand-painted in the local style. The kitchen and bathroom tiles have been painted by José's artist wife; the bedrooms are countrified and simple. There's a pool, a rustic bar and a dining room where the food is good. Your hosts are friendly, educated people who readily share their enthusiasm for this region.

- Tile-making: History & Painting: in English.
- Wine-tasting: 12km, in English.
- Alentejo Cookery: in English.
- Archaelogical sites, 10km.
- Wine & cheese production, 3km.
- Birdwatching.

rooms	9 self-catering apartments for 2-8.
price	€ 65-€ 90 per room. Singles € 50. Weekly rates available.
meals	Lunch/dinner from € 18.
closed	Rarely.
directions	On A2 from Lisbon, southbound, A6 eastbound; exit at Estremoz & join N4. Follow signs to Gloria & then to Rio de Moinhos. Monte Branco signed to right.

The Medeiros family

tel	+351 214 830834
fax	+351 214 863403
e-mail	montebranco@netcabo.pt
web	pwp.netcabo.pt/0218645001

Self-catering

map 9   entry 122

Quinta do Barranco da Estrada

7665-880 Santa Clara a Velha, Portugal

On the shore of one of the Alentejo's largest freshwater lakes, the Quinta is ideal if you're looking for a real hideaway. The whole area has a micro-climate which nurtures an amazing range of plant and animal life. Lulu and Frank spent a decade renovating the original low house and added a row of guest rooms. They are light, cool and uncluttered and their terraces look towards the lake. Lounge, dining room and bar share one large room and embrace Portuguese and English styles. There is also a vine-festooned terrace where you spend your time when it's warm.

- Well Being Retreats: March, May, June, Sept, from € 450 (4 days).
- Birdwatching: in English.
- Cookery: in English.
- Sauna on site.
- Swimming in clear, safe waters of lake.
- Mountain biking.

rooms	8: 7 twins/doubles, 1 family.
price	€ 90–€ 300. Singles from € 75.
meals	Cooked breakfast € 10. Lunch € 15. Dinner € 25.
closed	Mid-November–mid-February.
directions	From S. Martinho das Amoreiras, head towards Portimão. At T-junc., left to Monchique; after 8km left to Cortes Pereiras; after 8.5km right to Quinta.

Lulu & Frank McClintock

tel	+351 283 933065
fax	+351 283 933066
e-mail	paradiseinportugal@mail.telepac.pt
web	www.paradise-in-portugal.com

B&B

Quinta das Achadas

Estrada da Barragem, Odiáxere, 8600-251 Lagos, Portugal

The approach to the Quinta is a delight, a winding drive through groves of olive, almond and orange trees which give way to a wonderful subtropical garden; there's a heated, salt-water pool, a *cabana*, a jacuzzi and a small children's playground. The bedrooms are Algarve-rustic, with modern art and beautiful country antiques. Gorgeous bathrooms come with Santa Katerina tiles and swish showers. You can self-cater in the apartments. Dinners are eclectic and very good. Your hosts, Júlio and Jill, combine professionalism with a warm, human touch.

- Horse-riding: 3km.
- Walking & Birdwatching Trips.
- Watersports & Deep-sea Fishing: 5km.
- Painting with Local Artist.
- Golf Tuition: 5km.
- Scuba-diving: 5km.

rooms	3 doubles/twins. Also 3 self-catering apartments for 2-4.
price	€ 70–€ 90. Apartment (minimum stay 3 days), € 95–€ 160.
meals	Dinner with wine, from € 25 (2-3 times a week).
closed	Rarely.
directions	From Portimão, N125 for Lagos. In Odiáxere, right at sign for *barragem*. House signed on right after 1.2km.

Jill & Júlio & Isabella Pires

tel	+351 282 798425
fax	+351 282 799162
e-mail	info@algarveholiday.net
web	www.algarveholiday.net

B&B & self-catering

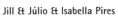

map 9   entry 124

Pedras Verdes Guesthouse

Sítio da Boavista, CP 658 T Quelfes, 8700 Olhão, Portugal

The house is north-African style, surrounded by carob and olive trees. The bedrooms are sensational, each with a theme: baroque, African, Asiatic, zen, Arabic. There are funky walk-in showers, minimalist décor, Portuguese antiques and some modern pieces. The humour in the décor reflects the character of the owners – Muriel and André are genuinely enthusiastic about creating a beautiful space. There is an overriding sense of calm and peace here. Dinner, French and delicious, is served on a beautiful wooden table and the cocktails are sublime.

- Swimming pool in garden.
- Gothic churches, 2km.
- Olhao fishing port & market.
- Fuseta beach, 5km.
- Nature Reserve 'Rio Formosa', 5km.
- Roman ruins, 5km.

rooms	6 twins/doubles.
price	€85–€95.
meals	Lunch €6–€7. Dinner €11–€14. Closed Mondays.
closed	Rarely.
directions	From Faro airport EN125-10 to Sâo Bras; on to N2 A22 to Spain; exit 15 Olhão O "Quelfes". Entering village, sharp left-hand bend at white building with red base; sharp right, follow green stones (or phone & André will meet you).

Muriel & André Mandi

tel	+351 289 721343
fax	+351 289 721343
e-mail	info@pedrasverdes.com
web	www.pedrasverdes.com

B&B

Quinta da Lua

Bernardinheiro 1622-X, S. Estevão, 8800-513 Tavira, Portugal

Miguel and Vimal love looking after people. The food is especially good; Vimal is a professional chef who cooks imaginative 'global kitchen' and Mediterranean. Breakfast is different every day and guests are asked their preferences. The house is surrounded by orange trees and vineyards and there is a lovely pool with shaded verandas. Inside is a blend of modern and traditional, with rough terracotta floor tiles and beamed ceilings throughout. It is a delightful surprise to find such a special place so close to the island beaches run by such nice people.

- Portuguese Language: 4km, in English, French & Dutch.
- Golf Tuition: 10km, in English.
- Rio Formosa National Park, 4km.
- Capo do Golfo, 10km.
- Beaches, 10-minute drive.
- Bike trails.

rooms	8: 6 twins/doubles, 2 suites.
price	€ 55-€ 120.
meals	Lunch/dinner € 10-€ 18.
closed	10 November-15 December.
directions	From Faro, IP1 to Spain, exit Tavira. At 2nd r'bout, N125 for Olhão. Right to S. Estevão. 1st left & next right, & look for arch over Quinta gateway.

Miguel Martins & Vimal Willems

tel	+351 281 961070
fax	+351 281 961070
e-mail	quintadalua@iol.pt
web	www.quintadalua.com

B&B

map 9   entry 126

france

Photography by Michael Busselle

france

Les Draps d'Or

152 rue Lambert d'Ardres, 62610 Ardres, Pas-de-Calais, France

The 'Cloths of Gold' has been an inn since 1640 and Christine's open, joyful welcome fits the tradition – she will receive you like old friends. She uses colour well too: the warm, bright little guest dayroom is a reflection of her dynamic personality; the bedrooms are equally fresh and bright, with good modern furniture and some pretty fabric effects. Three of them give onto the street but Ardres, a delightful little town, is extremely quiet at night while the green and gentle garden gives a country feel at the back. Breakfasts are delicious.

- Sailing on Lake: in French, in school holidays only.
- Watercolours, Pastels & Calligraphy: 2km, in French, in school holidays only.
- Ardres Tour of Former Bastion, Ramparts & Granary: 2km.
- Eperlecques, Mimoyecques & Coupole war museums.
- Nausicaa National Sealife Centre, Boulogne, 20km.
- Horse-riding, Nortkerque, 4km.

rooms	3: 1 twin, 1 double, 1 family room.
price	From €48.
meals	Restaurants within walking distance.
closed	Rarely.
directions	From Calais A16, exit 17; N43 to Ardres; right after church; house on corner on left.

Christine & François Borel

tel	+33 (0)3 21 82 20 44
fax	+33 (0)3 21 82 20 44
e-mail	christine@drapsdor.com
web	www.drapsdor.com

B&B

Le Manoir

40 route de Licques, 62890 Bonningues lès Ardres, Pas-de-Calais, France

Sylvie is restoring her old house, painstakingly and very well. Built in 1839 and known in the village as 'le château', it's not really big but, with so many original details intact, it's an architectural historian's delight. Stained glass, marble fireplaces, *trompe l'œil* wall paintings on the stairs, superb green and white tiling in the kitchen, original colours. Some of the bedrooms have spectacular carved wardrobes and beds. This is a house with a great atmosphere and a delightful young family at the helm. The food is good, too.

- Gourmet Cookery using Local Produce: in English.
- Golf Tuition.
- Walking & mountain bike trails.
- Eperlecques, 5km & La Coupole 25km war museums.
- Arc International, Arques - crystal factory & shop.
- Boat trip to Audomarois marshlands, St Omer.

rooms	5: 3 doubles, 1 triple, 1 suite for 4.
price	From € 58.
meals	Dinner with wine, from € 23.
closed	Rarely.
directions	From A26 exit 2; left D217 for Zouafques, Tournehem then Bonningues; house on right just after entering village.

Sylvie & Pierre Breemersch

tel	+33 (0)3 21 82 69 05
fax	+33 (0)3 21 82 69 05
e-mail	pierre.breemersch@wanadoo.fr
web	www.lemanoirdebonningues.com

B&B

map 12   entry 128

Station Bac Saint-Maur

La Gare des Années Folies77 rue de la Gare, 62840 Sailly sur la Lys, Pas-de-Calais, France

Vincent, *chef de gare*, and his young crew of conductors man this 1921 bistro-converted, red-bricked train station filled with vintage suitcases and trunks. There are miniature tin trains and a paraphernalia of reminders of the golden era of train travel. Your first-class *couchettes* are in the carriage of an authentic 'PLM' that travelled the Paris, Lyon, Mediterranean lines; retire to dreams of the Orient Express. A playground, a children's menu and antique highchairs make this a super place for kids. Take a barge tour along the La Lys; the lock is 400m from the station.

- Pottery: 500m, in French.
- Horse-riding: 2km, in French.
- Sailing: 4km, in French.
- Lace-making: 6km.
- Distillery, 15km.
- Lille - old town & markets, 15km.

rooms	6 Pullman compartments with 2 singles each.
price	€30–€60.
meals	Breakfast from €6. Lunch & dinner in train station €8–€24; served on board €28–€50. Children's meals from €6.50.
closed	2-16 January.
directions	From A25 exit 9 for Erquinghem to Sailly. At Bac St Maur 2nd left immediately after Havet factory.

Vincent & Valérie Laruelle

tel	+33 (0)3 21 02 68 20
fax	+33 (0)3 21 02 74 37
e-mail	chefdegare@wanadoo.fr
web	www.stationbacsaintmaur.com

Restaurant with rooms

La Vallée Saint Pierre

Chemin des Moines, Valloires, 80120 Argoules, Somme, France

Through the gate and into a vast other world of green and watery peace beside the Authie. The superlative modern house marches round an astonishing courtyard of 'giant bonsais' and sculpted creatures. Living is done in a huge fan-beamed room with marble floor, rich rugs, super antiques and doors to the veranda for breakfast. You sleep upstairs in the guest wing: original rooms, great use of colour, wood and exotica, fine bathrooms. Two lakes, two rowing boats, paddocks and woods. Your hosts are lively, interesting and fun – so is Shogun their dog.

- Horse-riding: on estate.
- Lake & river fishing.
- Mountain Biking.
- Walking trails.
- Valloires Abbey & Gardens.
- Marquenterrs Bird Sanctuary, 15km.

rooms	5: 3 doubles, 2 suites.
price	€80-€90.
meals	Dinner with wine, from €30. Restaurants 300m-5km.
closed	Rarely.
directions	From A16 exit 24 N1 to Vron; right D175 to Argoules; left D192 for Nempont; in Valloires Abbey car park: Chemin des Moines; gate 150m on left.

Michèle Harfaux

tel	+33 (0)3 22 29 86 41
fax	+33 (0)3 22 29 86 48
e-mail	michele@vallee-st-pierre.com
web	www.vallee-st-pierre.com

B&B

`map 12   entry 130`

1 rue Génermont

80320 Fresnes Mazancourt, Somme, France

A dazzling house whose hill-shaped roof becomes a timbered vault way above swathes of natural stone floor. The Picardy sky pours in and fills the vast minimally-furnished living space and your hostess shows shy pleasure at your amazement… then serves you superb food and intelligent conversation. Bedrooms are pure too: white walls, patches of colour, stone floors, excellent beds and bathrooms, 1930s antiques and touches of fun. Gourmet weekends can be arranged, and the First World War battlefields are at your door. Exceptional.

- Cookery Demo with Local Produce: in English & French.
- The Art of Wine Tasting: in English & French.
- Tour of Somme Battlefields: 15km, in English, from €20.
- Walking trails & fishing in Somme valley, 10-minute drive.
- Military & Industrial Railways Museum, 25-minute drive.
- Amiens Cathedral.

rooms	4: 2 twins, 1 family, 1 suite for 4.
price	€48–€50.
meals	Dinner with wine, €20–€23.
closed	Rarely.
directions	From A1 exit 13 on N29 for St Quentin; in Villers-Carbonnel, right at lights on N17 for 5km to Fresnes Mazancourt; house next to church.

Martine Warlop
tel +33 (0)3 22 85 49 49
fax +33 (0)3 22 85 49 59
e-mail martine.warlop@wanadoo.fr

B&B

La Tour du Roy

02140 Vervins, Aisne, France

Food is centre-stage, and resoundingly applauded. Monsieur, a delightful character, is wedded to his hotel, which he bought roofless 30 years ago and has renovated quite beautifully. You arrive in the attractive courtyard with its flowerbeds and stone fountain. The turrets – all that remain of the 11th-century town fortifications where the original building stood – have amazing semi-circular bedrooms, stained-glass windows, hand-painted basins, tapestries and old, carved beds. A place to spoil yourself with days of luxurious living and eating.

- Rifle-shooting.
- Fly-fishing on 13-hectare lake.
- Canoeing & kayaking on the l'Oise, 5km.
- Château-Fort, Guise.
- Museum of Barbarian History, Marle.
- Reims - cathedral & caves.

rooms	22: 14 twins/doubles, 8 suites.
price	€ 61-€ 92. Suites € 122-€ 229.
meals	Breakfast € 13. Picnic € 15. Lunch/dinner € 35-€ 80. Restaurant closed Monday & Tuesday lunchtimes except on request.
closed	Rarely.
directions	A26 exit 13 to Vervins on N2. Follow Centre Ville signs. Hotel directly on right. Parking through gate, past main building.

M & Mme Desvignes

tel	+33 (0)3 23 98 00 11
fax	+33 (0)3 23 98 00 72
e-mail	latourduroy@wanadoo.fr
web	www.latourduroy.com

Hotel

map 13   entry 132

Ferme de Ressons

02220 Mont St Martin, Aisne, France

A big, active farm out in the wilds, with an unspoilt house among rolling hills and champagne vineyards. Your hosts are hard-working, dynamic and good, even exciting, company; they also hunt. Madame, an architect, works from home, brings up three children *and* nurtures her guests. The deeply-carved Henri III furniture is an admirable family heirloom; rooms are colour-co-ordinated, beds are beautiful, views are stunning, dinners are excellent; bring rod and permit and you can fish in the pond. Arms are open for you in this civilised household. *Gîte also available.*

- Ceramic Painting Demonstration: in French.
- Calligraphy: 15km.
- French Wine-tasting: 5km, in French.
- Champagne Cellar Visits: 10km, in English, French & German.
- Fishing on lake.
- Reims Music Festival (July/August).

rooms	5: 1 double, 1 twin; 2 doubles, 1 twin, sharing bathroom.
price	€ 40–€ 48.
meals	Dinner from € 19.
closed	Rarely.
directions	From Fismes D967 for Fère en Tardenois & Château Thierry 4km. Don't go to Mont St Martin, but continue for 800m beyond turning; white house on left.

Valérie & Jean-Paul Ferry
tel	+33 (0)3 23 74 71 00
fax	+33 (0)3 23 74 28 88

B&B & self-catering

Ferme de Bannay

51270 Bannay, Marne, France

Bannay bustles with hens, ducks, guinea fowl, turkeys, donkey, sheep, cows, goats... the chatter starts at 6am. Children love this working farm and its higgledy-piggledy buildings; school groups come to visit. The house brims with beams, the rooms dance in swags, flowers and antique bits; the piano swarms with candles and photographs and one bathroom is behind a curtain. Our readers have loved the house, the family and the food. Little English is spoken but the welcome is so exceptional, the generosity so genuine, that communication is easy.

- The Life of a Farmer - Farm Tours: limited English.
- Taste & Aromas - Wine & Cheese-tasting & Rustic Meal: 15km, in English & French.
- Corn-dolly Making.
- Christmas Wreath Making.
- Table Decoration.
- Cookery.

rooms	4: 3 doubles ,1 suite.
price	€ 44–€ 53.
meals	Dinner with wine, from € 23; with champagne, from € 26.
closed	Rarely.
directions	From Épernay D51 for Sézanne; at Baye, just before church, right D343; at Bannay right; farm before small bridge.

Muguette & Jean-Pierre Curfs

tel	+33 (0)3 26 52 80 49
fax	+33 (0)3 26 59 47 78

B&B

map 12   entry 134

Habitation Beauvilliers

Port Aubry, 58200 Cosne sur Loire, Nièvre, France

You can do a day's canoeing on the Loire and disembark at the bottom of the garden for aperitifs and boules beneath the plane trees – pretty classy. Your hosts leave you the run of their fine French garden – box hedges and central pond – and classically symmetrical house with its unusual double stairway. Madame first came from Switzerland to study fine art and loves living here. Bedrooms are light and airy, one of them with a dreamy river view and a bathroom disguised as a cupboard. Breakfast is in the super kitchen, decorated with Monsieur's printed teacloths.

- Discover the Loire: in French.
- Canoeing & Kayaking: 15km, in French.
- Microlighting: 15km, in French.
- Vineyard Tours: 17km, in English & French.
- Porcelain Museum, 30km.
- Noirlac classical music festival.

rooms	3 suites.
price	€ 60–€ 75.
meals	Dinner from € 20.
closed	Rarely.
directions	From Cosne sur Loire for Bourges; at r'bout in front of bridge for Nevers (do not cross river); after 3km road turns to left; follow wall on right; gate on right.

Marianne & Daniel Perrier
tel   +33 (0)3 86 28 41 37
e-mail   habitationbeauvilliers@hotmail.com

B&B

Château Jaquot

2 rue d'Avallon, 89420 Ste Magnance, Yonne, France

It is as authentically 12th century as Madame can make it – she's passionate about the place and loves sharing it with like-minded visitors. The medieval flavour, called variously fascinating, stagey, strange, hits you as you enter: atmospherically low lighting, objects and artefacts, some as old as the Crusades, jostling for attention. Climb the winding stone turret stair, push the big oak door, choose your four-poster, wallow in the ingenious Gothicky bathroom, admire the brilliant bed hangings. A romantic retreat for convinced medievalists.

- Medieval Cookery: €10 per hour.
- Horse-riding, 2km.
- Rafting in Morvan nature park.
- Vézelay's Eternal Hill (World Heritage Site).
- Fontenay Abbey, 48km.
- Château de Tanlay, 55km - Renaissance château.

rooms	1 quadruple (2 four-posters).
price	€90 for 2; €130 for 3; €160 for 4.
meals	Dinner with wine, €35–€60.
closed	Rarely.
directions	From Avallon N6 for Saulieu. On entering Ste Magnance, 1st house on right, up drive.

Martine Costaille
tel   +33 (0)3 86 33 00 22

B&B

map 13   entry 136

Château de Créancey
21320 Créancey, Côte-d'Or, France

A breathtakingly beautiful 17th-century château, with a moat running past the kitchen door and, opposite, its very own 15th-century dovecote with resident owl. Fiona and her French husband have restored with impeccable taste: old oak doors and stairs, antique floor tiles, French linens and country furniture – this is one of the most seductive small hotels in Burgundy. If you prefer to self-cater there's a 14th-century tower in the grounds – relax on the terrace to the sound of the hoopoes as you quaff those Burgundy wines. *Children must be able to swim.*

- Wine-tastings: up to 50km, in English & French.
- Cookery.
- Karting & Aerodrome: 6km.
- Cycling: 10km.
- Horse-riding: 10km.
- Medieval villages.

rooms	5: 2 doubles, 2 twins, 1 suite. Also 1 self-catering cottage for 4.
price	€ 125-€ 215.
meals	Restaurant 4km.
closed	Rarely.
directions	A6 Paris-Lyon. Exit Pouilly en Anxois.

Fiona de Wulf

tel	+33 (0)3 80 90 57 50
fax	+33 (0)3 80 90 57 51
e-mail	chateau@creancey.com
web	www.creancey.com

Hotel & self-catering

La Monastille

21360 Thomirey, Côte-d'Or, France

Do pancakes or gingerbread for breakfast sound tempting? Traditionalists can stick to fresh bread and home-made jam. Supper might be *pot-au-feu*, with chicken from the farm next door, followed by a freshly-baked tart. Françoise will be happy to chat as she makes it, she is passionate about history, antiques and cooking and enjoys seeing her guests happy and relaxed. She is doing up the 1750 La Monastille herself. Bedrooms are a soothing mix of dark old furniture and crisp yellow and white, or perhaps flowery pink bed covers. Delightful.

- Cookery: in English, €15 per day.
- Wine cellar visits & wine-tasting.
- Bourgogne canal-boat trips.
- Autun Cathedral.
- Château de la Rochepot, 10-minute drive.
- Gallo-Roman monument & Norman church.

rooms	4 doubles.
price	From €60.
meals	Dinner with wine, from €23.
closed	Rarely.
directions	From Beaune D970 to Bligny sur Ouche; after village left to Écutigny; right to Thomirey; house with yellow flower pots by church.

Françoise Moine

tel	+33 (0)3 80 20 00 80
fax	+33 (0)3 80 20 00 80
e-mail	moine.francoise@wanadoo.fr
web	www.chez.com/thomirey

B&B

map 13 entry 138

Hôtel Britannique

20 avenue Victoria, 75001 Paris, France

The hotel is owned by an ex-naval man with a passion for Turner – the great man's *Jessica* greets you in the lobby. Do take the stair: elegantly pink and grey, it has handsome oak chests on each landing. The average-to-small rooms are all decorated with the same custom-made elements, boxes of pot-pourri for extra florality and very adequate bathrooms; higher floors have views over roofs and treetops. In the semi-basement, the breakfast room is prettily blue and yellow. A comfortable place with no ancient flourishes and staff in stripey waistcoats.

- Paris Fashion - personalized programmes: September-June (www.lamode-leclub.com).
- Notre Dame.
- George Pompidou Centre & National Centre for Modern Art.
- Ile St Louis – architecture, buskers, boutiques.
- Le Marais – boutiques, tea shops, antiques.
- Latin Quarter.

rooms	39: 23 doubles, 9 twins, 6 singles, 1 suite for 4.
price	From € 130. Suite from € 280.
meals	Buffet breakfast from € 12.
closed	Rarely.
directions	Metro: Châtelet (1, 4, 7, 11). RER: Châtelet-Les Halles. Bus Routes: 21 38 58 67 69 74 76 81 85. Car Park: Hôtel de Ville.

J. F. Danjou

tel	+33 (0)1 42 33 74 59
fax	+33 (0)1 42 33 82 65
e-mail	mailbox@hotel-britannique.fr
web	www.hotel-britannique.fr

Hotel

Grand Hôtel des Balcons

3 rue Casimir Delavigne, 75006 Paris, France

Owners and staff appear to work with lightness and pleasure, and breakfast (always a feast) is free on your birthday! Denise has decorated her Art Nouveau hotel by taking inspiration from the floral delights of the original 1890s staircase windows while her son Jeff manages – charmingly. Rooms are simple yet pleasing. The family rooms are big; other rooms are not but beds are firm, bathrooms good, colours and fabrics simple and pleasantly bright. Front rooms have balconies; at the back, you may be woken by the birds. *English and Spanish spoken.*

- Hemingway Walk: English, November-March, from € 10.
- Ile de la Cité & Notre Dame Walk: from € 10.
- Montmartre Walk: from € 10.
- Saints & Sinners Walk: from € 10.
- Palais & Jardins du Luxembourg.
- La Coupole - legendary brasserie.

rooms	50: 25 doubles, 14 twins, 6 singles, 5 quadruples.
price	€ 100–€ 180.
meals	Buffet breakfast from € 10.
closed	Rarely.
directions	Metro: Odéon (4, 10). RER: Luxembourg. Bus routes: 24 63 86 87 96. Car Park: École de Médecine.

Denise & Pierre Corroyer & Jeff André

tel	+33 (0)1 46 34 78 50
fax	+33 (0)1 46 34 06 27
e-mail	resa@balcons.com
web	www.balcons.com

Hotel

map 12   entry 140

Hôtel de l'Académie

32 rue des Saints Pères, 75007 Paris, France

On a bustling street a quiet retreat. Pass the *trompe-l'œil* dreamscape of classical damsels and exotic birds to the big *salon* furnished in Second Empire style – gildings and furbelows, tassels and bronze bits. In the bedrooms plain walls are a foil for old beams and some choice pieces. Some rooms are daringly done in rococo and crimson damask. Breakfast in the basement – you can have a caterer dinner here too. Bedrooms are biggish, by Paris standards, and storage space has been carefully planned. *English, German, Spanish & Portuguese tours available.*

- Paris Panoramic Tour: € 48.
- Tour of Versailles: € 65.
- Dinner on the Seine, € 48.
- Cabaret Shows - Lido & Moulin Rouge, € 185.
- The Louvre & Musée d'Orsay.
- Rue de Buci - street market & cafés.

rooms	35: 20 doubles, 10 twins, 5 suites.
price	€ 129-€ 299.
meals	Full buffet breakfast from € 15. Lunch & dinner from € 25.
closed	Rarely.
directions	Metro: St Germain des Prés (4). RER: Musée d'Orsay. Bus Routes: 48 63 86 95. Car Park: Consult hotel.

Gérard & Katia Chekroun

tel	+33 (0)1 45 49 80 00
fax	+33 (0)1 45 44 75 24
e-mail	academiehotel@aol.com
web	www.academiehotel.com

Hotel

New Orient Hôtel
16 rue de Constantinople, 75008 Paris, France

Behind a superbly renovated frontage the owners display their love of trawling country-house sales for furniture, pictures and mirrors. The mix of styles is sheer delight: brass beds and carved beds, little marble washstands, oriental and Mediterranean fabrics. The ground floor houses a carved dresser, a piano and a set of watercolours while a fine grandfather clock supervises the breakfast area. Note that some lift landings are awkward to negotiate with luggage. A human, pleasing place: pretty, original and fun. *English, Arabic, German, Hindi, Italian spoken.*

- Musée Jacquemart-André – townhouse museum & café.
- Marché Biologique, Saturday mornings.
- Rue de Lévis - gastronomy.
- Jogging in Parc Monceau.
- Saint Augustin Church.
- Wine bar, rue de Constantinople.

rooms	30: 15 doubles, 8 twins, 7 singles.
price	€85–€110.
meals	Breakfast from €8.
closed	Rarely.
directions	Metro: Villiers (2, 3), Europe (3). RER: Opéra-Auber. Bus routes: 30 53. Car Park: Europe.

Catherine & Sepp Wehrlé

tel	+33 (0)1 45 22 21 64
fax	+33 (0)1 42 93 83 23
e-mail	new.orient.hotel@wanadoo.fr
web	www.hotel-paris-orient.com

Hotel

map 12   entry 142

Manoir de Beaumont

76260 Eu, Seine-Maritime, France

In the old hunting lodge: a vast, boar- and stag's-headed dayroom with log fire, chandelier and rooms for seven – ideal for parties; in the main house: the huge room for three; from the garden: wide hilltop views. Monsieur manages the port and is a mine of local knowledge, Madame tends house, garden and guests, masterfully. Proud of their region, they are keen to advise on explorations: nature, hiking, historical visits, wet days, dry days... A delightful, welcoming couple of natural generosity, elegance and manners. *Gîte space for 4 people.*

- Bois l'Abbé, Forêt d'Eu, 1km - Gallo-Roman sanctuary.
- Walking trails.
- Château d'Eu, 2km.
- Horse-riding, 5km.
- Boat trips, Tréport, 5km.
- Museum of Old Tréport, 5km.

rooms	2: 1 double, 1 triple. Also 1 apartment for 5.
price	From € 45.
meals	In Eu 2km, Le Tréport 4km. Self-catering in apartment.
closed	Rarely.
directions	D49 to Eu. Before Eu left for Forest of Eu & Route de Beaumont. House 3km on right.

Catherine & Jean-Marie Demarquet

tel	+33 (0)2 35 50 91 91
e-mail	cd@fnac.net
web	www.demarquet.com

B&B & self-catering

Les Ombelles

4 rue du Gué, 27720 Dangu, Eure, France

The cottagey garden runs down to the River Epte, which Monet diverted at nearby Giverny for his famous *Nymphéa* ponds – it bestows the same serenity here. The old house is beautifully furnished with family antiques and Madame shares her great knowledge of all things Norman, including food. She has even devised her own detailed tourist circuits. Rooms are stylish and quiet; one has a majestic Art Deco brass bed designed by *Grand-père* and a hand-painted carved *armoire*. Both have total individuality.

- Historic tour: 'Les Templiers': in English, €45.
- Monet tour - Paris & Giverny: in English, €45.
- Fishing: in French.
- Pony club: 7km, in French.
- Goat's cheese factory, 6km.
- Doll museum, 20km.

rooms	2 doubles.
price	€55-€60.
meals	Dinner with wine, from €20.
closed	16 December-14 March.
directions	From Dieppe D915 to Gisors. Cross Gisors; D10 for Vernon. In Dangu, Rue du Gué is beside River Epte.

Nicole de Saint Père

tel	+33 (0)2 32 55 04 95
fax	+33 (0)2 32 55 59 87
e-mail	vextour@aol.com
web	vextour.ifrance.com

B&B

map 12   entry 144

Le Coquerel

27560 St Siméon, Eure, France

Ten years ago, this was a cottage in need of love. Jean-Marc transformed it into a floral, country gem to stay, meet, eat – and have fun in. It's a mix of the sober and the frivolous – old and modern pieces, rustic revival and leather, contemporary art and *brocante*. The maturing garden will become exuberant, too. The bedrooms stand out in their uncomplicated good taste and plain fabrics but it's Jean-Marc who makes the place: candlelit dinners and sporting events, strawberry soup and laughter, home-made bread and jam, flowers in your room. Amazing.

- Creative Writing.
- Cookery.
- French Language.
- Honfleur, 25-minute drive.
- Medieval Rouen & Pont Audemer, Normandy's 'Venice'.
- Château Beaumésnil & Gardens.

rooms	5: 1 twin, 1 double, 1 triple, 2 family.
price	From € 50.
meals	Dinner with wine, from € 19. Picnic possible.
closed	Rarely.
directions	From Pont Audemer D810 for Bernay 12km; right through St Siméon; up hill for Selles; house on left at top.

Jean-Marc Drumel

tel	+33 (0)2 32 56 56 08
fax	+33 (0)2 32 56 56 08
e-mail	moreau-drumel@wanadoo.fr
web	perso.wanadoo.fr/chambreshotes/

B&B

Les Gains

Survie, 61310 Exmes, Orne, France

There's home-made elderflower cordial if you arrive on a hot day – or the smell of hot bread may greet you: this converted manor farm with its pigeon tower and duck stream has a lived-in family atmosphere. Your hosts have 800 sheep, 300 apple trees (*Normandie oblige!*), work hard and are thoroughly integrated, as are their daughters. Bedrooms in the old dairy are light, soberly furnished with touches of *fantaisie* and Diana's very decorative stencils. Breakfast is varied, dinner, an occasion to linger over under the pergola in fine weather.

- Guided Tours of Region: up to 100km, in English & French.
- Camembert, 3km.
- D-day landing beaches.
- Mont Ormel Museum, 4km.
- Musée de la Tapisserie de Bayeux.
- Monet's Garden, Giverny.

rooms	3: 1 double, 1 twin, 1 triple.
price	€50–€55.
meals	Dinner with wine & aperitif, from €25.
closed	December–February.
directions	From Vimoutiers D916 for Argentan. Just outside Vimoutiers fork left D16 for Exmes; D26 for Survie & Exmes.

Diana & Christopher Wordsworth

tel	+33 (0)2 33 36 05 56
fax	+33 (0)2 33 35 03 65
e–mail	christopher.wordsworth@libertysurf.fr
web	www.lesgains.tk

B&B

map 12   entry 146

La Grange

La Boursaie, Tortisambert, 14140 Livarot, Calvados, France

A superb cluster of half-timbered buildings restored by English owner Peter and his German wife. La Grange, with its stupendous views over the courtyard, duck pond and lush valley beyond, was formerly the hayloft, and has been attractively converted into a split-level first-floor apartment for four. Downstairs Peter has his watercolour studio – you'll spot his work in the other cottages – and there's a dining room where he and Anja, both ex-catering, entertain guests to a weekly feast: Norman cuisine – and cider – at its best. *Four other cottages available.*

- Watercolours & Pastels: Eng. & German, spring & autumn, € 395 half-board (4 days).
- Normandy Cuisine: in English, spring & autumn, € 450 half-board (3 days).
- Horse-riding Deauville Beach: 35km, in French.
- Normandy Heritage Tours: in English & German, spring & autumn, € 150 (for 2-4).
- Cheese factory, museum & market, 4km.
- Participate in cider-apple harvest.

rooms	2 twins, with shower room & bathroom.
price	€ 580-€ 865 per week.
meals	Self-catering. Meals from € 25.
closed	Rarely.
directions	D579 to Livarot, take D4 towards St Pierre s/Dives, after 1km left onto D38 through Heurtevent then, after 800m, left at crossroads.

Anja & Peter Davies

tel	+33 (0)2 31 63 14 20
fax	+33 (0)2 31 63 14 28
e-mail	laboursaie@wanadoo.fr

Self-catering

Les Fontaines

Barbery, 14220 Bretteville sur Laize, Calvados, France

A solid, elegant Norman mansion with walled garden and summer house, billiards and *two* dining rooms. Andrew receives you in relaxed style, dynamic Elizabeth is present at weekends. On the airy first floor, your sleeping and sitting rooms have generous light, glowing parquet, French and English antiques against pale walls. Downstairs, the dining room is unusually frescoed and the oak-panelled, many-windowed dining room is beamed and fireplaced; both have seriously big tables. Andrew continues his restoration in excellent taste. *Gîte space for 7 people.*

- Drawing: weekends.
- French Language: weekends.
- Bikes for forest trails.
- Snooker on site.
- Musée de la Tapisserie de Bayeux.
- Musée Mémorial, Bayeux.

rooms	5: 2 doubles, 2 family, 1 single.
price	€60–€65.
meals	Dinner with wine, from €21.
closed	Christmas & New Year.
directions	From Caen ring road exit 13 for Falaise; 9km, right to Bretteville sur Laize; on to Barbery. House behind field on right, with high, green gates.

Elizabeth & Andrew Bamford

tel	+33 (0)2 31 78 24 48
fax	+33 (0)2 31 78 24 49
e-mail	lesfontaines@free.fr
web	lesfontaines.free.fr

B&B & self-catering

map 12 entry 148

Ferme de la Rançonnière

Route d'Arromanches, 14480 Creully, Calvados, France

A matronly farmer was unloading eggs from a wrinkled grey Deux Chevaux as we drove through the crenellated carriage gate, past the 15th-century tower into the vast grassy courtyard. Some went into a tiny corner store to sit with local cheeses and cream; others were whisked into the oak-beamed, vaulted restaurant laid beautifully for lunch. The comfortable bedrooms have small windows and rustic furniture, but the new rooms in the old farmhouse down the road might be quieter at weekends; book ahead for the best. A wonderful old place.

- Guided Tour of D-Day Landing Beaches.
- Guided Tour of Mont St Michel.
- Arromanches, 5km - man-made harbour.
- Musée de la Tapisserie de Bayeux, 12km.
- Golf at Omaha Beach, 25km.
- Umbrella-making studio, Creully, 3km.

rooms	48: 35 doubles/twins; in 'manoir' 7 doubles/twins, 6 suites.
price	€ 50–€ 150.
meals	Breakfast from € 11. Lunch € 16–€ 40. Dinner € 24–€ 40. Restaurant closed 1st three weeks January.
closed	Rarely.
directions	From Caen exit 7 to Creully on D22 for 19km. There, right at church for Arromanches on D65. In Crépon, hotel 1st on right.

Mme Vereecke & Mme Sileghem

tel	+33 (0)2 31 22 21 73
fax	+33 (0)2 31 22 98 39
e-mail	ranconniere@wanadoo.fr
web	www.ranconniere.com

Hotel

Ferme-Manoir de la Rivière

14230 Géfosse Fontenay, Calvados, France

Breakfast by the massive fireplace may be oil-lamp-lit on dark mornings in this ancient fortress of a farm. It also has a stupendous tithe barn and a little watchtower (turned into a perfect gîte for two). Madame is proud of her family home, its flagstones worn smooth, its fine country antiques so suited to the sober, immensely high second-floor rooms – one has a shower in a tower, another looks over the calving field. The farm lies in a little coastal village near the Normandy landing beaches, a short drive from Caen and Bayeux. *Gîte also available.*

- Archery: 1km, in English, French, Dutch, German, € 12.50.
- Mosaics: 1km, June-September, € 45 (for 2).
- Cider Tastings: 1km, in English, French, Dutch, German, € 1.50 (for 2).
- Pétanque: in English, French, Dutch, German, € 5 per hour.
- Mickey Mouse Museum in neighbouring house.
- Dairy Co-operative, Isigny - farm visits.

rooms	3: 2 triples, 1 double.
price	From € 50.
meals	Dinner with cider or wine, from € 20.
closed	Rarely.
directions	From Bayeux N13 30km west; exit on D514 to Osmanville & on for Grandchamp, 5km; left for Géfosse Fontenay; house 800m on left before church.

Gérard & Isabelle Leharivel

tel	+33 (0)2 31 22 64 45
fax	+33 (0)2 31 22 01 18
e-mail	manoirdelariviere@mageos.com
web	www.chez.com/manoirdelariviere

B&B & self-catering

map 11   entry 150

Hôtel Restaurant Le Mesnilgrand

Négreville, 50260 Bricquebec, Manche, France

Deep in the countryside lies a converted 18th-century cider farm, restaurant, small hotel and creative activity centre in one. The owner and chef – both English – provide rare opportunities: you could find yourself, chef by your side, seeking the finest fish, cheese or cider from the local market. Then recline in the English-style long bar at the end of the day. Bedrooms are comfortable, quiet and simply decorated and have good bathrooms. You eat in a setting to match Michael's culinary skills – his reputation is big and his organic menu varies from day to day.

- Cookery: in French & English, end-October-November.
- Yoga: in English.
- Ayurvedic Treatments: in French & English, November & December.
- Reiki Courses & Treatments: in French & English.
- Horse-riding.
- Wild Mushrooming & Nature Trails.

rooms	6 doubles.
price	From €80. Children under 3 free. Half-board €125.
meals	Dinner, organic whenever possible, €25-€30.
closed	Rarely.
directions	From Cherbourg RN13 exit St Joseph on D146 for Rocheville. Hotel signposted 5km after dual carriageway (not in Négreville itself).

Tina Foley

tel	+33 (0)2 33 95 09 54
fax	+33 (0)2 33 95 20 04
e-mail	mesnilgrand@wanadoo.fr
web	www.lemesnilgrand.com

Hotel

La Bergerie

La Valette, 50580 Saint Rémy des Landes, Manche, France

After a day on the dunes, cook your dinner, Norman-style, in the great inglenook fireplace, then wash it down with a flask of local cider. All is wooden inside this ancient farmhouse, from the gorgeous panelling around the hearth to the inviting oak settle and heavy ceiling beams. High-quality furnishings make this feel like a much-loved home. Enjoy serene views across the fields from the huge, sunny master bedroom; children will be happy in the carpeted dorm. There's a games room if it's wet. Ideal for two families (it sleeps 8) holidaying together.

- Beach, 1.5km.
- Sailing, 5km.
- Horse-riding, 5km.
- World War II museums & beaches.
- Château at Pirou, 15km.
- Musée de la Tapisserie de Bayeux, 1-hour drive.

rooms	4: 2 doubles; 1 double, 1 quadruple sharing bathroom.
price	£300–£675 per week.
meals	Self-catering.
closed	Rarely.
directions	Directions given on booking.

Oriana Lea

tel	+44 (0)1963 359234
fax	+44 (0)1963 351433
e-mail	oj.lea@btinternet.com

Self-catering

map 11   entry 152

Les Hauts de la Baie du Mont Saint Michel

7 avenue de la Libération, 50530 Saint Jean Le Thomas, Manche, France

You will either love or hate the inside of this house; everyone, however, will love the spot: perched in a beautiful garden above the sea, with wonderful views across the bay to Mont St Michel. Madame Leroy is warm, bubbly and chatty. The beach, 400 metres away, is pebbled but there are others nearby. The bedrooms range from big to delicately pretty in pale pink, with blue-green paintwork, chintz curtains and bed covers. One room is bold black with white and brown patterns. Breakfasts are a feast of fruits, cheeses, charcuterie and twelve types of jam!

- Horse-riding across Baie du Mont St Michel at low tide.
- Cookery: €25 half-day (with meal & wine).
- Beaches.
- Bikes for hire.
- Golf, 30m.
- Jogging.

rooms	8: 5 doubles, 2 twins, 1 family (1 double/1 twin).
price	€56–€180.
meals	Picnic with wine, €16. Good restaurants a 5-minute walk.
closed	Rarely.
directions	From Cherbourg, N13 to Valognes; D2 to Coutances; D971 to Granville; D911 (along coast) to Jullouville & on to Carolles & St Jean Le Thomas (6.5km from Jullouville).

André & Suzanne Leroy

tel	+33 (0)2 33 60 10 02
fax	+33 (0)2 33 60 15 40
e-mail	contact@chateau-les-hauts.com
web	www.chateau-les-hauts.com

Hotel

La Haute Gilberdière

50530 Sartilly, Manche, France

Generous, artistic and young in spirit, the Champagnacs are a privilege to meet. Their 18th-century *longère* bathes in a floral wonderland: roses climb and tumble, narrow paths meander and a kitchen garden grows your breakfast – wander and revel or settle down in a shady spot. Inside, bedrooms are cosy with handsome antiques, pretty bed linen and polished floors or modern with pale wood and bucolic views. The honey-coloured breakfast room is all timber and exposed stone – pots of home-made jam roost between the beams.

- Wood-turning.
- Guided Walk, Baie du Mont St Michel: 5km.
- Coastal walks, cycle & horse-rides.
- Mont St Michel & Baie du St Michel spring tide (le Mascaret).
- Jardin des Plantes d'Avranches.
- St Malo, 1-hour drive.

rooms	2 doubles. Also 1 self-catering apartment for 4.
price	€ 78–€ 120.
meals	Good restaurants 5-25km.
closed	November-March.
directions	From Avranches D973 for Granville & Sartilly; left at end of village D61 for Carolles; 800m house on left.

Édith Champagnac

tel	+33 (0)2 33 60 17 44
e-mail	champagnac@libertysurf.fr
web	www.champagnac-farmhouse.com

B&B & self-catering

map 11 entry 154

Le Brittany

Boulevard Sainte-Barbe, 29681 Roscoff, Finistère, France

A convenient stopover if you're travelling to or from Plymouth or Cork. This is an old Breton manor house with a rather austere looking façade which overlooks the harbour and is far enough from the terminal buildings to have views of the lovely Ile de Batz. The entrance from the carpark is quite a surprise: a mezzanine on the first floor overlooks the reception area, with a huge chandelier, an expanse of marble floors and lovely rugs and curtains hanging down two storeys. In the bedrooms, maybe a jug of fresh flowers or a bowl of strawberries.

- Painting.
- Fishing.
- Sailing.
- Thalassotherapy.
- Golf: 15km.
- Boat trips to Ile de Batz.

rooms	27: 25 doubles, 2 suites.
price	€79–€136. Suites €120–€183. Special half-board prices for thalassotherapy treatments.
meals	Breakfast €12. Dinner €30–€54.
closed	4 November–21 March.
directions	Exit Morlaix from N12. From ferry terminal right for 300m.

Patricia Chapalain
tel	+33 (0)2 98 69 70 78
fax	+33 (0)2 98 61 13 29
e-mail	info@hotel-brittany.com
web	www.hotel-brittany.com

Hotel

Château du Launay

Launay, 56160 Ploërdut, Morbihan, France

A dream of a place beside a pond and quiet woods. Launay marries austere grandeur with simple luxury, fine old stones with contemporary art, minimalism with exotica. The staircase sweeps up, past art on the huge landing, to big light-filled rooms. The second floor is more exotic, the rooms slightly smaller but rich. For relaxation, choose the gilt-edged billiard room, the library or the stupendous drawing room with piano (concerts are given). A house of a million marvels where fabulous parties are thrown by charming young hosts.

- Pony-trekking: in English & French.
- Walking Trails: in English & French.
- Fishing: in English & French.
- Local History & Heritage: 50km, in English & French.
- Outdoor pool with music.
- Balneotherapy pool.

rooms	10 twins/doubles.
price	€ 100–€ 125.
meals	Breakfast from € 6. Dinner from € 26.
closed	January-February.
directions	From Pontivy D782 (21km) to Guémené; D1 for Gourin to Toubahado, 9km. Don't go to Ploërdut. In Toubahado right on C3 for Locuon, 3km. Entrance immediately after 'Launay' sign.

Bogrand Family

tel	+33 (0)2 97 39 46 32
fax	+33 (0)2 97 39 46 31
e-mail	info@chateaudulaunay.com
web	www.chateaudulaunay.com

Hotel

map 11   entry 156

Château des Briottières

49330 Champigné, Maine-et-Loire, France

This heavenly *petit château*, sitting in 50 hectares of gardens, has been in the family for 200 years: *la vieille France* is alive and well. A magnificent library/billiard room leads into a small sitting room, and you share a pre-dinner aperitif with Monsieur in the huge, and hugely aristocratic salon. replete with family portraits and fine antiques. Sweep up the marble staircase to the fancy bedrooms on the first floor, whence park and lake views. In the grounds is a delightful country-style orangery, let as a *gîte*, and a large pool.

- Cookery: in French & English.
- Hot-air ballooning: from grounds, small groups.
- Loire wine & cointreau tastings.
- Pony Club in grounds (July & August).
- Bikes free of charge.
- Solesmes Abbey - Benedictine monks.

rooms	15: 12 doubles, 3 suites. Also 1 cottage for 12.
price	€ 140-€ 320. Cottage € 700, breakfast included.
meals	Breakfast from € 11. Dinner from € 46. Restaurant closed December-mid-March.
closed	Two weeks in February.
directions	From Paris A11 exit 11 at Durtal onto D859 & D770 to Châteauneuf sur Sarthe, then D770 to Champigné. Follow hotel signs.

François de Valbray

tel	+33 (0)2 41 42 00 02
fax	+33 (0)2 41 42 01 55
e-mail	briottieres@wanadoo.fr
web	www.briottieres.com

Hotel & self-catering

La Gilardière

53200 Gennes sur Glaize, Mayenne, France

The old stairs wind up through the subtly-lit interior to fairly sophisticated rooms with lovely furniture, beams and low doorways, sitting areas, rooms off for your children or your butler. The French-Irish Drions' beautiful restoration of this ancient priory is a marvel (famous people get married in the chapel). They are friendly and humorous, horse and hunting enthusiasts who greatly enjoy their B&B activity. The huge grounds lead to unspoilt open country, that big pond is full of carp for keen fishers, and there's tennis, swimming and a barbecue.

- Fishing on Lake: May-October.
- Game Shooting: September-February.
- Tennis court & swimming pool.
- Wildlife walks.
- Cycle routes.
- Golf, 30km.

rooms	4: 2 doubles, 2 family.
price	€55-€90.
meals	Dinner with wine, from €23.
closed	November-April. (Open weekends Nov-Feb for game shooting.)
directions	From Château Gontier D28 for Grez en Bouère; at Gennes right D15 for Bierné; in St Aignan right before church; house 2km on left.

Ghislain & Françoise Drion

tel	+33 (0)2 43 70 93 03
fax	+33 (0)2 43 70 93 03
e-mail	ghislain.drion@wanadoo.fr

B&B

map 11   entry 158

Auberge du Roi René

53290 Saint Denis d'Anjou, Mayenne, France

Monsieur is the original *bon viveur*, and looks the part. He's also a fund of culture and wit. Madame has no airs and graces either: she is chief gastronome, has passed muster with several top chefs and cooks a *cuisine d'amour*. The stately Auberge, which dates from the 15th century, lies in the centre of St Denis, a delightful village (let Monsieur be your guide). The narrow, cosy bedrooms on the first floor are reached via ancient stone stairs in the tower and have magnificent old oak doors and terracotta floors. Everything that an auberge should be, and more.

- Cookery: in English.
- Guided Tour of Village & Surrounds: in English.
- Carriage-driving: 1km, in English & French.
- Solesmes Abbey.
- Earthenware & Ceramics Museum.
- Le Mans race track.

rooms	4: 3 doubles, 1 suite.
price	€65–€85.
meals	Breakfast from €8. Dinner €15–€40.
closed	Rarely.
directions	From Sablé sur Sarthe D309 to St Denis d'Anjou. Auberge in centre of village.

Marie-Christine & Pierre de Vaubernier

tel	+33 (0)2 43 70 52 30
fax	+33 (0)2 43 70 58 75
e-mail	info@roi-rene.fr
web	www.roi-rene.fr

Inn

Château de Monhoudou

72260 Monhoudou, Sarthe, France

Your hosts are the nicest, easiest of aristocrats, determined to keep the ancestral home alive in a dignified manner – 19 generations on. A jewel set in rolling parkland, sheep grazing, horses in the paddock, swans on a bit of the moat, peacock, deer, boar... there are antiques on parquet floors and modern beds; bathrooms and loos in turrets, cupboards, alcoves; an elegant dining room with family silver, a sitting room with log fire, family portraits, a small book-lined library – and do ask to see the chapel upstairs. Hunting trophies, timeless tranquillity, genuine people.

- Bike hire on site.
- 400km walking & biking trails.
- Horse-riding, 10km.
- Golf, 20km.
- Le Mans race track, 40km.
- Castles & manor houses of Perche.

rooms	6: 4 doubles, 1 twin, 1 suite for 3.
price	€85–€140.
meals	Dinner from €37; from €64 with wine.
closed	Rarely.
directions	From Alençon N138 S for Le Mans about 14km; at La Hutte left D310 for 10km; right D19 through Courgains; left D132 to Monhoudou; signed.

Michel & Marie-Christine de Monhoudou

tel	+33 (0)2 43 97 40 05
fax	+33 (0)2 43 33 11 58
e-mail	monhoudou@aol.com
web	www.monhoudou.com

B&B

map 12   entry 160

Maison JLN

80 rue Muret, 28000 Chartres, Eure-et-Loir, France

The whole world comes to enjoy this gentle, polyglot family and the serene vibes of their old Chartrain house. Up two steep spirals to the attic, across the family's little prayer room (your sitting room), past the stained-glass window, the lovely bedroom feels a bit like a chapel with beds. Lots of books; reminders of pilgrimage – properly so, yards from the great Cathedral; perfect hosts: Madame knowledgeably friendly, Monsieur a charmer who enjoys a chuckle, their children, genuinely interested in your travels. An unusual place in a timeless spot.

- Stained-glass Window-making: 300m, in English & French.
- Guided tours of Chartres.
- Chartres Cathedral.
- Maison Picassiette – house of mosaics.
- Le Compa Agricultural Museum, Pont de Mainvilliers.
- Museum of Education.

rooms	1 twin with private shower & wc on floor below.
price	From € 45.
meals	Choice of restaurants on doorstep.
closed	Rarely.
directions	Arriving in Chartres follow signs for IBIS Centre; park by Hotel IBIS (Place Drouaise); walk 20m along Rue de la Porte Drouaise to Rue Muret (approx. 100m car to house).

Jean-Loup & Nathalie Cuisiniez

tel	+33 (0)2 37 21 98 36
fax	+33 (0)2 37 21 98 36
e-mail	jln.cuisiniez@wanadoo.fr

B&B

Le Fleuray Hôtel

37530 Cangey - Amboise, Indre-et-Loire, France

Peter and Hazel have created a haven of peace. A solid, handsome old manor house with duck pond, barns and mature trees was all that was needed to persuade them to settle. The rooms in the barn, slightly cut off from the rest, are just right for families, and French windows open onto the garden. The Newingtons are unstuffy and easy-going, genuinely enjoying the company of visitors. They have created a slightly English mood, with lightly floral sofas, bookcases, flowers and prints. The bedrooms are big and fresh; Hazel's cooking is superb.

- French Language: Amboise, 12km.
- Cookery & Wine: Tours, 35km.
- Hot-air ballooning.
- Vineyards to visit.
- River cruises.
- Aquarium.

rooms	15: 9 doubles/twins, 6 family.
price	€70–€100.
meals	Breakfast from €11. Dinner €25–€35. Children's meals from €13.
closed	One week February; one week November; Christmas & New Year.
directions	From A10 exit 18 Amboise & Château Renault. D31 to Autrêche. Left on D55 to Dame Marie Les Bois. Right on D74 for Cangey.

The Newington Family

tel	+33 (0)2 47 56 09 25
fax	+33 (0)2 47 56 93 97
e-mail	lefleurayhotel@wanadoo.fr
web	www.lefleurayhotel.com

Hotel

map 12   entry 162

Le Chat Courant

37510 Villandry, Indre-et-Loire, France

Traditional materials – soft Touraine stone, lime render, wood – and old furniture, pale colours and lots of light make the slate-topped house a welcoming haven by the Cher where the birdsong drowns out the trains. Here live Anne, Éric, their four children and various animals. They have lots of local lore for you, and concoct wonders from their mini-Villandry flower and vegetable garden. Anne adores looking for new recipes, new bits of antiquery (your bedhead in the lovely guest room is an adapted Breton *lit clos*) and attends lovingly to every detail.

- Personalized Tour Inventory to Touraine.
- Horse-riding, 7km.
- Golf: 12km.
- Horse-harnessing in Troglodyte Village: 7km.
- Basketry in Troglodyte Village: 25km.
- Château de Villandry: 1km.

rooms	1 family room.
price	From €45–€90.
meals	Dinner with wine, €18.
closed	Rarely.
directions	From Tours D7 to Savonnières; right across bridge; left for 3.5km; on right.

Anne & Éric Gaudouin
tel +33 (0)2 47 50 06 94
e-mail lechatcourant@netcourrier.com
web www.le-chat-courant.com

B&B

Manoir de la Rémonière

37190 Cheillé - Azay le Rideau , Indre-et-Loire, France

Come for the authentic 15th-century château. There are regal rooms, genuine antiques, four-poster beds. Rémonière stands on 2,000 years of history: the lovely stable block overlooks the fourth-century Gallo-Roman remains so its guest spaces have mosaics and murals of Roman scenes. A delight, in brilliant contrast to the main house (where you breakfast): equally enchanting, perfectly restored. Views are unsurpassed, the quiet is broken only by birds, the owl wheezing behind the children's turret and the friendly Thai pig trotting round the courtyard. A dream.

- Tours of Loire Châteaux: 15-23km.
- Horse-riding: 10km.
- Tennis, 600m.
- Hot-air ballooning.
- Château de Villandry.
- Route des Arts.

rooms	9: 6 twins/doubles, 1 suite for 4, 2 duplexes in stable block.
price	€86-€122. Duplexes & suite €100-€162.
meals	Gourmet restaurants 1km & 4km.
closed	Open all year & by reservation only November-Easter.
directions	A10 exit Joué les Tours, D751 for Chinon. Through Azay past Château to Cheillé. Left on D17; entrance 250m on left. Signposted.

Carole & Chantal Pecas

tel	+33 (0)2 47 45 24 88
fax	+33 (0)2 47 45 45 69
e-mail	pcarole@wanadoo.fr

Hotel

map 12   entry 164

Château de la Bourdaisière

25 rue de la Bourdaisière, 37270 Montlouis sur Loire, Indre-et-Loire, France

A superlative experience, the Château is a member of the National Tomato Conservatory. The brothers grow 200 aromatics and 500 types of tomato – taste some in salad with a glass of home-grown wine. There are formal gardens, a Renaissance château, remnants of a medieval fortress, a little boudoir and a bright, floral breakfast room. One guest room has a bathroom the size of a bedroom; some are gorgeously feminine; cheaper rooms are less grand. The drawing room is the Princes' own – they drop by, their books lie around and family antiques furnish it.

- Horse-riding.
- Château de Villandry.
- Château de Chenonceau, 19km.
- Château d'Amboise, 12km.
- Fine Art Museum, Tours, 12km.
- Route des Vignobles.

rooms	19: 11 doubles, 2 suites in château; 6 doubles in pavilion.
price	€115–€199. Suites €148–€207.
meals	Breakfast from €12. Light lunch from €15 (April-September). Dinner €30.
closed	Rarely.
directions	From A10 exit Tours Centre for Amboise, then D751 to Montlouis sur Loiret. Signposted.

Prince P.M. de Broglie

tel	+33 (0)2 47 45 16 31
fax	+33 (0)2 47 45 09 11
e-mail	contact@chateaulabourdaisiere.com
web	www.chateaulabourdaisiere.com

Hotel

Le Belvédère

24 rue des Déportés, 37150 Bléré, Indre-et-Loire, France

From plain street to stately courtyard magnolia to extraordinary marble-walled spiral staircase with dome atop – it's a *monument historique*, a miniature Bagatelle Palace, a bachelor's folly with a circular *salon*. The light, airy, fadingly elegant rooms, small and perfectly proportioned, are soft pink and grey; lean out and pluck a grape from the vine-clad pergola. Monsieur was a pilot; Madame was an air hostess and English teacher and is casually sophisticated and articulate about her love of fine things. Wonderful, and a stone's throw from Chenonceaux.

- Discover Local Wine & Cheese: in English & French.
- Flying Club: flights over the châteaux of the Loire: 5km.
- Hot-air ballooning.
- Rowing, Bléré.
- Chaumont sur Loire - International Garden Festival, June-October.
- Châteaux d'Amboise & de Chenonceaux.

rooms	2: 1 double, 1 suite for 4.
price	From € 76. Suite from € 122.
meals	Good restaurant opposite, book ahead.
closed	Rarely.
directions	From Amboise D31 to Bléré through Croix en Touraine; over bridge (Rue des Déportés opposite is one-way): left, immediately right, 1st right, right again. OR collection from private airport 5km.

Dominique Guillemot

tel	+33 (0)2 47 30 30 25
fax	+33 (0)2 47 30 30 25
e-mail	jr.guillemot@wanadoo.fr
web	www.multimania.com/lebelvedere

B&B

map 12   entry 166

Le Village aux Potiers

37460 Loché-sur-Indrois, Indre-et-Loire, France

Sit out among the lavender bushes and absorb the deep peace of this pretty village on the poplar-lined banks of the river Indrois. James, the English owner, teaches art and design and his colourful paintings compliment the delightful furnishings and old oak beams of the three properties – farmhouse, cottage (pictured, with private courtyard garden) and working studio. On the cookery weekends you're met at Tours, taken to the wonderful market at Loches to shop for dinner, then back to all cook and eat together. *Shared pool for those on courses only. Children's courses too.*

- Cookery Weekends: £240 full-board.
- Painting, Drawing, Watercolours: in English & French, £440 full-board.
- Yoga: summer, £440 full-board.
- Music: summer, £440 full-board.
- Silk Painting: in English & French, £440 full-board (+ cost of materials).
- Pottery: in English & French, £440 full-board.

rooms	House: 2 doubles, 1 quadruple. Cottage: 2 doubles, 1 twin.
price	Cottage only, €422–€677 per week.
meals	Meals included in price of course, otherwise self-catering.
closed	Term times.
directions	Directions given on booking.

Flora & James Cockburn

tel	+44 (0)1732 357022 (term) or +33 (0)2 47 92 61 79 (holidays)
e-mail	mrsfscockburn@aol.com
web	www.pbase.com/jamescockburn

Self-catering

The Cottage, La Grande Metairie
Leugny, 86220 Leugny, Vienne, France

Rose was bewitched by La Grande Metairie which she thought looked like an illustration by Arthur Rackham; 10 years and 200 rose bushes on, this ancient farm keeps its enchantment. The stone buildings surround a courtyard shaded by fruit trees. Inside: friendly old armchairs around a woodburner, and dark, gnarled beams. Upstairs are ancient iron bedsteads (and modern mattresses) and gabled beamed ceilings. In summer, dine out on a private terrace in the large dreamy garden. Your hosts are often there to help. *Studio for 2-3 also available.*

- Rose Pruning: in English & French, Oct-Nov & Feb-Mar, £35 (coffee, lunch, wine inc.).
- Pool & tennis in garden.
- Local bike hire.
- Château de la Guerche, 1km.
- Château du Grand Pressigny & Museum of Prehistory.
- Le Grand Pressigny Festival (July/August).

rooms	3: 1 double, 1 twin, 1 single on landing, all sharing bathroom.
price	£340-£580 per week.
meals	Self-catering.
closed	Rarely.
directions	Directions given on booking.

Richard & Rose Angas

tel	+44 (0)208 743 1745
fax	+44 (0)208 743 1745
e-mail	angas@freeuk.com

Self-catering

map 12   entry 168

Le Relais du Lyon d'Or

4 rue d'Enfer, 86260 Angles sur l'Anglin, Vienne, France

Each room was rebuilt round its old flagstones, doors and beams, then decorated in warm natural colours with Heather's beautiful paint effects and stencils – she now gives courses in paint finishes, using her rooms as living examples. Marvellous they are too, small, not overdone, with delicious bathrooms. It's like staying in a country house with delightfully relaxed and friendly hosts. The menu is varied and breakfasts are served in the pretty yard in summer. Steam baths on site; massage, face and body care a short drive away. Your pet is most welcome, too.

- Birdwatching in Brenne National Park: 20-minute drive, spring & autumn.
- Special Effects Painting: in English & French, spring & autumn.
- Romanesque Architecture: in English & French, autumn.
- Wine Harvest & Tasting: 30-minute drive, in English & French, October.
- Le Jardin des Rosiers, 10-minute drive.
- L'Abbaye de St Savin, 10-minute drive.

rooms	10: 9 doubles, 1 suite for 4.
price	€ 55-€ 100.
meals	Breakfast from € 6. Lunch from € 17. Dinner from € 25.
closed	January-February.
directions	A10 exit Châtellerault Nord D9/D725 east through La Roche Posay onto D5 to Angles sur l'Anglin; hotel in village centre.

Heather & Guillaume Thoreau	
tel	+33 (0)5 49 48 32 53
fax	+33 (0)5 49 84 02 28
e-mail	thoreau@lyondor.com
web	www.lyondor.com

Hotel

Hôtel les Orangeries

12 avenue du Doctuer Dupont, 86320 Lussac les Châteaux, Vienne, France

Even before you step inside, the fabulous pool will convince you that these people have the finest sense of how to treat an old house and garden: the harmony of the deep wooden deck, raw stone walls, giant baskets and orange trees draw you in. The young owners applied all their talent – he's an architect – to giving it an authentic 18th-century elegance in contemporary mood. Indoors, oak doors, stone walls and floors of warm wood are radiant with loving care. The rooms over the road are soundproofed. The Gautiers' enthusiasm is unquestionable.

- Nautical Centre - aquatic fitness, sauna, water-chute: 8km.
- Fresco Restoration & Painting: 15km.
- Gardening: 25km.
- Fishing - all types: 30km.
- Formula 3000 Driver-training & 4x4 Off-roading: 25-40km.
- Calligraphy; Illumination; Ceramics; Embroidery: 15km.

rooms	10 doubles/triples. Also 3 apartments for 4-5.
price	€ 60-€ 120. Suite € 100-€ 160.
meals	Breakfast from € 9. Dinner from € 28.
closed	Mid-December–mid-January.
directions	Exit Poitiers for Limoges on N147 to Lussac les Châteaux, 35km from Limoges. Ask for directions via Châtellerault if arriving from north.

Olivia & Jean-Philippe Gautier

tel	+33 (0)5 49 84 07 07
fax	+33 (0)5 49 84 98 82
e-mail	orangeries@wanadoo.fr
web	hotel-lesorangeries.com

Hotel

map 15   entry 170

Château de Tennessus

79350 Amailloux, Deux Sèvres, France

Moat, drawbridge, dreams. Two stone spirals to "the biggest bedroom in France": granite windowsills, giant hearth, canopied bed, shower snug in the old *garde-robe*; high in the keep, the stunning medieval family room: vast timbers, arrow slits and real windows. Furniture is sober and fires are always laid and you breakfast under the guardroom vault, feet on 14th-century flagstones. The whole place is brilliantly authentic, the gardens glow and Pippa is eager and attentive – flowers, bubbly, fishing in the moat, all on the house! *Gîte also available.*

- Medieval Workshops.
- Punting on the moat.
- Birdwatching.
- Fishing.
- Horse-riding, 5km.
- Golf, 20km.

rooms	2: 1 double, 1 suite for 2-4.
price	€ 110–€ 135.
meals	Restaurant 4km; choice 9km.
closed	Christmas & New Year.
directions	From A10 exit 29 on N147; N149 W to Parthenay; round Parthenay northbound; continue on N149 for Bressuire; 7km north of Parthenay right at sign for château.

Nicholas & Philippa Freeland

tel	+33 (0)5 49 95 50 60
fax	+33 (0)5 49 95 50 62
e-mail	tennessus@csi.com
web	www.tennessus.com

B&B & self-catering

Château de Saint Loup sur Thouet

79600 Saint Loup Lamairé, Deux Sèvres, France

This château inspired Perrault to write *Puss in Boots*! It is so inspiring that both château and gardens are open to the public. The count, charming and passionate about his home, is painstakingly restoring the house and the grounds, using early 18th-century plans. If you are a gardener, you won't know where to turn: to the orchard with 75 ancient varieties or to the enormous *potager*. The guestrooms are full of atmosphere with beautiful old beds and fine antiques. Dinner, after an aperitif in the library, is taken in the medieval keep.

- Gardening: in English.
- Cookery: in English.
- Fontevraud Abbey, 30-minute drive.
- Punting under willows, Marais Poitevin, 45-minute drive.
- Wine-tasting at château's suppliers, Chinon, 45-minute drive.
- Golf courses, 30-minute drive.

rooms	15: 2 singles, 13 doubles. Entire château can be rented.
price	€ 130–€ 190. Singles from € 100.
meals	Breakfast € 11–€ 15. Dinner with wine, from € 55.
closed	Rarely.
directions	From Airvault D46 to St Loup Lamairé. Château visible on entering village.

Comte Charles-Henri de Bartillat

tel	+33 (0)5 49 64 81 73
fax	+33 (0)5 49 64 82 06
e-mail	chdb@compuserve.com
web	www.chateaudesaint-loup.com

Hotel

map 12   entry 172

Le Manoir Souhait

7 rue du Chateau d'Eau, 17490 Gourvillette, Charente-Maritime, France

The majestic arched Charentais porchway promises something grand and you're not disappointed: a stunning 17th-century manor house with original washhouse, *pigeonnier* and large garden. There's a homely kitchen with a massive table, plenty of space and a lovely L-shaped pool to share with guests from the two-bedroom cottage in the grounds. Camaraderie between the two houses is encouraged and guests at both are invited to an aperitif on the day they arrive. Liz and Will run B&B next door. This is wonderful walking and cycling country.

- Cognac distillery tours, 20-minute drive.
- Heated swimming pool with children's section.
- Games area with snooker, table tennis, badminton & swings.
- Bike hire.
- Horse-riding, 30-minute drive.
- Golf, 30-minute drive.

rooms	7: 3 doubles; 1 triple; 1 single; 2 twins; shower & wc; 2 bathrooms & wcs.
price	€ 1,085–€ 3,300 per week. B&B € 48–€ 55 per room per night.
meals	Self-catering. Dinner € 19.
closed	Rarely.
directions	Directions given on booking.

Will & Liz Weeks

tel	+33 (0)5 46 26 18 41
fax	+33 (0)5 46 24 64 68
e-mail	willweeks@aol.com
web	www.manoirsouhait.com

B&B & self-catering

Château Le Lout

Avenue de la Dame Blanche, 33320 Le Taillan - Medoc, Gironde, France

If the dusky pink walls and first-floor *loggia* give the look of an Italian villa, this is because it was originally designed by an architect from Siena. A flight of stone steps leads into a white stone hall, sparsely decorated with tapestries and the odd old chest. The dining room has fine *chinoiserie* wallpaper framed by soft green panelling and well-polished wood floors. A stone staircase leads to the bedrooms; all have wooden floors and maybe rich orange or soft cream walls. Colette will cook you a five-course dinner while Olivier knows all about wine and golf.

- Dinner with Special Wines: in English, €65 (min 10 people).
- Chateaux Route with Wine-tastings: in English, from €5.
- Wine Appreciation: 10km, in English.
- Horse-riding, 3km.
- 36-hole golf course, 6km.
- Tennis, 3km.

rooms	7: 5 twins/doubles, 2 suites for 3.
price	€95–€135. Suites €155–€195.
meals	Breakfast €13. Hosted dinner with wine, €43.
closed	Rarely.
directions	Rocade for Bordeaux & Merignac (airport). Exit 7 N215 to Eysines & Leverdon. After 1km on D2 for Blanquefort & Pauillac. After 2.5km, left at lights to N33 for Le Taillan 1km. Signposted.

Colette & Olivier Salmon

tel	+33 (0)5 56 35 46 47
fax	+33 (0)5 56 35 48 75
e-mail	chateau.le.lout@wanadoo.fr
web	http://pro.wanadoo.fr/chateau.le.lout/

Hotel

 map 14 entry 174

Hôtel Laminak

Route de Saint Pée, 64210 Arbonne (Biarritz), Pyrénées-Atlantiques, France

The style is country cottage, with floral designs, stripes and neatly controlled flourishes… almost English. The setting is gorgeous, with the lush greenery of the Basque countryside at your feet and mountain views. The hotel is on a quiet road outside Arbonne; in summer it is a delight to eat breakfast on the terrace. Rooms are neat and attractive, carpeted, wallpapered and with antique pine furniture. It is but a hop to the throbbing vitality of Biarritz. Those mountains are worth a week's effort in themselves; just below them, the fish await your line.

- Golf Tuition: 6km.
- Horse-riding: 3km.
- Surfing: 5km.
- Biarritz-Bidart beach, 4km.
- Basque Museum, 8km.
- St Jean de Luz, 15km.

rooms	12 twins/doubles.
price	€53–€91. Children up to 10 free.
meals	Breakfast from €9. Dinner €8–€15.
closed	Mid-November–mid-December.
directions	A63 exit 4 La Négresse & follow signs to Arbonne; signposted.

M & Mme Proux

tel	+33 (0)5 59 41 95 40
fax	+33 (0)5 59 41 87 65
e-mail	info@hotel-laminak.com
web	www.hotel-laminak.com

Hotel

Maison L'Aubèle

4 rue de la Hauti, 64190 Lay-Lamidou, Pyrénées-Atlantiques, France

The Desbonnets have completely renovated their grand 18th-century village house in this sleepy village in the Pyrenean foothills; both house and owners are quiet, elegant, sophisticated and full of interest, and the furniture a feast for the eyes. Dinner is a chance to pick their well-stocked brains about the region and to delve into their tempting library (she binds books). The light, airy bedrooms have interesting furniture on lovely wooden floors. La Rose is very chic, La Verte is a dream – enormous and colourful with mountain views and a 'waltz-in' bathroom.

- Bookbinding Demonstration: in English & French, no charge.
- Talk on Old Books & Documents of Village: in English & French, no charge.
- Walking trails & mountain bike trails.
- Horse-riding.
- Rafting, 5km.
- Parapenting, 5km.

rooms	2 doubles.
price	From € 50.
meals	Dinner with wine, from € 20.
closed	Rarely.
directions	From Navarrenx D2 for Monein to Jasses; right D27 for Oloron Ste Marie; in Lay-Lamidou, left, 1st right, 2nd house on right.

Marie-France Desbonnet

tel	+33 (0)5 59 66 00 44
fax	+33 (0)5 59 66 00 44
e-mail	desbonnet.bmf@infonie.fr
web	www.ifrance.com/chambrehote/

B&B

map 14   entry 176

Manoir du Soubeyrac

Le Laussou, 47150 Monflanquin , Lot-et-Garonne, France

High, wrought-iron gates lead you to white paving, a central statue, climbing and potted plants. Stroll into the garden and there's an infinity pool. Most bedrooms have that same beautiful hillside view; décor is opulently traditional with chintzy touches and rugs on wooden or tiled floors. Bathrooms have all the cosseting extras: jacuzzi-type massage sprays, dressing gowns and essential oils. The courteous Monsieur Rocca cooks gastronomic dinners too. Exposed beams and an open fireplace in the dining room set the scene for those candlelit meals. *Gîte for 6.*

- Painting.
- Pottery.
- Canoeing & kayaking.
- Horse-riding.
- Bastide towns of Monpazier & Monflanquin.
- Vineyards at Cahors, Bergerac & Monbazillac.

rooms	5: 4 doubles, 1 suite.
price	€ 70-€ 120. Suite from € 140.
meals	Breakfast from € 8. Dinner from € 28.
closed	October–April.
directions	From Villeneuve sur Lot D676 to Monflanquin, then D272 for Laussou. After bridge, left to Envals for 3km; left for Soubeyrac.

Claude Rocca

tel	+33 (0)5 53 36 51 34
fax	+33 (0)5 53 36 35 20
web	www.manoir-du-soubeyrac.com

Hotel & self-catering

Château de Rodié

47370 Courbiac de Tournon, Lot-et-Garonne, France

Paul and Pippa did this triumphant restoration themselves, with two small children and a passionate commitment to the integrity of the ancient building, so brash modernities are hidden. It is breathtaking: an elaborate *pisé* floor set in cabalistic patterns and lit only with candles, two stone staircases, patches of fresco, a vast hall with giant fireplace and table. The tower room is unforgettable, so is the pool. This family is pro-organic; dinner may feature home-reared lamb and last for hours. You – and your pet – will be happy here. *Gîte also available.*

- Helicopter tours from grounds.
- Canoeing & kayaking: 15km.
- Parachuting: 7km.
- Walks in own 54-hectare nature reserve - one of the smallest in France.
- Château de Bonaguil.
- Musée du Foie Gras.

rooms	5: 3 doubles, 2 suites.
price	€ 70-€ 100.
meals	Dinner with wine, € 18.
closed	Rarely.
directions	From Fumel D102 to Tournon; D656 for Agen 300m; left to Courbiac, past church, right at cross for Montaigu 1km; house on left.

Paul & Pippa Hecquet

tel	+33 (0)5 53 40 89 24
fax	+33 (0)5 53 40 89 25
e-mail	chateau.rodie@wanadoo.fr

B&B & self-catering

map 15   entry 178

Le Petit Tilleul

Montillou, La Rivière, 24250 Domme, Dordogne, France

The river is just yards from the door (great for swimming) and busy, beautiful Domme is up the hill, but here is total peace. Friendly owners Mary – she an art teacher – and Alan live in another farm building along the lane where they do B&B. Old beams and stone walls are all intact and there's a woodburner in the lovely stone fireplace in the living room. The well-lit kitchen has white formica worktops and French windows onto the terrace and garden; bedrooms are simple, with shutters and open hanging space. *Two more self-catering properties avaiable.*

- Drawing & Painting: in English, May–September, €575 full-board.
- Canoeing: 150m.
- Fishing: 150m.
- Horse-riding: 7km, in English & French.
- Hot-air ballooning: 4km.
- Châteaux of Beynac & Castlenaud.

rooms	2: 1 double, 1 twin, sharing shower & wc.
price	€350–€650 per week.
meals	Self-catering.
closed	November–March.
directions	On south side of Dordogne, across bridge at Vitrac, 9km south of Sarlat.

Alan & Mary Johnson

tel	+33 (0)5 53 29 39 96
fax	+33 (0)5 53 29 39 96
e-mail	montillou@hotmail.com

B&B & self-catering

Pauliac

Celles, 24600 Ribérac, Dordogne, France

The overflowing stone plunge-pool in the tumbling terraced garden is unforgettable. John and Jane's talent is a restful atmosphere, their conversion a brilliant marriage of cottage simplicity – simple décor with sparks from African throws and good paintings – and contemporary style. Delightful, energetic Jane offers superb food in the new veranda or the bright, rustic dining room with its limed walls and ticking chair covers, and early supper for children. John "is a joy to be with". Lovely people and a house in a view-drenched spot. *Gîte space for 4 people.*

- Stone Carving & Sculpture: in English, 9-15 June & September, £450 full-board.
- Painting & Drawing: in English, 16-27 June & 1-12 Sept, £700 full-board (11 days).
- Creative Writing: in English, 1 week in October, half-board.
- Cookery: in English.
- Orchid Trail: in English, French & German, May.
- Tennis - all levels: in English & French.

rooms	5: 2 doubles, 1 twin; 1 double, 1 twin sharing bathroom.
price	€ 46–€ 53.
meals	Dinner € 17.
closed	Rarely.
directions	From Angoulême D939 for Périgueux 29km; right D12 for Ribérac to Verteillac; left D1 for Lisle 5km; right D99 for Celles for 400m; sign to left.

Jane & John Edwards

tel	+33 (0)5 53 91 97 45
fax	+33 (0)5 53 90 43 46
e-mail	pauliac@infonie.fr
web	www.pauliac.fr

B&B & self-catering

map 15   entry 180

Le Noyer

24340 Saint Felix de Bourdeilles, Dordogne, France

Sheep graze lazily in the surrounding seven acres of fields and woods, and life continues much as it always has in the pretty village of St Felix across the valley. Bridget and Pete, who live nearby during British school holidays, have restored with taste and skill. Warm beams, Shaker-style green-painted cupboards and a terracotta tile floor give a welcoming atmosphere to the kitchen/dining room, prettily decorated with English china and country antiques. Bedrooms are high vaulted and pine-boarded. Enjoy the serene views, dine on the terrace. Marvellous for families.

- Canoeing on River Dronne.
- Medieval Brantôme with Friday market.
- Grottes de Villars Prehistoric Caves.
- Cycling & walking routes.
- France's oldest belltower, Brantôme.
- Château de Mareuil, 8km - outdoor theatre & concerts.

rooms	3: 1 double; 1 double, 1 room with bunkbeds, sharing bathroom.
price	£450-£550 per week.
meals	Self-catering.
closed	Winter months.
directions	Directions given on booking.

Bridget & Pete Jones
tel +44 (0)1491 682834
e-mail bridget@rcol.org.uk

Self-catering

Main House

Fleuret , 19500 Curemonte, Corrèze, France

The setting of this 17th-century farmhouse is breathtaking: Fleuret, once a hamlet of 12 families, stands in its own secret valley. A sensitive restoration by Gilly and her architect husband Tim, who live in another part of the house – walls are thick, space is plentiful. The kitchen/dining room has a woodburner in the ancient fireplace and a wonderful table for family feasts; the sitting room has terracotta-washed walls and sofas to lounge in. One double bedroom is downstairs, the others are in the gabled attic. *Cottage for four also available.*

- Landscape Photography.
- Pool & games room.
- Curemonte market (July/Aug), 3km.
- Collonges la Rouge, 12km.
- Canoeing, 9km.
- Rocamadour, 35-minute drive.

rooms	5: 2 doubles; 1 twin, 1 triple, 1 single, sharing bathroom.
price	€ 1,250–€ 2,000 (£790–£1,250) per week.
meals	Self-catering.
closed	Rarely.
directions	Directions given on booking.

Tim & Gilly Mannakee

tel	+33 (0)5 55 84 06 47
fax	+33 (0)5 55 84 05 73
e-mail	info@fleuretholidays.com
web	www.fleuretholidays.com

Self-catering

map 15   entry 182

Château de Maulmont

Saint Priest Bramefant, 63310 Randan, Puy-de-Dôme, France

This extraordinary place, built in 1830 by Louis Philippe, has long views, medieval crenellations, neo-Gothic windows, even real Templar ruins. The Dutch owners cultivate a certain 'formal informality'. Bedrooms go from small to very big, from plain with simple shower room to draped and four-postered château-romantic with marble bathroom (the *luxe* rooms are worth the difference). And do visit the King's Room, a round blue and white (original paint!) 'tent' in a tower. There are evening entertainments – wine-tasting, music, spit-roast dinner…

- 4x4 Mountain Trip: 35km, in English & French.
- Horse-riding.
- Tennis: 12km.
- Hot-air ballooning: 35km.
- 'Vulcania' European Volcanic Centre, 45km.
- Golf.

rooms	16: 15 twins/doubles, 1 suite for 4. Also 3 apartments for 4-6.
price	€ 70-€ 165. Suite from € 215. Apartments € 215-€ 245.
meals	Breakfast from € 10. Lunch & dinner € 18-€ 49.
closed	January-mid-February.
directions	A719, then N209 for Vichy. Then Hauterive & St Yorre. Leave Hauterive on D131, D55 to St Priest Bramefant Les Graveyrons (signed) right on D59 to château.

Mary & Théo Bosman

tel	+33 (0)4 70 59 03 45
fax	+33 (0)4 70 59 11 88
e-mail	hotel.chateau-maulmont@wanadoo.fr

Hotel

Raymond, Mandailles St Julien

Raymond, Mandailles St Julien, 15590 Aurillac, Cantal, France

Walk out of the door into stupendous countryside and glorious views of the cone-shaped *puys*. The 200-year-old house used to be two cottages. One half retains the family quarters and has the original wooden beams, a long table and a fireplace where you can toast your toes. The other half has a modern feel with extra windows to make it light. Bedrooms are a mix of crannied and characterful, and modern; one leads to a terrace. Buy fresh milk and cheese from the farmer next door. A travelling shop comes three times a week – listen out for his horn.

- Guided Mountain Walks: 2km, May-October.
- Paragliding: 22km, May-October.
- Adventure Sports for Adults & Children: 18km, May-October.
- Walking with Donkeys: 13km, May-October.
- Horse-riding: 22km, May-October.
- Bilberry- & mushroom-picking.

rooms	3: 2 doubles, 1 twin/double, sharing 2 showers & wcs.
price	€ 400 per week.
meals	Self-catering. Restaurant 2km.
closed	December-Easter.
directions	D17 from Aurillac to Puy Mary. At Mandailles on for 2km. Left just past Benech to Raymond. Last house on right.

Ann & Stephen Haine

tel	+44 (0)207 267 8936
fax	+44 (0)207 813 5573
e-mail	annhaine@blueyonder.co.uk

Self-catering

map 15   entry 184

Auberge de Concasty

15600 Boisset, Cantal, France

Half a mile high stands the river-ploughed plateau: the space immense. Here stands the 300-year-old family mansion, proud beneath its curvy shingle roof. Over 40 years the family has restored it, bringing everything thoroughly up to date: jacuzzi, Turkish bath and organic or local-grown produce to keep you blooming. The dining room and the covered patio overlooking the valley are the backdrop for wonderful food and wine. Guest rooms, some here, some in a barn, are stylish-rustic and you'll warm to the smiling, attentive staff and the family atmosphere.

- Cookery: in English & French.
- Outdoor pool.
- Jacuzzi & Turkish bath.
- Walking trails.
- Maison de la Chataigne, 15km.
- Lac de St Etienne Cantales, 15km.

rooms	13: 9 doubles, 4 suites.
price	€ 55–€ 88. Suite with terrace, € 92–€ 108.
meals	Breakfast from € 14. Picnic available. Dinner € 28–€ 38.
closed	Mid-December–mid-March.
directions	From Aurillac for Figeac N122, left to Manhès on D64; from Figeac N122 then D17 after Maurs.

Martine & Omar Causse Adllal

tel	+33 (0)4 71 62 21 16
fax	+33 (0)4 71 62 22 22
e-mail	info@auberge-concasty.com
web	www.auberge-concasty.com

Inn

Brezou Main House & Lodge

Feneyrols, 82140 Saint Antonin Noble Val, Tarn-et-Garonne, France

Follow in the steps of the stars: many have stayed here, which gives you some idea of the luxurious style of this gorgeous 1901 manor house. It has spectacular views, an acre of garden, an inviting (fenced) pool, sumptuous furnishings. Families holidaying together can feast at the long antique dining table. The huge open-plan kitchen/dining room, with beech work surfaces and great oak beams, is immaculately equipped, and there's a comfortable sitting room and well-stocked library, too. *Lodge House available independently for rest of year (sleeps 4).*

- Choral Singing: 8km, in French.
- Painting & Sculpture: 8km, in French.
- Piano Tuition: 8km, in French.
- Pony & Donkey-trekking: 12km, in French.
- Guided Tours of Medieval Town.
- Canoeing through Aveyron Gorge.

rooms	4: 2 doubles; 1 double, 1 twin sharing bathroom & wc. 2 more rooms available.
price	£1,875-£2,450 per week for Main House & Lodge.
meals	Self-catering.
closed	Main House available July/August only; Lodge all year.
directions	Directions given on booking.

Jayne & Rod Millard

tel	+33 (0)5 63 30 68 89
fax	+33 (0)5 63 30 68 97
e-mail	rod@brezou.com
web	www.brezou.com

Self-catering

map 15 entry 186

Setzères

Scieurac et Flourès, 32230 Marciac, Gers, France

Setzères is an 18th-century Gascon manor, square and generous in its large lush garden – boules, badminton, tranquil pool. Beautifully restored, decorated with English antiques and oriental mementos, breathing charm and peace, it has heart-stopping views to the Pyrenees. Christine cooks local dishes and dinner conversation on the star-lit terrace is both cosmopolitan and fun. This is hidden France: old stone hamlets scattered across wide empty countryside, fascinating architecture, fabulous food. A highly civilised place to stay. *Two gîtes also available.*

- French Cookery: in French, May.
- Jazz, 12km (August).
- Eauze Archaeological Museum.
- Woad production at Blue de Pastel, Lectoure - 1-hour drive.
- Skiing in Pyrenees, 2-hour drive.
- White-water rafting, 2-hour drive.

rooms	3: 1 double, 1 twin, 1 suite for 4.
price	From € 110.
meals	Dinner from € 40; good wine list.
closed	2 weeks December-January.
directions	From Auch N124 for Vic Fézenac 5km; left D943 to Barran, Montesquiou, Bassoues (32km); D943 left for Marciac, sign for Scieurac & Flourès; in village left by church; house on right.

Christine Furney

tel	+33 (0)5 62 08 21 45
fax	+33 (0)5 62 08 21 45
e-mail	setzeres32@aol.com
web	www.setzeres.com

B&B & self-catering

Château de Garrevaques

81700 Garrevaques, Tarn, France

The 15th generation of Ginestes are in charge and Marie-Christine has all the charm and passion to make a go of such a splendid place – slightly faded in parts but stuffed with interest. Huge reception rooms hold magnificent antiques and some original 18th-century wallpaper, bedrooms are charming and stylish, bathrooms are modern if not luxurious. The Pavillion in the grounds has been renovated and houses 15 fine bedrooms; there's a spanking new relaxation centre, too. The garden is as grand as the château, and the *orangerie* is perfect for weddings.

- Flying lessons: next door.
- French Cookery.
- Spa & Herbal Massages.
- Portrait Painting.
- Tai Chi, Spa, Jacuzzi.
- Sculpture, Marquetry & Painting on Wood: 4km, in French.

rooms	23: 7 doubles, 1 suite for 4-5; 15 rooms in Pavillion.
price	From € 130. Suites from € 230. Half-board from € 95 p.p.
meals	Buffet lunch from € 15. Dinner with drinks, from € 30. Excellent restaurants nearby.
closed	Rarely.
directions	From Revel D1 for Caraman. Opposite 'gendarmerie' in Revel, D79F to Garrevaques, 5km. Château at end of village on right.

Marie-Christine & Claude Combes

tel	+33 (0)5 63 75 04 54
fax	+33 (0)5 63 70 26 44
e-mail	m.c.combes@wanadoo.fr
web	www.garrevaques.com

Hotel

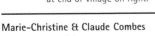

map 15   entry 188

Montarsés de Tayrac

12440 La Salvetat Peyralés, Aveyron, France

Easy to understand why the friendly Riebens upped sticks from Picardy for this huge old farmhouse and barn on the top of a hill. Jacques indulges his passion for pure-bred horses, Jo runs B&B. Rooms are big and properly old-fashioned. A large if sombre living/dining room has great beams and a compact kitchen area at one end; bedrooms have stripped wooden floors, cream walls and open hanging space. The area is rich in *bastide* towns with perfectly preserved arcaded market squares. *Gîte space available for further 4 or 6 people.*

- Lake fishing.
- Forest trails.
- Horse-riding on estate.
- Château du Bosc, 15km.
- Villefranche de Rouergue, 30km.
- Albi, 50km.

rooms	2: 1 double & 1 twin sharing bathroom. Also 2 showers, 3 wcs.
price	€270–€530 per week. B&B €45 per room per night.
meals	Self-catering.
closed	In winter.
directions	Directions given on booking.

Jo & Jacques Rieben

tel	+33 (0)5 65 81 46 10
fax	+33 (0)5 65 81 46 10
e-mail	chantelouve@club-internet.fr
web	www.ifrance.com/aveyronvacances

Self-catering & B&B

La Grande Combe

12480 St Izaire, Aveyron, France

An energetic, lovable couple live in this astonishing old place, built on a hillside before a heart-stopping view. The ancient timber frame holds brilliantly restored rooms done in a simple, contemporary style that makes the old stones glow. The emphasis is on communal living, of course – superb dining and sitting rooms with original paving, huge organic potager, great atmosphere – but there are little terraces and a library for quiet times. Lovely guest rooms are big (except the singles), pale or bright. Exceptional. *Children over 4 welcome. Gîte space for 6 people.*

- Fit for the Gods Cookery: in English, April, May, October.
- Four Valleys 6-day Walking Tours: in English.
- Combe Culinary & Cultural Week - visits to medieval towns: in English, November.
- Knights Templar Cities Tour.
- Caves of Roquefort & sheep farm, 45km.
- Millau Viaduct, 55km.

rooms	7: 5 twins; 2 singles with shower & separate wc.
price	From € 70.
meals	Dinner with wine, € 20.
closed	Rarely.
directions	From Millau D992/D999 for Albi; at St Pierre D902 right for Réquista; 4km after Faveyrolles before bridge over Tarn, two times left; signed.

Hans & Nelleke Versteegen

tel	+33 (0)5 65 99 45 01
fax	+33 (0)5 65 99 48 41
e-mail	grande.combe@wanadoo.fr
web	www.la-grande-combe.nl

B&B & self-catering

map 15   entry 190

Château de Grézan

34480 Laurens, Hérault, France

Exotic vegetation, stunning architecture, a touch of theatre. "Vast, amazing" – the brochure lies not. Towers, turrets, troubadour style – yet a simple welcome from Marie-France, daughter of Victor Lanson from the Champagne house of Lanson. Chandeliers, grand piano, original wallpapers, cavernous rooms with beamed ceilings. Marie-France has organised her wine trail especially for English speakers – it's quite an experience and you'll find out all about the wines, the people and the passion behind them. *Gîtes for 4 and 6 also available.*

- Wine and Country Trails: in English & French, March–November, except August.
- Holistic Treatments: in English & French.
- Watercolours/Calligraphy: in English & French.
- Honey Eco-Museum, 10-minute drive.
- Olive mill, 20-minute drive.
- Pezenas crafts, 20-minute drive.

rooms	3: 2 doubles, 1 twin.
price	€98–€108.
meals	Dinner/lunch €25 (restaurant in grounds).
closed	Rarely.
directions	From A75 exit 35 Béziers N112 NW10km; right D909 for Bédarieux 17km; right to Grézan.

Mme Marie-France Lanson

tel	+33 (0)4 67 90 28 03
fax	+33 (0)4 67 90 05 03
e-mail	chateau-grezan.lanson@wanadoo.fr

Self-catering & B&B

Le Vieux Relais

1 rue de l'Étang, 11700 Pépieux, Aude, France

With all her energy, Sally has turned her 17th-century coaching inn into a balanced marriage of solid old French base and modern inspiration. Having lived in England and America, then adopted France, her sense of style permeates the old house in a comfortable mix of antique and contemporary. She is also a superb cook, making delicious Mediterranean-inspired dishes with the best local produce, and provides all possible goodies in her big, well-furnished bedrooms. She loves to share her passion for, and books on, history and travel. *Min. 2 nights June-September.*

- Watercolours: in English, May, September, October, £900 per week full-board.
- Canal du Midi, 2km.
- Minerve - historic village, 8km.
- Olonzac market, 1km.
- Narbonne Cathedral.
- Wine-tasting.

rooms	3: 2 doubles, 1 suite for 4.
price	From € 61. Suite € 106.
meals	Dinner with wine, from € 30.
closed	Rarely.
directions	From Carcassonne N113 to Trèbes; left D610 to Homps; left D910 to Olonzac; follow signs to Pépieux; next to church.

Sally Worthington

tel	+33 (0)4 68 91 69 29
fax	+33 (0)4 68 91 65 49
e-mail	worthingtonjane@wanadoo.fr
web	perso.wanadoo.fr/carrefourbedbreakfast/

B&B

map 15   entry 192

La Terrasse au Soleil

Route de Fontfrède, 66400 Céret, Pyrénées-Orientales, France

A place for a splurge of activity and delicious indulgence. It has space: a four-hectare garden, a terrace with olive and mimosa trees, a vineyard; and a big pool, a tiny golf course and a tennis court. Deep green views to Mont Canigou, too. It's a retreat of "luxurious simplicity" in four connecting villas with fresh colour schemes; suites have terraces and two bathrooms. Delicious meals and an inviting bar between the indoor and outdoor dining rooms. A path has been cut to Céret so that you can avoid the road. Monsieur Leveillé is very attentive.

- Cultural Excursions.
- Modern Art at Céret.
- The Art of Cooking.
- Sauna, jacuzzi, massage.
- Swimming pool, tennis, putting, jogging circuits.
- Walking trails.

rooms	38: 31 doubles, 7 suites.
price	€159–€265. Suites €190–€296.
meals	Picnic available. Dinner from €43.
closed	Rarely.
directions	From Perpignan A9 south to Le Boulou; D115 south-west to Céret. 2km beyond Céret on road to Fontfrède.

M Leveillé Nizerolle

tel	+33 (0)4 68 87 01 94
fax	+33 (0)4 68 87 39 24
e-mail	terrasse-au-soleil.hotel@wanadoo.fr
web	www.la-terrasse-au-soleil.com

Hotel

Le Mas Bleu

07260 Rosières, Ardèche, France

Spot your neighbours through the mists of the steam bath or the bubbles of the jacuzzi. This old stone farmstead, run by an energetic and welcoming German couple, is beautifully decorated and supremely peaceful, despite the presence of up to 30 other residents. It's slightly alternative, with a 'writer's café' in the grounds and some nude pool-bathing. Estourel is the largest apartment, sleeping seven: two storeys and a covered terrace with magnificent views of vineyards and mountains. The highlight inside is a vast antique table, once used to cut lengths of local silk.

- Watercolours: in English, German & French.
- Ayurveda; aqua-wellness; massage; yoga.
- Southern France Discovery.
- Daily markets in surrounding villages.
- Sandpit, table-tennis, outdoor games & bikes.
- Trout & carp fishing in river Beaume.

rooms	7 apartments.
price	€ 450–€ 1,100 per week. Spa weeks € 700–€ 1,200 p.p.
meals	Self-catering.
closed	Rarely.
directions	Directions given on booking.

Anna Niedeggen

tel	+33 (0)4 75 39 93 75
fax	+33 (0)4 75 39 92 79
e-mail	info@thebluehouse.net
web	www.thebluehouse.net

Self-catering

map 16   entry 194

Les Jardins de Longsard

Château de Longsard, 69400 Arnas, Rhône, France

Orange trees in the *orangerie*, an obelisk amid the topiary, two spectacular Lebanon cedars, estate wine, 17th-century beams... Your hosts, much-travelled, sophisticated and informal, are working hard to return the estate to its former glory. They also love sharing their enthusiasm for the area and its wines and will organise tastings, including their own. Bedrooms, pure château from pastel to bold with hints of modernity, some with fine carved door frames, are eclectically furnished (Olivier's brother is an antique dealer). Breakfast jams are delicious.

- Horse-riding: in French, €12 per hour.
- Wine-tasting: in English & French.
- The Study of Wine: in English & French.
- Cookery: 20km, in English & French.
- Golf Tuition: 9km, in French.
- Cross-Country Cycling Centre, 10km.

rooms	5: 3 doubles, 2 suites.
price	€96–€101.
meals	Dinner with wine, from €32.
closed	Rarely.
directions	From north A6 exit 'Belleville'; N6 for Lyon 10km; right D43 to Arnas. Through village; château on right after 1.5km.

Alexandra & Olivier du Mesnil

tel	+33 (0)4 74 65 55 12
fax	+33 (0)4 74 65 03 17
e-mail	longsard@wanadoo.fr
web	www.longsard.com

B&B

Château de Pramenoux

69870 Lamure/Azergues, Rhône, France

Climb up the Mont du Beaujolais hills above Lyon. Rivers pulse down and a great pine forest cleans the air. As you round a curve, Gothic pepperpot turrets pop into view. The château sits in a natural clearing and views from the terrace and bedrooms sweep splendidly down the valley. Bits date from the 10th century up to the Rennaissance, including the mullioned windows along the gallery that links the towers. You'll find a panelled room, a gold and white striped bed, Louis XVI chairs, a canopied bed; all rooms are big and comfortable with simply elegant bathrooms.

- Cookery: 5-minute drive.
- Wrought-iron Workshops: 15-minute drive.
- Wine-tasting: 20-minute drive, in French.
- Jam-making: 30-minute drive, in French.
- Watercolour Painting: 30-minute drive.
- Classical music concerts & opera master classes.

rooms	4 doubles.
price	€ 110–€ 125.
meals	Dinner with drinks, from € 30.
closed	Rarely.
directions	From Paris A6 exit Belleville; D37 Beaujeu, at St Vincent left for Quincié en Beaujolais & Marchampt D9 for Lamure. Almost through village of Lamure, take lane in front of 'terrin de sport' marked Pramenoux & climb.

Emmanuel Baudoin & Jean-Luc Plasse

tel	+33 (0)4 74 03 16 43
fax	+33 (0)4 74 03 16 28
e-mail	pramenoux@aol.com
web	www.chateau-de-pramenoux.com

Hotel

map 16   entry 196

Château Lambert

69840 Chénas, Rhône, France

Marty's passion for textiles, his talent as an upholsterer and his eye for detail make this small 17th-century château especially beautiful. It sits in Beaujolais country on a hill overlooking the village of Chénas. Vines and more vines stretch over the Sâone plain and sometimes the snow-topped Alps are visible. A fine library takes up one wall in the huge apartment on the ground floor and a pair of *vieux rose* antique armchairs render a curvy touch of elegance. A magnificent canopied bed in the alcove has matching *toile de Jouy* drapes and bedspread.

- Grape-picking & Wine Tasting: in English, French, German & Dutch, September.
- Cookery Weekends: in English, French, German & Dutch.
- Wine hamlet, 4km.
- Cellars of the Beaujolais wine estate.
- Chateau de Cormatin, 30km.
- Pouilly-Fumé wine, 10km.

rooms	4: 2 doubles, 2 suites for 2.
price	€98–€129.
meals	Hosted dinner €26.
closed	January.
directions	A6 exit Macon Sud or A40 exit Replonges. N6 for Lyon. After 12km at La Chapelle de Guinchay, right for Chénas. At church, right. Signposted.

Marty Freriksen

tel	+33 (0)4 74 06 77 74
fax	+33 (0)4 74 04 48 01
e-mail	contact@chateau-lambert.com
web	www.chateau-lambert.com

Hotel

Hôtel Auberge Camelia

, 74570 Aviernoz, Haute-Savoie, France

The inn was thoroughly modernised by Roger and Sue some years ago: a small, intimate restaurant in the old kitchen, and bedrooms, carpeted and larger than average, straightforwardly comfortable with white walls, unfussy furnishings and good big bathrooms. Your happy hosts will take you to the start of some glorious walks. See the spectacular flower meadows, taste wine, ski at all levels – you can even watch the Alpine cattle stroll past your window, their great bells ringing nostalgically. A very welcoming inn with delightful owners and friendly staff.

- Golf Tuition: 15km, in English & French.
- Guided Alpine Walking: 15km, in French, €200.
- Historical Tour, Plateau de Glière: in English & French, no charge.
- Seminar facility.
- Cross-country & downhill skiing, 17km & 30km.
- Fishing, 4km.

rooms	12: 5 doubles, 6 triples, 1 quad.
price	€60-€98. Half-board €100-€130 (for 2).
meals	Breakfast from €9. Picnic from €7. Lunch/dinner from €15.
closed	Rarely.
directions	Annecy-Chamonix; Mt Blanc; LaRoche; N203. Right at mini r'bout Pont de Brogny, under r'way bridge. After 4km right for Villaz on D175. There, keep left, then left for Aviernoz; on left.

Suzanne & Roger Farrell-Cook

tel	+33 (0)4 50 22 44 24
fax	+33 (0)4 50 22 43 25
e-mail	info@hotelcamelia.com
web	www.hotelcamelia.com

Inn

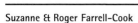

map 16   entry 198

Hôtel Le Cottage Fernand Bise

Au Bord du Lac, 74290 Talloires, Haute-Savoie, France

Watch the sun set over the 'Roc de Chère' across the Lac d'Annecy from the terrace. Fabulous. Monsieur and Madame Bise run this relaxed place with a quiet Savoyard efficiency, which, at its heart, has a proper concern for the comfort of guests. *Douillette* – that lovely word which is the French equivalent of 'cosy' – perfectly describes the atmosphere in the bedrooms. This is a wonderfully adult holiday centre, offering multifarious activities for the sporty and inspiration for the arty who wish to follow in the footsteps of Cézanne or Lamartine.

- Guided Mountain Biking & Walking: 4m.
- Golf Tuition: 3km.
- Tennis & Watersports: 4km.
- Guided visit to Roc de Chère nature reserve.
- Annecy.
- Reblochon cheese-making.

rooms	35 doubles.
price	€ 125–€ 220.
meals	Breakfast from € 14. Lunch/dinner € 35–€ 60.
closed	10 October-20 April.
directions	In Annecy follow signs Bord du Lac for Thônes D909. At Veyrier du Lac D909A to Talloires. Signposted in Talloires.

Jean-Claude & Christine Bise

tel	+33 (0)4 50 60 71 10
fax	+33 (0)4 50 60 77 51
e-mail	cottagebise@wanadoo.fr
web	www.cottagebise.com

Hotel

Salivet

26460 Truinas, Drôme, France

Breathtaking mountain views, a lovely owner and a fascinating building: the honey-stone house stands where the oxen sheds and haylofts used to be. Jane, an artist who specialises in silk-screen printing, lives next door; she and her architect partner have restored the place simply but beautifully with old beams, terracotta tile floors, stone fireplaces and antique furniture. Sit on the terrace, snooze on the lawn under the willow, cool off in the (shared) pool. On summer nights you can sleep on the roof terrace. *House for 4-6 also available.*

- Design & Decoration of Silk with Tour: on site & 35km, in English & French, from 2004.
- Qi-Gong & Shiatsu: on site & 5km, in English & French.
- Cookery, Farm to Table - Regional Recipes & Visits: in English & German.
- Guided Mountain Walk Week: in English.
- Own swimming pool.
- Local markets (Tuesdays-Fridays).

rooms	4: 2 singles, 1 double; 1 twin & 1 twin with cot, sharing 2 bathrooms.	
price	€650–€1,200 per week. Full-board & course €620–€696 p.p. per week.	
meals	Self-catering.	
closed	November-April.	
directions	Directions given on booking.	

Jane Worthington

tel	+33 (0)4 75 53 49 13
fax	+33 (0)4 75 53 37 31
e-mail	worthingtonjane@aol.com

Self-catering

map 16   entry 200

La Roche Colombe

26450 Charols, Drôme, France

If you like the idea of socialising with other Anglophone families, you'll love it here. Bob and Celia also run a B&B, and in the evenings everyone dines out in the huge courtyard under the plane trees. Your swish self-catering apartment has a bedroom with four-poster bed and pure white drapes, and a large living room with kilims and big fireplace. The children's room is furnished in pine and primary colours. Book meals; or if you prefer to eat *en famille* you can sit on the balcony and revel in the views. A discreet swimming pool is shared with B&B guests.

- Provencal Furniture Making & Painting: 1km, 10km, in English.
- Provencal Cookery: 3km, in English.
- Watercolours & Painting in Oils: 1-5km, in English.
- Wood sculpture; pottery: 1km, in English.
- Cotes du Rhône Wine Tour: in English.
- Pony trekking through river gorges.

rooms	2: 1 double, 1 twin sharing bathroom. B&B: 5 doubles/twins.
price	€928 per week. B&B €77 per room per night.
meals	Self-catering. Dinner €28.
closed	November-March.
directions	Directions given on booking.

Bob & Celia Christmas
tel	+33 (0)4 75 90 48 22
e-mail	rochecolombe@hotmail.com
web	www.bbfrance.com/xmas.html

B&B & self-catering

Domaine du Bois de la Cour

Route de Carpentras, 84290 Cairanne, Vaucluse, France

A great spot for exploring Provence. The big old house, surrounded by its vineyards and within harmless earshot of a road, is very handsome and Madame brings it to life with her special sparkle and enthusiasm for what she has created here. The decoration is all hers – more 'evolved French farmhouse-comfortable' than 'designer-luxurious'. She loves cooking, herbs and flowers; you may be offered her elderflower aperitif and have home-made cakes at breakfast. Nothing is too much trouble – walkers' luggage can be transferred, picnics can be laid on.

- Cookery: 8km, in English, French & German, January & February.
- Horse-riding.
- Wine Cellar & Wine-Tasting.
- Painting.
- Roman Amphitheatre, Orange, 18km.
- Avignon, 40km.

rooms	5: 2 doubles, 1 triple, 1 suite for 4, 1 apartment for 6.
price	From €90. Singles from €75.
meals	Dinner from €23.
closed	Rarely.
directions	A9 exit Bollène for Carpentras 18km; exit Cairanne, towards Carpentras 1.5km; house on right-hand turn.

Élisabeth & Jerry Para

tel	+33 (0)4 90 30 84 68
fax	+33 (0)4 90 30 84 68
e-mail	infos@boisdelacour.com
web	www.boisdelacour.com

B&B

map 16   entry 202

Auberge de la Fontaine

Place de la Fontaine, 84210 Venasque, Vaucluse, France

A place with a difference, sitting discreetly behind the central fountain of one of the most beautiful hill towns of Provence. Enter through a small bistro, then follow a tiny, wonky staircase to the restaurant where you'll find a grand piano in the middle of the room. Then up to bed to a suite furnished with modern pieces from young designers of zen-like sobriety; some of their small private terraces are up on another level. All rooms have cleverly hidden kitchens (with dishwashers) and sound systems for cassettes and CDs. Outstanding.

- Cookery: in English, French & German.
- Drawing: in village.
- Tennis, 1km.
- Botanical trails.
- Pony-trekking.
- 'Bâteaux de Provence' trips to Avignon.

rooms	5 suites.
price	From € 125.
meals	Breakfast € 10. Lunch & dinner € 18 in bistro (closed Sunday evening & Monday). Dinner € 38 in restaurant (closed Wednesday).
closed	Rarely.
directions	From Carpentras D4. Hotel opposite fountain, 7-minute walk from parking area. Tiny streets of hill town are pedestrian.

M & Mme Soehlke

tel	+33 (0)4 90 66 02 96
fax	+33 (0)4 90 66 13 14
e-mail	fontvenasq@aol.com
web	www.auberge-lafontaine.com

Inn & self-catering

entry 203   map 16

La Bastide de Voulonne

84220 Cabrières d'Avignon, Vaucluse, France

In splendid isolation in the lavender fields beneath the ancient hilltop villages of the Luberon mountains, the 18th-century farm was rescued from years of neglect. Sophie and Alain have done a fantastic job, sticking to natural, local colours. The bedrooms are huge. The garden – more like a park really – has a big pool not far from the house. It's a great place for children; Sophie and Alain have young twins. They plan to grow vegetables in the garden and menus already centre round local food. Lots of places around for lunch, or Sophie will do you a picnic.

- All about Truffles: in grounds & 3km, in English & French, January & February.
- Wine-tasting: on site & 5km, in French, October.
- Lavender Museum, Coustellet, 2km.
- Corkscrew Museum, Ménerbes, 6km.
- Antique dealers' village & market, Isle sur la Sorgue, 12km.
- Villages of Gordes & Bories.

rooms	8: 7 doubles, 1 suite.
price	€ 125–€ 150.
meals	Breakfast from € 11. Dinner from € 29.
closed	Mid-November–mid December; can open by arrangement, January & February.
directions	After Avignon A7 on N100 for Apt. At Coustellet x-roads to Gordes; at r'bout (Collège de Calavon) for Gordes. After 1km right, Bastide 600m on left.

Sophie & Alain Rebourg

tel	+33 (0)4 90 76 77 55
fax	+33 (0)4 90 76 77 56
e-mail	sophie@bastide-voulonne.com
web	www.bastide-voulonne.com

Hotel

map 16 entry 204

Mas de Cornud

Route de Mas Blanc, D31, 13210 Saint Rémy de Provence, Bouches-du-Rhône, France

Guest house and cookery school combine successfully in a typical farmhouse where majestic plane trees stand guard and the scents and light of Provence hover. Nito and David have done a superb restoration where every object is clearly the best. Bedrooms are big and varied, all beautifully decorated yet warmly simple. The atmosphere is convivial and open: you are a member of a family here, so join the others at the bar, choose a book from the library, bask in the pool and jacuzzi. The kitchen is country-traditional, with cast-iron range and long wooden table.

- Home Cooking in Provence: spring & autumn, week-long residential.
- Single-session Cookery.
- Cuisine au Feu Outdoors: July, 5-day residential.
- Cooking & Hiking in Provence: spring & autumn, 5-day residential.
- Wine-tasting excursions in Rhone Valley.
- Fête de la Transhumance repast: Whit Monday.

rooms	6: 5 doubles, 1 suite.
price	€ 130–€ 220. Suite € 240–€ 350.
meals	Picnic available. Lunch € 20–€ 45. Hosted dinner from € 40–€ 55.
closed	January–March.
directions	3km west of St Rémy de Provence on D99 for Tarascon. Left on D27 for Les Baux; after 1km left at sign Château des Alpilles D31. Mas 200m on left.

David & Nitockrees Tadros Carpita

tel	+33 (0)4 90 92 39 32
fax	+33 (0)4 90 92 55 99
e-mail	mascornud@compuserve.com
web	www.mascornud.com

Hotel

Hostellerie Bérard

Rue Gabriel-Péri, 83740 La Cadière d'Azur, Var, France

The Hostellerie is made up of an 11th-century monastery and an old *bastide* and 'painter's house'. Danièle and Michel Bérard grew up in this ancient village, in sight of a mountain called the Grand Bérard. In the old convent each bedroom is a surprise: you might find a delicate four-poster, with *toile de Jouy* curtains or shutters opening onto the olive- and vine-covered hills, or onto the swimming pool. Michel is a Maître Cuisinier de France, while Danièle is an expert in the local wines. Those on the cookery course are taken to local producers and markets.

- Cookery: in English.
- Watercolour Painting: in English.
- Kitchen Gardening: in English.
- Roman museum, 5km.
- Honey farm, 4km.
- Oil mill, 2km.

rooms	40: 36 doubles, 4 suites.
price	€ 79–€ 148. Suites € 224–€ 290.
meals	Buffet breakfast from € 15. Lunch à la carte. Dinner € 40–€ 99.
closed	January.
directions	A50 towards Toulon exit 11. Hotel in centre of village.

M & Mme Bérard

tel	+33 (0)4 94 90 11 43
fax	+33 (0)4 94 90 01 94
e-mail	berard@hotel-berard.com
web	www.hotel-berard.com

Hotel

map 16 entry 206

La Maison Blanche

Route de Claviers, Quartier le Lauron, 83830 Bargemon, Var, France

You're outside one of the prettiest and most fashionable villages of east Provence but here you see no-one. Surrounded by lawns, flower-filled meadows and orchards, the old farmhouse in the mountains has been completely renovated, with old beams instact. Furniture is mostly antique French and English, and the lovely end bedroom, once the hayloft, has a vine-clad balcony. As bedrooms are reached by two staircases, the house is ideal for two families holidaying together. Eat on the huge terrace under the shade of the limes, bask by the heavenly pool.

- French Language: in village, every Thursday, 2pm.
- Boules, table tennis & croquet in garden.
- Thursday village market - short walk uphill.
- Weekly hiking party in village, Wednesdays.
- Wine tasting, 10-12km.
- Rock climbing, kayaking & rafting, Gorge du Verdon.

rooms	5: 3 twins; 1 twin, 1 double sharing bathroom.
price	£470-£2,050 per week.
meals	Self-catering.
closed	Rarely.
directions	Directions given on booking.

Janet Hill

tel	+44 (0)1628 482579
fax	+44 (0)1628 482579
e-mail	dsimons@onetel.net.uk

Hôtel Paris-Rome

79 Porte de France, 06500 Menton-Garavan, Alpes-Maritimes, France

The Paris-Rome was built by Gil's grandfather and has been run as a family hotel for many years. Friendly Gil has put together a programme for visiting the coastal gardens – from Ellen Willmott's Hanbury, to an afternoon with the head gardener at Lawrence Johnston's Serre de la Madone and a tour of a rarely-opened botanical garden. Gil also offers fishing holidays when your catch will be cooked to your liking. Rooms are comfortable and traditional and some have sea views. There's a private beach, too.

- Art & Painting: in English & French, Saturday afternoons.
- Garden Tours: in French.
- Fishing Trips: in French.
- Private beach.
- Tours of old Menton.
- Tours of Maria Serena Gardens.

rooms	22: 17 doubles, 2 singles, 3 triples.
price	€ 55–€ 85.
meals	Breakfast from € 8.50. Lunch from € 25. Dinner from € 35.
closed	November-January.
directions	A8 exit Menton, proceed to waterfront & towards Italian border. Hotel at traffic lights opposite Port of Garavan, 100m before Italian border.

Gil Castellana

tel	+33 (0)4 93 35 73 45
fax	+33 (0)4 93 35 29 30
e-mail	paris-rome@wanadoo.fr
web	www.hotel-paris-rome.com

Hotel

map 1   entry 208

england, scotland
& wales

Photography by Michael Busselle

england, scotland & wales

Apsley House

141 Newbridge Hill, Bath , Bath & N. E. Somerset, BA1 3PT, England

The Duke of Wellington is thought to have lived here, though if he did, the tempo was probably a little stiffer than it is now. The house is full of great furniture, tallboy porter chairs, gilt mirrors and rich Colefax & Fowler fabrics. Take a drink from the bar, then collapse into one of the sofas in the drawing room and gaze onto the garden through the huge, arched window. The dining room shares the same, warm elegance, with fresh flowers on all the tables. Bedrooms are big; breakfasts are memorable. *Private car park. Children over five welcome.*

- Roman Baths.
- Royal Crescent.
- Theatre Royal, Bath.
- River Avon & canal.
- Pulteney Bridge.
- Stonehenge.

rooms	10: 3 doubles, 5 twins/doubles, 1 four-poster, 1 family.
price	£75-£140. Singles £60-£85.
meals	Restaurants in Bath.
closed	Christmas.
directions	A4 west into Bath. Keep right at 1st mini-r'bout. On for about 2 miles, then follow 'Bristol A4' signs. Pass Total garage on right. At next lights, branch right. On left after 1 mile.

Claire & Nicholas Potts

tel	+44 (0)1225 336966
fax	+44 (0)1225 425462
e-mail	info@apsley-house.co.uk
web	www.apsley-house.co.uk

B&B

Paradise House

Holloway, Bath, Bath & N. E. Somerset, BA2 4PX, England

The magical 180-degree panorama from the garden, which draws you out as soon as you enter the house, is a dazzling advertisement for Bath. Most of the rooms make full use of the view – the best have bay windows. All have a soft, luxurious country feel, with drapes, wicker and good bathrooms. There are also two garden rooms in an extension in keeping with the original Bath stone house – David is justly proud. The whole place uses glass in all the right places; the sitting room has lovely stone-arched French windows that draw in the light. *Seven-minute walk from centre.*

- Thermae Bath Spa, opens 2003.
- Roman Baths, Bath.
- The Cotswolds.
- Stonehenge.
- Avebury.
- Stourhead House & Gardens (NT).

rooms	11: 4 doubles, 4 twins, 1 family, 2 four-posters.
price	£75–£155. Singles £55–£95.
meals	Restaurants in Bath.
closed	Christmas.
directions	From train station one-way system to Churchill Bridge. A367 exit from r'bout up hill. After 0.75 miles left at Andrews estate agents. Left down hill into cul-de-sac. On left.

David & Annie Lanz

tel	+44 (0)1225 317723
fax	+44 (0)1225 482005
e-mail	info@paradise-house.co.uk
web	www.paradise-house.co.uk

Hotel

map 17 entry 210

Corston Fields Farm

Corston, Bath, Bath & N.E. Somerset, BA2 9EZ, England

The Addicotts have given over a generous swathe of their farm to the creation of a natural habitat for indigenous wildlife and have a Gold Award under the Duke of Cornwall's Habitat Award 2002 scheme. Utterly committed to the environment, they use flax from the vibrant blue linseed crops to heat their sturdy listed house. There are stone mullion windows, dressers with old china, Chinese rugs on wooden floors, open fires, a smattering of Africana and big bedrooms. Your affable hosts manage the mix of B&B-ing and farming with easy-going humour.

- Conservation Education: no charge.
- Wildlife Watch - mobile shepherd's hut in grounds.
- Roman Baths, Bath, 5 miles.
- Horse-riding, 5 miles.
- Golf, 1 mile.
- Thermae Bath Spa, 5 miles.

rooms	4: 1 double, 1 twin; 2 doubles sharing bath/shower.
price	£60-£72. Singles £36.
meals	Lunch/dinner from £12.
closed	Christmas & New Year.
directions	From A4 west of Bath, A39 through Corston. 1 mile on, just before Wheatsheaf Pub (on right), right. Signed 200yds along lane on right.

Gerald & Rosaline Addicott

tel	+44 (0)1225 873305
fax	(0)1225 874421
e-mail	corston.fields@btinternet.com
web	www.corstonfields.com

B&B

Honey Batch Cottage

Railway Lane, Wellow, Bath, Bath & N.E. Somerset, BA2 8QG, England

Our inspector loved the way this place manages to combine elegance with cosiness. Logs burn in the fireplace, the colours are warm, the dresser is Welsh, the stones are flagged. The kitchen – with Aga and terracotta tiles – is beamed and cheerful with a cherrywood refectory table. There is peace and comfort among the quirky internal touches, the winding stairs and old bread oven. Angharad is an aromatherapist (book a treatment in advance). The bedroom is "pure magic", with gorgeous furniture. Wellow is delightful. *Children over five welcome.*

- Aromatherapy.
- Life Coaching & Stress Management.
- Painting & Drawing.
- Embroidery, Beading & Sewing.
- Garden Tours.
- Guided Tour of Bath.

rooms	2: 1 double, 1 single.
price	£55-£60. Singles from £35.
meals	Lunch from £8. Dinner from £15.
closed	Rarely.
directions	From Bath A367 Exeter road. After 3 miles, left opp. Strydes Inn, signed 'Wellow 3 miles'. Park in square by Fox & Badger pub. House 2 doors down in Railway Lane.

Angharad Rhys-Roberts
tel   +44 (0)1225 833107
e-mail angharad@waitrose.com

B&B

map 17   entry 212

Claremont House Hotel

13 Second Avenue, Hove, Brighton & Hove, BN3 2LL, England

This handsome Victorian villa is being gently renovated by its new owners. They're not aiming for opulence, although 19th-century chandeliers, fireplaces and cornices survive in many rooms. What Russell and Michael are passionate about is making guests feel cared for in their home, and they are seriously keen on food – fresh, local and seasonal; no special diet is too much trouble. Flowers – outside and in – smell gorgeous. High-ceilinged bedrooms have good beds and linen, pristine bathrooms and little extras, and the whole place feels hugely cared for.

- Windsurfing: 0.5 miles.
- Cricket: 0.25 miles.
- Safe beach.
- Sussex County Cricket Ground, 0.25 miles.
- Brighton Pier & Pavilion, 1 mile.
- Glyndebourne Festival (May–August).

rooms	12: 6 doubles, 5 singles, 1 four-poster.
price	From £70–£150. Singles from £45.
meals	Dinner from £18.50; local restaurants, too.
closed	Rarely.
directions	M23/A23 to Brighton. At seafront r'bout opp. pier, right on A259 Kings Rd/Kingsway for 1.5 miles, then right into Second Ave. Hotel near top of road on right.

Russell Brewerton & Michael Reed

tel	+44 (0)1273 735161
fax	+44 (0)1273 735161
e-mail	claremonthove@aol.com
web	www.claremonthousehotel.co.uk

Hotel

Model Farm

Little Gransden, Cambridgeshire, SG19 3EA, England

One cosy yet large and very private bedroom is up its own spiral staircase – it is a lovely conversion and sure winner of first prize in any Loo With A View competition. In the main house is a fresh blue and white bedroom; those that like their independence will be happy in either room, as the Barlows' relaxed 'take-us-as-you-find-us' approach pervades the whole house. There are fruit trees and bees in the garden and home-made jam and honey for breakfast and, although this is now an arable farm, sheep still graze the land. Perfectly quiet, and close to Cambridge.

- Guided Walking Tour of Cambridge: 15 miles.
- Duxford Imperial War Museum.
- Shuttleworth Aircraft Collection.
- Anglesea Abbey.
- Wimpole Hall.
- Ely.

rooms	3 doubles.
price	From £50. Singles from £30.
meals	Pub/restaurant 3 miles.
closed	Christmas.
directions	Exit A1198 at Longstowe onto B1046. House on right after 3 miles, before Little Gransden.

Sue Barlow

tel	+44 (0)1767 677361
fax	+44 (0)1767 677883
e-mail	bandb@modelfarm.org.uk
web	www.modelfarm.org.uk

B&B

map 18   entry 214

Penzance Arts Club

Chapel House, Penzance, Cornwall, TR18 4AQ, England

Amusing, quirky and original... the Arts Club has brought a little fun to old Penzance. Belinda has created an easy-going but vital cultural centre. Fall into bed after a combination of poetry and jazz in the bar – comfortable sofas hug an ancient wooden floor that fills with people as the laid-back party atmosphere warms up. Presiding over all in his unassuming way is Dave the barman, ready to pour a pint; the local organic beer is superb. Upstairs, attractive and colourful bedrooms are as charmingly flamboyant as the bar is raffish. Not luxurious, but good value.

- Painting: £100 per day, inc. B&B.
- Writing: £100 per day.
- Gallery on site.
- Tate St Ives, 20-minute drive.
- Penlee Museum, 5-minute drive.
- Eden Project.

rooms	7: 2 doubles; 1 double, with private bath; 1 double, 3 family, all with shower, sharing wc.
price	£70–£100. Singles from £35.
meals	Lunch from £5. Dinner from £12.50. Restaurant closed Sundays, plus Mondays in winter.
closed	Rarely.
directions	Drive along harbourside sea on left. Opp. docks, right into Quay St (Dolphin pub). Up hill; house on right opp. St Mary's Church.

Belinda Rushworth-Lund

tel	+44 (0)1736 363761
fax	+44 (0)1736 363761
e-mail	reception@penzanceartsclub.co.uk
web	www.penzanceartsclub.co.uk

Inn

Pine Cottage

Portloe, Truro, Portloe, Cornwall, TR2 5RB, England

What a treat! Catch a tantalising glimpse of the sea from your B&B and wake to the sound of a bubbling stream. Clare's generous, sunny nature is reflected in her lovely home, with its shelves of books, rose-strewn wallpapers and delicious smells of baking. She used to run a restaurant and is a superb cook who loves to treat guests to locally-caught fish. Bedrooms are filled with light; the double has a glimpse of the sea. All this, a garden full of birdsong, a (real) fishing village 500 yards below and the Eden project close by. *Children by arrangement.*

- Safe secluded beaches.
- Cornish Coastal Path.
- St Just in Roseland Church.
- Eden Project.
- National Maritime Museum, Falmouth.
- Lost Gardens of Heligan.

rooms	2: 1 twin/double; 1 double with private bath/shower.
price	£70-£90. Singles from £45.
meals	Dinner £25-£30.
closed	Rarely.
directions	From Tregony, A3078 to St Mawes. After 2 miles left to Portloe at Esso garage. Through village until Ship Inn. Right fork after pub car park. Immed. on left between white gate posts up drive under trees.

Clare Holdsworth

tel	+44 (0)1872 501385
web	www.pinecottage.net

B&B

map 17   entry 216

Polsue Manor

Ruan High Lanes, Truro, Cornwall, TR2 5LU, England

A footpath leads from the garden to a big sandy beach – a perfect spot for seaside holidays. There's no shortage of spare welly boots for the children either; a sense of fun echoes around Polsue. Rooms are huge, bedrooms have country eiderdowns, comfy beds and views; there are wooden floors and rugs in the dining room. Annabelle has cooked professionally and her breakfasts are special. Outside: big trees, camellias, a pond, green field views and a real sense of space. You are close to the Eden Project, and there are lots of fine gardens nearby.

- Lost Gardens of Heligan, 20-minute drive.
- Eden Project, 40-minute drive.
- Trelissick, a ferry ride.
- Trewithan Gardens (NT), 15-minute drive.
- Trebah Gardens, 45-minute drive.
- Glendurgan Gardens, 45-minute drive.

rooms	3 twins/doubles.
price	From £80. Singles from £40.
meals	Pub 1 mile.
closed	Rarely.
directions	A3078 south from Tregony. In Ruan High Lanes, 2nd right (for Philleigh & King Harry Ferry). House 1 mile up on left.

Annabelle Sylvester

tel	+44 (0)1872 501270
fax	+44 (0)1872 501177
web	www.polsuemanor.co.uk

B&B

Penellick

Pelynt, Nr. Looe, Cornwall, PL13 2LX, England

You are at the head of the old smuggling route and an ancient right of way leads you to Polperro's little harbour. The Macartneys have breathed new life into the 14th-century Grade II*-listed hall house and the ancient charm blends perfectly with added comforts. There are three dressing-gowns in descending order of size and you have your own cosy, timbered A-frame sitting room with woodburner, candles, wild flowers; it's stylish, memorably special, and very good value. Food is organic and free-range where possible and always cooked with enormous care.

- Eden Project.
- Lost Gardens of Heligan.
- Lanhydrock (NT).
- Cotehele House & Gardens (NT).
- Cornish Coastal Path.
- Caerhays & many other gardens nearby.

rooms	2: 1 double, 1 single, sharing private bath & sitting room.
price	£50–£70. Singles £25–£35.
meals	Dinner from £21.50.
closed	Rarely.
directions	A387 through Looe & approx. 3 miles beyond, then B3359 for Pelynt. Less than a mile on, second of 2 turnings on left. After 0.5 miles, left at T-junc.tion then fork left, signed.

Michael & Ann Macartney

tel	+44 (0)1503 272372
fax	+44 (0)1503 272372
e–mail	penellick@hotmail.com

B&B

map 17   entry 218

Glynn Barton Cottages

Cardinham, Bodmin, Cornwall, PL30 4AX, England

Like the Pied Piper, Andy leads the visiting children away – to collect eggs and meet the animals. And there's great planting in progress in the 13 acres of these thoughtfully renovated farm buildings with amazing views. The single-storey cottages, sleeping from two to six, have open-plan living rooms with comfy sofas, gas 'woodburners' and beams. Furniture is spotless pine. On the brick terrace or the lawns children are wonderfully safe, and there's so much to keep them happy: swimming, tennis, table-tennis, barbecue, games, videos, books, company.

- Indoor swimming pool.
- Tennis & games barns.
- Children's play area.
- Eden Project, 8 miles.
- Sandy beaches, 8-12 miles.
- Surfing beaches, 12 miles.

rooms	6 cottages, sleeping 2, 4, 4, 4, 6, 6.
price	£200-£1,100 per week.
meals	Self-catering.
closed	Rarely.
directions	Directions given on booking.

Andy & Lucy Orr

tel	+ 44 (0)1208 821375
fax	+ 44 (0)1208 821104
e-mail	cottages@glynnbarton.fsnet.co.uk
web	www.glynnbarton.co.uk

Self-catering

Old De Lank Farm

St. Breward, Bodmin, Cornwall, PL30 4ND, England

It is thought that the origins of this 13th-century hall house were ecclesiastical. It was added to in the early 19th century, and the Castles have completely restored the period Regency look: one guest commented that it was like living on a Jane Austen set! Slate flagstones with oriental rugs, an oak-panelled drawing room and a classic Regency dining room with inglenook fireplaces. History is blended with modern comfort upstairs: new period bathrooms have roll-top baths and/or power showers, pretty bedrooms have leaded windows and very comfortable beds.

- Cookery Demonstrations: winter.
- Sailing Trips: 50-minute drive, summer.
- Horse-riding, 5-minute drive.
- Bicycle hire, 5-minute drive.
- Lanhydrock (NT), 20-minute drive.
- The Eden Project, 30-minute drive.

rooms	3: 2 doubles, 1 twin/double.
price	From £60. Singles £40.
meals	Picnic lunch £9.95. Dinner £13.50–£22.50.
closed	Rarely.
directions	10 minutes from A30 taking Blisland & Breward turning. Precise directions given at time of booking.

John & Marcia Castle

tel	+44 (0)1208 851366
fax	+44 (0)1208 851829
e-mail	olddelankfarm@aol.com

B&B

map 17   entry 220

Gillthwaite Rigg, Heathwaite Manor

Lickbarrow Road, Windermere, Cumbria, LA23 2NQ, England

The Grahams are passionate about conservation, their house and the wildlife which populates the 14 acres of private woodland and grounds. The Edwardian Arts & Crafts-style house has beautifully made oak doors with wooden latches, motifs moulded into plasterwork, stone fireplaces, green Lakeland slate roof and great round chimneys. Bedrooms, reached via a spiral staircase, are simple and, like the panelled sitting room, allow the architecture to breathe. Distant views of mountains and lakes are stupendous. *Babies & children over six welcome.*

- Fell-walking.
- Guided wildlife tours of own woodland.
- Levens Hall & Topiary Gardens.
- Beatrix Potter's Home at Sawrey (NT).
- Sailing & windsurfing, Lake Windermere.
- Blackwell Arts & Crafts House.

rooms	3: 1 double, 1 twin; 1 further double for members of same party.
price	£55–£64. Singles from £37.50.
meals	Excellent pubs/restaurants locally.
closed	Christmas & New Year.
directions	From M6, junc. 36, A590/A591 to r'bout, then B5284 for Hawkshead (via ferry) for 6 miles. After golf club, right for Heathwaite. Bear right up hill past nursery. Next drive on right; central part.

Rhoda M. Graham

tel	+44 (0)15394 46212
fax	+44 (0)15394 46212
e-mail	tony_rhodagraham@hotmail.com

B&B

Low Fell

Ferney Green, Bowness-on-Windermere, Windermere, Cumbria, LA23 3ES, England

Louise and Stephen are bubbly and fun and give a big, generous welcome with not a hint of stuffiness. Bedrooms are sunny and bright with huge comfy beds, fat pillows and super quilted throws, and overlook a wonderful variety of trees – open the windows and let the birdsong. You'll find it easy to relax by the fire in the winter with a glass of wine, or in the secluded garden in summer. After a splendid breakfast – lots of choice and home-made bread and Aga pancakes too – stroll to lake, fells or village, just five minutes away.

- Sailing: 0.5 miles.
- Guided Walks - all levels.
- The Mountain Goat - guided mini-bus tours.
- Lake Windermere.
- Watersports on lake.
- Hot-air ballooning.

rooms	3: 1 twin/double, 1 family suite (1 double, 1 twin).
price	£56-£72. Single £36-£40.
meals	Picnic lunch from £6.
closed	Christmas & New Year.
directions	From Kendal, A591 to Windermere & follow signs to Bowness. There, bear left at bottom of hill & 1st left opposite church. Follow road past garage on left. House 50yds on, on right.

Louise & Stephen Broughton

tel	+44 (0)15394 45612
fax	+44 (0)15394 48411
e-mail	lowfell@talk21.com
web	www.low-fell.co.uk

B&B

map 17 entry 222

Rose Cottage

Snelston, Ashbourne, Derbyshire, DE6 2DL, England

Lush greenness surrounds this house, up a tiny country lane. It has views over the Dove Valley and there's a fine garden. An ancestor of Peter was Lord Mayor of London in 1681, hence the memorabilia. Cynthia is Australian and they are a delightful and genuinely friendly couple. Although elegant, the house is primarily a home. Guests are treated as friends and there is a small, book-lined sitting room just for you. The hall sets the tone: white tiles, Indian rugs, woodburning stove and ancestral paintings. The bedrooms are impeccable.

- Chatsworth, 20 miles.
- The Potteries, 20 miles.
- Tissington Trail with bike hire, 4 miles.
- Sudbury Hall (NT), 8 miles.
- Alton Towers, 6 miles.
- Dovedale & Manifold Valley, 9 miles.

rooms	2: 1 double; 1 double with private bathroom.
price	£52–£56. Singles from £35.
meals	Good pub 2 miles.
closed	Christmas.
directions	From Ashbourne, A515 Lichfield road. After 4 miles, right onto B5033. After 1 mile, 2nd lane on right. Cottage 0.5 miles on, on right.

Peter & Cynthia Moore

tel	+44 (0)1335 324230
fax	+44 (0)1335 324651
e-mail	pjmoore@beeb.net

B&B

South Hooe Mine

Hole's Hole, Bere Alston, Yelverton, Devon, PL20 7BW, England

The house swims with light. The Tamar is magnetic and there's a ruin of an ivy-clad engine house and mine count house from the days when lead and silver were mined here. The lovely Trish makes bread and will procure beef and lamb, or salmon fresh from the river below. Martha the donkey helps Trish win the battle with nature but prefers to have her front feet in the kitchen. Sail in, through the SSSI and AONB: there are moorings and a jetty. A characterful backdrop to writer Roselle's inspirational writing classes. *Young children beware mine shaft and tidal river.*

- Creative Writing Workshops with Roselle Angwin: from £195 (2 days) full-board.
- Cotehele House & Gardens (NT).
- Buckland Abbey & Gardens (NT).
- Dartmoor, 7 miles.
- Eden Project, 1-hour drive.
- Boating on the Tamar.

rooms	5: 1 double; 1 twin/double with extra single/dressing room; 3 singles.
price	£50-£55. Singles £25-£27.50.
meals	Picnic from £5. Supper from £12.50. Dinner from £15.
closed	Rarely.
directions	B3257 Bere Alston, left for Weir Quay. Over x-roads. Hole's Hole sign, right for Hooe. Fork left for South Hooe Farm. 300yds on, turn sharply back to left & down track.

Trish Dugmore

tel	+44 (0)1822 840329
e-mail	southhooe@aol.com
web	www.roselle-angwin.co.uk

B&B

map 17   entry 224

The Yeoman's Country House

Collaton, Salcombe, Devon, TQ7 3DJ, England

The house is one of the few remaining thatched Devon longhouses in the area and it sits at the head of its own valley with wonderful walking and beaches nearby. It is more like a hotel than a private house: lots of attention to detail – a fridge for drinks, Molton Brown toiletries in the bathroom, boxed stationery, lavender-scented linens and afternoon tea on arrival. Every window is dressed with swags, tails and tie-backs. Breakfast will be free-range, organic, local and seasonal; bread is baked daily and jam and muesli are home-made. *Children by arrangement.*

- Antique Auction Sales: 2 miles, 8 May, 10 July, 18 September, 20 November.
- Sailing, Salcombe Estuary: 2 miles.
- Bridge, Duplicate/Rubber: 2 miles, Monday-Friday.
- Bee-keeping: 5 miles.
- Writing: 2 miles, Tuesday, fortnightly.
- Yoga: 3 miles.

rooms	3: 1 double, 1 twin/double, 1 four-poster.
price	£80–£130. Singles from £65.
meals	Picnic from £7.50. Candlelit dinner from £30 (min. 6).
closed	Christmas.
directions	In Marlborough, turn opp. Texaco garage into Collaton Rd. Approx. 0.3 miles on, left for Collaton. Keep left at grass island, for Higher Collaton. At end of private lane.

Mark Andrews

tel	+44 (0)1548 560085
fax	+44 (0)1548 562070
e-mail	yeomanshouse@easicom.com
web	www.yeomanshouse.com

B&B

Vogwell Cottage
Manaton, Newton Abbott, Devon, TQ13 9XD, England

The house is small, cosy, unpretentious, plain and fits around you like a well-worn glove. Christina is welcoming and plies you with tea and well-travelled companionship. The valleys of the Teign river are a marvellous part of Devon to explore – take your binoculars and watch the birds; your hostess will name paths to follow. Bedrooms have good sheets, cottagey curtains and bedspreads. There are fabulous bedroom views: the garden and stream from one and the open moor from another. Slightly chaotic and worn around the edges but there's real warmth here.

- Carriage-driving: 30-minute drive.
- Falconery.
- Archaeological Walks - Bronze Age to Industrial Revolution.
- Birdwatching: on site & on estuary.
- Pony-trekking: Widecombe-in-the-Moor.
- Hunting: own stables & field.

rooms	2 doubles both with private bathroom.
price	From £40.
meals	Light supper from £12. Dinner from £20.
closed	May-mid-October.
directions	From Bovey Tracey follow signs to Manaton/Becky Falls. From Kestor Inn in Manaton follow signs to Moretonhampstead for 3.3 miles. Lane to house is 2nd on left after Heatree Cross.

John & Christina Everett
tel   +44 (0)1647 221302

B&B

map 17   entry 226

The Hoops Country Inn & Hotel

Horns Cross, Bideford, Devon, EX39 5DL, England

Blissfully out of kilter with the outside world, Hoops Inn has changed little in 800 years – there are just fewer smugglers rubbing shoulders with the local gentry at the bar these days. The bar has a mellow tick-tock atmosphere, with irregular beams, snug corners and blazing fires in winter. Above, baroque-style bedrooms are magnificent; pass a pretty courtyard to more bedrooms in an old coachhouse. They're smaller but have the same period feel. Fresh fish, an ample vegetarian menu and the friendliest welcome.

- Falconry: weekly, £90 per day.
- Painting: £90 per day.
- Coarse & Sea Fishing: 3 miles, weekly.
- Diving: 3 miles, weekly.
- Horse-riding: 5 miles.
- Birdwatching on Lundy Island.

rooms	12: 4 doubles, 2 twins/doubles, 1 twin, 3 four-posters, 1 family, 1 suite.
price	£90–£170. Singles from £50.
meals	Lunch £4.50–£10. Dinner £7.50–£23.
closed	Christmas Day.
directions	From Bideford, A39 for Bude (North Devon coastal road) for 6 miles. Just past Horns Cross, road dips. Inn on right.

Gay Marriott

tel	+44 (0)1237 451222
fax	+44 (0)1237 451247
e-mail	sales@hoopsinn.co.uk
web	www.hoopsinn.co.uk

Inn

Combe House Hotel & Restaurant

Honiton, Nr. Exeter , Devon, EX14 3AD, England

Ruth and Ken have distilled their worldly experience to create a sublime place to stay. What makes this place so special is the modest way they apply themselves to every task, big or small. Try the best Devon produce, local as can be, with the chef finishing your main course on the huge, restored wood-burning range. The rest of the house is just as fabulous – Elizabethan and Restoration eras meld into one: mullioned windows, oak panelling, oils, luxurious bedrooms and *trompe l'œil*. The long, wooded drive that brings you here will unravel all.

- Masterchef Cookery.
- Wine Appreciation.
- Floral Workshops.
- Walking Jurassic coast: 20 minute-drive.
- Exploring the thatched village of Gittisham.
- Honiton's lace & antique shops.

rooms	15: 11 twins/doubles, 1 four-poster, 3 suites.
price	£138–£265. Singles from £99.
meals	Lunch from £16.50. Dinner from £34.
closed	Rarely.
directions	A30 south from Honiton for 2 miles; A375 for Sidmouth & Branscombe. Signed through woods.

Ruth & Ken Hunt

tel	+44 (0)1404 540400
fax	+44 (0)1404 46004
e-mail	stay@thishotel.com
web	www.thishotel.com

Hotel

map 17   entry 228

West Colwell Farm

Offwell, Honiton, Devon, EX14 9SL, England

Privacy and stylish comfort in stunning surroundings: after a lot of travelling, these ex-TV producers had a clear vision of what made a perfect place to stay. Each bedroom is self-contained and has a private 'deck' dotted with pots; the woodland views are glorious. No expense has been spared: chrome shower heads are the size of dinner plates, the beds firm, the linen luxurious. They have used local craftsmen and materials in the renovation. Judging by Frank's nut torte, breakfasts will be excellent. Valley, woodland and bluebell walks start from your terrace.

- Walks from door - with written guide.
- Offwell Woodland & Wildlife Trust.
- Honiton.
- Jurassic coast.
- Lyme Regis.
- Dartmoor, 40-minute drive.

rooms	3 doubles.
price	From £70. Singles from £35.
meals	Picnic from £7.50. Restaurants in Honiton.
closed	Christmas.
directions	Offwell is 3 miles from Honiton & signed off A35 Honiton–Axminster road. In centre of village, at church, down hill. Farm 0.5 miles on.

Frank & Carol Hayes

tel	+44 (0)1404 831130
fax	+44 (0)1404 831769
e-mail	stay@westcolwell.co.uk
web	www.westcolwell.co.uk

B&B

Gray's Farmhouse

Toller Porcorum, Dorchester, Dorset, DT2 0EJ, England

The house is set in a maze of paths that run through ancient wildflower meadows and medieval woodland; the views from the ramparts of Eggardon's hill fort are superb. From up there you can gaze down on the soft stone farmhouse and sleepy flower-decked lanes. The former shooting lodge has enormous flagstones, stripped floors, chunky studded doors and exposed beams. The tranquillity of the bedrooms complements Rosie's decorative paintings. Explore the secret valleys and bumpety hills of West Dorset and the spectacular World Heritage coast. Enchanting.

- Painting.
- Art & Imagework.
- Digital Cameras - How to Use Creatively.
- World Heritage coastline, 9 miles.
- Wildlife reserves adjoining grounds.
- Walking the Jubilee Trail.

rooms	2: 1 family, 1 twin.
price	£48-£64. Singles from £30.
meals	Full-board available for those on courses. Pub, 3 miles.
closed	Rarely.
directions	On A37, then A356 from Dorchester, left at 1st sign for Toller Porcorum. Through village & up hill for 1 mile. At x-roads, right for Powerstock, under bridge. Track 0.5 miles on left, opp. white post by lane. At end, on left.

Rosie & Roger Britton
tel +44 (0)1308 485574
e-mail rosieroger@farmhousebnb.co.uk
web www.farmhousebnb.co.uk

B&B

map 17   entry 230

Bridge House Hotel

3 Prout Bridge, Beaminster, Dorset, DT8 3AY, England

There is much here to make one happy – good food, award-winning hospitality and the inestimable beauty of Hardy country. At the heart of Bridge House is the food – traditional and as local as possible, and probably not for slimmers. You eat in the panelled, Georgian dining room, with a fine Adam fireplace and the palest of pink linen. The bedrooms, too, are solidly traditional, with padded headboards, floral duvet covers and curtains – no surprises but stacks of space. Peter is very much the convivial host: he has won many accolades and rightly so.

- Jurassic coast, 6 miles.
- Forde Abbey, 8 miles.
- Mapperton Gardens, 2 miles.
- Broadwindsor Craft & Design Centre.
- Llama-trekking & horse-riding.
- Golf, tennis & fishing.

rooms	14: 3 doubles, 9 twins/doubles, 1 single, 1 family.
price	£102–£134. Singles £54–£96. Half-board (min. 2 nights) from £75 p.p.
meals	Lunch from £11. Dinner from £23.50.
closed	Rarely.
directions	From Yeovil, A30 west, then A3066, signed Bridport, for 10 miles to Beaminster. Hotel at far end of village, as road bends to right.

Peter Pinkster

tel	+44 (0)1308 862200
fax	+44 (0)1308 863700
e-mail	enquiries@bridge-house.co.uk
web	www.bridge-house.co.uk

Hotel

Whitfield Farm Cottage

Poundbury Road, Nr. Dorchester, Dorset, DT2 9SL, England

The well-travelled Jackie and David make light of the practicalities of B&B; they and their 200-year-old cottage have much character and charm. Breakfast in the large, stone tiled, beamed kitchen or in the walled courtyard in summer. The twin bedroom, with garden access, is immaculate in fresh blue and white checks. The sitting room, with comfy sofas and pretty red checked cushions, has an inglenook fireplace and window seats. The River Frome – a chalk stream favoured by local fishermen – is within 150 yards. Convenient for the A35, yet peaceful.

- Fly-fishing: April-October, approx. £20 per day.
- Guided Tour of Dorchester: 1 mile.
- Heritage coastal walk, 9 miles.
- Dorset Country Museum, 1 mile.
- Thomas Hardy's Cottage, 3 miles.
- Athelhampton House & Gardens, 5 miles.

rooms	3: 1 twin with (downstairs) shower; 1 twin with private bath. 1 single also available.
price	£50-£54. Singles from £25.
meals	Pub/restaurant 1.25 miles.
closed	Easter & Christmas.
directions	From r'bout at top of Dorchester, west on B3150 for 100yds. Right onto Poundbury Rd (before museum). 1 mile, over another road, 2nd track on right beyond Whitfield Farmhouse sign.

Jackie & David Charles

tel	+44 (0)1305 260233
fax	+44 (0)1305 260233
e-mail	dc.whitfield@clara.net
web	www.dc.whitfield.clara.net

B&B

map 17　entry 232

The Old Vicarage
Milborne Port, Sherborne, Dorset, DT9 5AT, England

Altogether surprising – the austere Gothic exterior doesn't prepare you for the exuberance of the interior. It's a pleasant surprise – striking mixtures of fabrics and furniture that blend east and west. Anthony, from Hong Kong, is an excellent chef – at weekends, when he cooks, you really must eat in. Much of his food is Mediterranean with an oriental influence: Thai crabmeat cake with stir-fried veg, wild sea bass with shitake mushrooms. The Chinese bedroom is luxurious and wonderfully showy. Splendid views, too. *Children over five welcome.*

- Portraiture: 2 miles.
- Multi-media Drawing: 2 miles.
- Calligraphy: 2 miles.
- Life Drawing: 2 miles.
- Optical Colouring: 2 miles.
- Stourhead Gardens (NT) & Montacute House (NT), 30-minute drive.

rooms	6: 3 doubles, 3 family.
price	£58–£102. Singles £45–£73.
meals	Dinner £19.50–£25, Friday & Saturday only. Pub/restaurant 200 yds.
closed	January.
directions	From Sherborne A30 to Milborne Port. House 2nd on right on entering village.

Mr Anthony Ma & Jorgen Kunath

tel	+44 (0)1963 251117
fax	+44 (0)1963 251515
e-mail	theoldvicarage@milborneport.freeserve.c
web	www.milborneport.freeserve.co.uk

B&B

Munden House

Alweston, Sherborne, Dorset, DT9 5HU, England

The Benjamins worked in the States and have imported the country's high standard of B&B. Bedrooms are more 'grand luxe' than cottagey and the beds are big and of the finest quality; the four-poster has steps up to it. Lovely *toile de Jouy* curtains throughout and a feeling of opulence. State-of-the-art bathroom fittings, power showers (of course) and fluffy towels. The garden was professionally designed and they have space for wedding party marquees, too, so just ask. Sylvia's other passion is antiques – you can buy some if you wish.

- De-stressing Weekends - pilates, massage, reflexology.
- Bridge - all levels.
- Wedding receptions.
- Minton Gardens on Digby Estate, 20-minute drive.
- Stourhead House & Gardens (NT), 25-minute drive.
- Antique shops in Sherbourne, 5-minute drive.

rooms	6: 4 doubles, 2 twins. Also 1 studio with double, campbeds, cot, kitchenette & shower.
price	£72-£90. Singles £42-£52. Studio £75-£85 for 2; extra beds £15.
meals	Good pub within walking distance.
closed	Rarely.
directions	From Sherborne to A3030, then to Alweston, 2 miles. Past Post Office on right, parking sign on left, next left into Munden Lane. Behind Oxford Bakery.

Sylvia & Joe Benjamin

tel	+44 (0)1963 23150
fax	+44 (0)1963 23153
e-mail	sylvia@mundenhouse.demon.co.uk
web	www.mundenhouse.demon.co.uk

B&B & self-catering

map 17   entry 234

The Old Forge, Fanners Yard

Compton Abbas, Shaftesbury, Dorset, SP7 0NQ, England

This converted forge was built in the 1700s and the wheelwright and carriage-builder from the local estate used to work here. Tim is a classic-car restorer and has rebuilt a 1934 Lagonda; Lucy rides long-distance on her Arab horse. The attic bedrooms are snug, with Lucy's quilts, antiques and sparkling bathrooms. Breakfasts include organic sausages and bacon and eggs from the Kerridges' free-ranging chickens and ducks. The Downs beckon keen walkers. A lovely setting. Master baker Paul Merry runs the popular courses at nearby watermill, Cann Mills.

- Breadmaking: 0.75 miles, from £90.
- Stourhead House & Gardens (NT).
- Local hill forts.
- Cranborne Chase.
- Fontmell & Melbury Downs.
- Kingston Lacy House (NT).

rooms	3: 1 family; 1 double, 1 single (let to same party) sharing bathroom. Also 2 self-catering cottages for 2.
price	From £50–£70. Singles from £40.
meals	Pub/restaurant 1 mile.
closed	Rarely.
directions	From Shaftesbury, A350 to Compton Abbas. House 1st on left before Compton Abbas sign. Left; entrance on left through 5-bar gate.

Tim & Lucy Kerridge

tel	+44 (0)1747 811881
fax	+44 (0)1747 811881
e-mail	theoldforge@hotmail.com

B&B & self-catering

Number 34

The Bank, Barnard Castle, Durham, DL12 8PN, England

This Georgian townhouse stands impressively horizontal on The Bank in 'Barney'. There you can meet Digby, Eva, Ian and George – in that order. Digby's an Old English sheepdog and George is the resident ghost whose manners are unfailingly polite. Eva and Ian merely run the place. Ian cooks the breakfasts; Eva arranges them artistically. They love their guests and provide beautiful rooms. After breakfast stagger forth to see the rest of Barney on the Tees: castle, antique shops and restaurant next door where Cromwell really stayed.

- English Language, Business & General: price negotiable.
- German Language, Business & General: price negotiable.
- Cultural Visits, Walks & Talks: price negotiable.
- Bowes Museum, Abbey & Castle, Durham.
- Antique shops, Durham.
- Fishing, canoeing, walking, riding & bike hire.

rooms	2: 1 double; 1 twin with private bathroom.
price	£50–£60. Singles from £35.
meals	Lunch & dinner can be arranged.
closed	Rarely.
directions	At A1 Scotch Corner, A66 west for 7 miles. Then 1st dual carriageway; right for Barnard Castle. At lights right over bridge, left at T-junction to Butter Market. Left down bank, house on left.

Ian & Eva Reid

tel	+44 (0)1833 631304
fax	+44 (0)1833 631304
e-mail	evasreid@aol.com

B&B

map 17 entry 236

Boot & Shoe Cottage

Waterside Cottage, Wycliffe, Barnard Castle, Durham, DL12 9TR, England

Pure *Wind in the Willows*: the waters of the River Tees pass the bottom of your garden. The 300-year-old cottage was once a cobbler's home, hence the name. All is simple, fresh and immaculate within – pale walls and crisp white woodwork blend beautifully with country antiques. The kitchen is compact but perfect; the dining end with woodburner opens onto a terrace with roses, barbecue and steps to the river (do watch little ones). Groups of six may also use the Peats' own spare room. Rustle up a picnic from the farm shop and walk the glorious Teesdale Way.

- Cookery for Children & Aga Demonstrations: £15.
- Fly-fishing on River Tees.
- Bowes Museum, Durham & Raby Castle.
- Walks on North Pennines & Teesdale Way.
- Frozen meal service.
- Farm shop, 2 miles.

rooms	2: 1 double, 1 twin, sharing bathroom & wc.
price	£295-£360 per week.
meals	Self-catering.
closed	Rarely.
directions	3 miles north of A66. Take either Hutton Magna or Greta Bridge turn. In Wycliffe continue on to private road following river upstream for about 500 yards.

Mrs Rachel Peat

tel	+ 44 (0)1833 627200
fax	+ 44 01833 627200
e-mail	info@bootandshoecottage.co.uk
web	www.bootandshoecottage.co.uk

Self-catering

Heaven's Above at The Mad Hatters

3 Cossack Square, Nailsworth, Gloucestershire, GL6 0DB, England

Mike and Carolyn are inspiring – they've opened a fully organic restaurant above which sits an absolutely charming B&B. "We do it for spirit, not money," says Carolyn and it's a place that we are delighted to include. Each room is delightful – huge, like a studio, with oak floors or seagrass matting and lovely art on the walls. They've used local craftsmen to make the beds, light fittings, fire baskets, tables and crockery and you have your own entrance opposite the Herb Wheel. Nailsworth is a fascinating Gloucestershire town, perfect for an afternoon's amble.

- Sunday Painting with Anthony Hodge: £180.
- Essentially You Beauty Packages: next door.
- Horse-riding.
- Painting pottery in Town Studio.
- Creative Writing with Sue Limb: Sundays, 10-4, £180 for 1, 2 or 3 people.
- Ruskin Mill Education & Craft centre.

rooms	3: 1 twin; 2 doubles sharing bathroom.
price	£60-£70. Singles £35-£40.
meals	Lunch, 3 courses, from £17.50. Dinner £25-£30.
closed	Last 2 weeks of January.
directions	M5, junc. 13, A419 to Stroud; A46 south to Nailsworth. Right at r'bout & immed. left; restaurant & house opposite Britannia Pub.

Carolyn & Mike Findlay

tel	+44 (0)1453 832615
fax	+44 (0)1453 832615
e-mail	mafindlay@waitrose.com

Restaurant with rooms

map 17   entry 238

The Pinetum Lodge

Churcham, Gloucestershire, GL2 8AD, England

Come in spring and the nightingale's song is the only sound that could disturb your slumber; but this is a year-round, soothing retreat, a hunting lodge with views over the rolling Cotswold Hills. You enter an enchanted wood surrounded by a RSPB sanctuary and a pine arboretum which was planted by Thomas Gambier Parry in 1844. Your hosts, Carol and David, are friendly, unobtrusive and knowledgeable about organic gardening, as reflected in the 13-acre grounds. The bedrooms with new beds and bathrooms have the most wonderful garden views.

- Growing & Cooking Your Own Food: £75 (includes lunch).
- Heated swimming pool, May–Sept.
- Gloucester Cathedral.
- Tewkesbury Abbey.
- Cheltenham Spa.
- Walking in Forest of Dean & Wye Valley.

rooms	2 twins/doubles.
price	£50–£65. Singles from £25.
meals	Dinner from £17.50.
closed	Rarely.
directions	From Gloucester A40/A48 r'bout follow A40 (Ross) for 0.7 miles. At brow of hill right up drive of black & white cottage; follow track for 0.75 miles into woods. House at top through iron gates. Drive round house to front door.

David & Carol Wilkin

tel	+44 (0)1452 750554
fax	+44 (0)1452 750402
e–mail	c.wilkin@amserve.net
web	www.pinetumlodge.ik.com

B&B

Whitelands

Whitehall Lane, Rudford, Gloucestershire, GL2 8ED, England

Petrina is a natural and imaginative cook (a eulogy from a French chef in the visitors' book endorses this) and both she and James thrive on the bustle and conversation of their guests. The place is an oasis of comfort and ease, and very early risers can help themselves to tea and coffee. There's also plenty of space – the bedrooms are large and airy, and the beds are emperor-size, no less. Large gardens and sweeping views of May Hill and the Malverns, combined with the attractive and elegant house, create an atmosphere to which the Pughs bring a real sense of fun.

- Gloucester Cathedral.
- Royal Forest of Dean.
- Wye Valley.
- The Severn Bore.
- The Cotswolds.
- Walking & cycling in Malvern Hills.

rooms	3: 2 twins/doubles; 1 double with private shower.
price	£60. Singles from £40.
meals	Dinner from £20.
closed	Very rarely.
directions	A40 from Gloucester for Ross-on-Wye, then B4215 (for Newent & Highnam). Whitehall Lane 2 miles on left. Approx. 0.75 miles down lane, on right, behind laurel hedge.

James & Petrina Pugh

tel	+44 (0)1452 790406
fax	+44 (0)1452 790676
e-mail	pughwhitelands@yahoo.co.uk

B&B

map 17   entry 240

Three Choirs Vineyards

Newent, Gloucestershire, GL18 1LS, England

A fondness for cooking and the wine-making process will thoroughly equip you for the full-bodied and very English experience of Three Choirs. Thomas has run the vineyard with thoughtful and gentle reserve for almost a decade. The hotel and restaurant evolved more recently as a natural addition to the winery. Bedrooms are crisply clean and functional and each has French windows, so relax with a glass of house wine and drink in the views that produced it. There's even wine with your breakfast smoked salmon and scrambled eggs – it's a house special.

- Cookery: monthly, from £75 per day.
- Wine-tasting.
- 75 acres of vineyard walks.
- Hereford & Gloucester cathedrals, 20-minute drives.
- Bike hire for Forest of Dean.
- Eastnor Castle, 15-minute drive.

rooms	8 twins/doubles.
price	£85–£105. Singles from £65.
meals	Lunch from £15. Dinner from £25.
closed	Christmas & New Year.
directions	From Newent, north on B4215 for 1.5 miles, following brown signs to vineyard.

Thomas Shaw

tel	+44 (0)1531 890223
fax	+44 (0)1531 890877
e-mail	info@threechoirs.com
web	www.threechoirs.com

Hotel

The Grove House

Bromsberrow Heath, Ledbury, Herefordshire, HR8 1PE, England

You sleep in the ancient heart of the house, among 12th-century timbers and 18th-century additions. Grove House is wonderfully warm and cosseting – the dark wood gleams and large, luxurious rooms glow in firelight. In the elegant guests' drawing room there are books by the fire and plump armchairs and sofas to sink into. In the bedrooms, window-seats, ornately carved canopied beds and Jacobean panelling. Michael is an excellent cook and dinner is a special occasion, so do eat in. Play tennis, swim in the neighbour's pool or walk the Malvern Hills.

- Tennis & outdoor pool.
- Horse-riding.
- Malvern Hills.
- Goodrich Castle.
- Eastnor Castle.
- The Cotswolds.

rooms	3: 1 twin/double, 2 four-posters.
price	£75–£85. Singles £50 (not Sat/Sun).
meals	Dinner £25–£30.
closed	Christmas & New Year.
directions	Leave M50 at junc. 2, for Ledbury. 1st left to Bromsberrow Heath. Right by Post Office & up hill. House on right.

Michael & Ellen Ross

tel	+44 (0)1531 650584
e-mail	rossgrovehouse@amserve.net
web	www.the-grovehouse.com

B&B

map 17   entry 242

Stowting Hill House

Stowting, Nr. Ashford, Kent, TN25 6BE, England

The Lathams are well-travelled, friendly and active, yet firmly attached to their home and its surrounding acres. The house has a mix of styles: Tudor, Georgian and modern co-exist in harmony. High ceilings and a conservatory with terracotta-tiled floor, brimming with greenery. You'll find good furniture, yet the house is homely; bedrooms are comfortable with traditional bathrooms. Guests have their own log-fired drawing room with wonderful views of all that countryside. You are 10 minutes from the Chunnel. *Children over 10 welcome.*

- Historic Buildings of East Kent Tours.
- World War II in East Kent Tours.
- Trenches in Northern France Tours (min. 6 people).
- Driven Pheasant Shooting.
- Canterbury, 9 miles.
- Dover Castle, 15 miles.

rooms	3: 2 twins; 1 double, for members of same party willing to share a bathroom.
price	£60-£70. Singles from £35.
meals	Dinner £20-£25.
closed	Christmas & New Year.
directions	From M20 junc. 11, B2068 north. After 4.6 miles, left opp. Jet garage. House at bottom of hill on left, after 1.7 miles. Left into drive.

Richard & Virginia Latham

tel	+44 (0)1303 862881
fax	+44 (0)1303 863433
e-mail	vjlatham@hotmail.com

B&B

The Woolhouse

Grove Lane, Hunton, Kent, ME15 0SE, England

The Wettons are genuinely smiley and easy and their house is lovely inside and out. The small manor house in the beautiful conservation village of Hunton was built in the 1600s by a wealthy wool merchant as a place for storage and display. It's a delightfully artistic, beamed home whose ancient character and architectural details have survived intact. Bedrooms are charming and lack nothing. Grand piano and open fire in the drawing room, a conservatory for breakfast and a garden with alpacas. Anne has been a professional framer for 27 years.

- Picture Framing: from £120, Tuesday-Friday (mornings) with sandwich lunch.
- Sissinghurst Castle Gardens (NT).
- Leeds Castle & Hever Castle.
- Chagall windows in Tudeley Church.
- Yalding Organic Garden & Iden Green herb garden.
- Emmetts Garden (NT).

rooms	3: 1 double, 2 twins.
price	From £56-£66. Singles £28-£33.
meals	Pub/restaurant 2 miles.
closed	Christmas & New Year.
directions	A229 Maidstone & Hastings. At lights at Linton x-roads, turn for Coxheath & through village. 1st left down Hunton Hill. Pass church, park & school, then right into Grove Lane.

Gavin & Anne Wetton

tel	+44 (0)1622 820778
fax	+44 (0)1622 820645
web	www.wetton.info

B&B

map 18 entry 244

The Inn at Whitewell

Whitewell, Clitheroe, Lancashire, BB7 3AT, England

Long ago, merchants stopped at this old deerkeeper's lodge to fill up with wine, food and song before heading north through notorious bandit country; superb hospitality is still assured but the most that will hold you up on the road today is a stubborn sheep. Richard, officially the Bowman of Bowland, peers over half-moon glasses with a smile on his face, master of all this informal pleasure. Bedrooms are a triumph of style, warm and fun, some with fabulous Victorian showers, others with deep cast-iron baths and Benesson fabrics. Book early – it's very popular.

- Bikes on site.
- Fishing – trout & salmon.
- Shooting.
- Broshoome Hall, 3 miles.
- Levens Hall, Kendal.
- Dove Cottage & Wordsworth Museum, Grasmere.

rooms	17: 11 twins/doubles, 5 four-posters, 1 suite.
price	£89–£133. Singles from £69.
meals	Bar meals from £12. Dinner, à la carte, from £23.50.
closed	Rarely.
directions	M6, junc. 31a, then B6243 east through Longridge, then follow signs to Whitewell for 9 miles.

Richard Bowman
tel   +44 (0)1200 448222
fax   +44 (0)1200 448298

Inn

6 Oakfield Street

Little Chelsea, London, SW10 9JB, England

This district of Little Chelsea dates from the mid-1660s and Simon, who knows his Chelsea onions, has maps to prove it. Bedrooms are at the top of the house: the twin, in blue and yellow, is smaller than the double, but being at the back is silent at night. The double has a big wooden bed and an 18th-century oak *armoire*, and the roof terrace – handy in the summer – sports a smart green umbrella. After bacon, eggs and excellent coffee for breakfast, hop on the Number 14 bus to Piccadilly – perfect. Restaurants on Hollywood Road are a 30-second stroll.

- V&A, Science Museum, Natural History Museum.
- Kensington Gardens.
- King's Road.
- Brompton Cemetery.
- Chelsea Physic Garden.
- West End theatres (25 minutes by bus).

rooms	2: 1 double, 1 twin.
price	£60–£70. Singles from £40.
meals	Dinner with wine, from £10.
closed	Rarely.
directions	Tube: Earl's Court (15-min walk); South Kensington (20-min walk). Bus: 14. Parking: Nearest car park £25 per 24 hrs.

Margaret & Simon de Maré
tel   + 44 (0)20 7352 2970
e-mail   demare@easynet.co.uk

B&B

 map 18   entry 246

24 Fox Hill

Crystal Palace, London, SE19 2XE, England

This part of London is full of sky, trees and wildlife; Pissarro captured on canvas the view up the hill in 1870 and the original painting can be seen in the National Gallery. There's good stuff everywhere – things hang off walls and peep over the tops of dressers; bedrooms are stunning, with antiques, textiles, paintings and big, firm beds. Sue, a graduate from Chelsea Art College, employs humour and intelligence to put guests at ease and has created a very special garden, too. Sue will cook supper (sea bass, maybe, stuffed with herbs); Tim often helps with breakfasts.

- Computing.
- Quilting & Patchwork.
- Silk-painting.
- Dulwich Picture Gallery.
- Horniman Museum.
- Crystal Palace Museum.

rooms	3: 1 twin/double; 1 double, 1 twin, sharing shower.
price	£80–£100. Singles from £50.
meals	Lunch £15–£20. Dinner from £20.
closed	Rarely.
directions	Trains from Victoria or London Bridge, 20 mins to Crystal Palace, then 7 mins walk. Sue will give you directions or collect you. Good buses to West End & Westminster.

Sue Haigh

tel	+44 (0)20 8768 0059
e-mail	suehaigh@foxhill-bandb.co.uk
web	www.foxhill-bandb.co.uk

B&B

Paddock Lodge

The Green, Hampton Court, London, KT8 9BW, England

The two acres of formal rose beds, borders, lawns and orchards sweep down to the Thames. What a magical secluded London base. For garden lovers, Hampton Court Palace (home to the International Flower Show) is next door and Windsor, Wisley and Kew a short drive away. This elegant Palladian house has fine moulded ceilings, portraits, books and flowers; bedrooms are sumptuous with fine fabrics, exquisite furniture and lovely views. Sonia serves delicious home-cooking including a fine repertoire of Jewish and continental recipes. *Minimum stay two nights.*

- Hampton Court Palace.
- Windsor Castle.
- Kew Gardens.
- Royal Horticultural Gardens, Wisley.
- Ham House.
- Syon House.

rooms	2 doubles.
price	£84-£100. Singles from £55.
meals	Dinner from £26.
closed	Rarely.
directions	From Hampton Court r'bout, A308, west, for 300 yds. Left through wrought-iron gates, house at end of drive. Hampton Court station 5 mins, 30 mins Waterloo.

Dr Louis & Sonia Marks
tel   +44 (0)20 89795254
e-mail   101723.1100@compuserve.com

B&B

map 18   entry 248

Rival

PO Box 4553, Henley-on-Thames, London, RG9 3XZ, England

Rival, a 1925 Luxmotor barge, spent her working life on Dutch canals, then fell into Michael's hands. She now shines: varnished mahogany interiors, the original wheel in the wheelhouse, a woodburner in the saloon, even heated towel rails in compact shower rooms. B&B out of season (October to March) at Chiswick Quay Marina. In summer, Rival heads to Henley and messes about on the river. Here you can B&B, or cruise from Henley to Hampton Court via Windsor: breakfast on deck, stop at pubs for lunch, see the sights. Wonderful.

- Barge Cruises - gardens, historic buildings, restaurants, pubs.
- The Barge Experience - handling, buying, converting.
- Hot-air ballooning.
- Go-karting & Cycling (bike hire).
- Golf at Henley & Cookham.
- Henley Royal Regatta (2-6 July).

rooms	3: 2 double cabins, 1 twin cabin. Also sofabed in saloon.
price	£75-£135. Singles from £60. Cruise prices on application.
meals	Lunch from £12. Dinner from £15.
closed	Rarely.
directions	Train: Henley-on-Thames. Rival moored next to River & Rowing Museum; parking small charge. Winter: Chiswick Station or Chiswick Park Tube (guests met by car). Free parking in marina.

Michael Clayton-Smith & Frances Northcott

tel	+ 44 (0)7976 390 416
e-mail	rivalbarge@orange.net
web	www.rivalbarge.com

B&B

College Farm

Thompson, Thetford, Norfolk, IP24 1QG, England

Mrs Garnier has become a legend among B&B-ers – she has been in the business for so long and looks after her stupendous Grade II*-listed house single-handedly. She tells colourful stories of the house and her family's long local history: from 1349 until the Dissolution of the Monasteries it was a college of priests; later, it was brought back to life from ruin. It has a stunning panelled dining room, big bedrooms (the sky-blue one is particularly pretty) and beautiful views. Incredible value for such a special house. *Children over seven welcome.*

- Swaffham Market, 12 miles.
- Oxborough Hall (NT), 15 miles.
- Medieval churches.
- Sandringham House, 24 miles.
- Norwich, 24 miles.
- Cambridge, 45 miles.

rooms	3: 1 twin, 1 twin/double; 1 double with private bath; extra shower & wc.
price	From £50. Singles from £25.
meals	Afternoon tea included. Pub 1 mile.
closed	Rarely.
directions	From Thetford A1075 north for Watton. After 9 miles, left to Thompson. After 0.5 miles 2nd left at red postbox on corner. Left again, house at dead end.

Mrs Garnier

tel	+44 (0)1953 483318
fax	+44 (0)1953 483318
e-mail	collegefarm@amserve.net

B&B

map 18   entry 250

Grove Farm

Back Lane, Roughton, Norfolk, NR11 8QR, England

Play croquet, find a cosy spot to read, doze – we applaud Clare's ease and willingness to share her home. The house has a contemporary barn feel and, with clever use of space, light and aspect, Clare has created varied sitting areas in the open-plan ground floor. In one bedroom there is coir matting and a double brass bedstead and striking fabric, and the twin is equally stylish, and large. Wood everywhere and lovely stone, a formal garden, ponds and a summer house. And nearby thousands of acres of sky, sea and sand. *Two self-catering barns, too.*

- English Language, Business & General: from £700 p.w.
- Felbrigg Hall (NT), 3 miles.
- Blickling House (NT), 3 miles.
- Ruston Garden, 7 miles.
- North Norfolk coast, 7 miles.
- Norfolk Broads, 9 miles.

rooms	3: 2 doubles, 1 twin.
price	£80-£100. Singles from €40.
meals	Lunch from £5. Dinner from £15.
closed	Rarely.
directions	From Norwich, A140. Enter Roughton & left into Back Lane. After 0.75 miles, pass 1 cottage on left. Farm 30yds on right.

Clare Wilson

tel	+44 (0)1263 761594
fax	+44 (0)1263 761605
e-mail	grovefarm@homestay.co.uk
web	www.grove-farm.com

B&B & self-catering

Glebe Farmhouse

Wells Road, North Creake, Fakenham, Norfolk, NR21 9LG, England

You can have a real fire in one of the bedrooms – Mary will light it if you ask. She runs a bustling, welcoming household with good humour. There's a natural, family feel – a homely kitchen with old, cream Aga, jade woodwork and bright china – and bold design, too. Much that is wooden has been painted and everything is draped in brightly coloured coverings. Upstairs, faded carpets, fresh flowers, good sheets, a lovely bathroom and A-frame ceilings. In the sitting room: deep sofas, a log-burner, wooden floor and beams.

- Decorative Paintwork & Stencilling: £75.
- Exploring Colour & Creative Expression: 2 miles, £65.
- Using Digital Video: £75.
- Editing Digital Video: £75.
- Sailing & Windsurfing: 8 miles.
- Horse-riding: 20 miles, from £15 per hour.

rooms	2: 1 double; 1 double with private shower.
price	£50–£60. Singles from £27.50.
meals	Pub 3-minute walk.
closed	Christmas.
directions	From Fakenham north on B1135 to centre of North Creake. Right at red phone box. 200m on right.

Mary & Jeremy Brettingham

tel	+44 (0)1328 730133
fax	+44 (0)1328 730444
e-mail	info@eastnortheast.co.uk

B&B

map 18   entry 252

Thistleyhaugh

Longhorsley, Morpeth, Northumberland, NE65 8RG, England

Enid seems to thrive on hard work and company, and that combination makes a perfect B&B hostess; you could not meet a nicer woman. You could choose any of her large homely bedrooms and stay a week: the house is awash with comfort, old paintings, silk fabrics, views... and there's masses to eat and drink. Stray downstairs past the log fire and the groaning table (dinner is good value). There are 600 acres of farmland around you and a few million more of the Cheviots beyond that. So much to explore.

- Alnwick Castle & Gardens.
- Craigside Hall, Rothbury.
- Bamburgh Castle on coast.
- Brinkburn Priory.
- Cambo village.
- Millennium Bridge & Baltic Centre for Contemporary Art, Newcastle.

rooms	5: 4 doubles, 1 twin.
price	£56–£64. Singles from £37.
meals	Dinner, 3 courses, from £14.
closed	Christmas.
directions	Exit A1 for A697 for Coldstream & Longhorsley; 2 miles past Longhorsley, left at Todburn sign. 1 mile to x-roads, then right. On 1 mile over white bridge; 1st right, right again, over cattle grid.

Henry & Enid Nelless

tel	+44 (0)1665 570629
fax	+44 (0)1665 570629
web	www.thistleyhaugh.co.uk

B&B

The Tankerville Arms Hotel

Cottage Road, Wooler, Northumberland, NE71 6AD, England

A warm, honest Northumbrian welcome awaits at this 17th-century inn. Anne has been involved in running the place for more than two decades and does so in a calm, friendly way. Once a posting house on the London-Edinburgh run, the inn lies at the foot of the Cheviot hills, just inland from miles of wild and unspoilt coastline. Inside, décor is warm and homely, paintings and prints give character, and carpeted bedrooms are done in a traditional style. Brighten winter nights next to an open fire, or choose a nice sheltered spot in the garden.

- Alnwick Castle & Gardens.
- Hadrian's Wall.
- Lindisfarne (NT).
- Northumberland National Park.
- Golf courses.
- Fishing on rivers Till & Glen.

rooms	16: 6 doubles, 6 twins, 2 singles, 2 family.
price	£85–£90. Singles from £49.
meals	Light lunch from £4.50. Dinner from £14.95.
closed	Christmas.
directions	From Newcastle, A1 north of Morpeth, then A697 to Wooler. Inn just north of village on right.

Anne Park

tel	+44 (0)1668 281581
fax	+44 (0)1668 281387
e-mail	enquiries@tankervillehotel.co.uk
web	www.tankervillehotel.co.uk

Hotel

map 19   entry 254

The Old Bank Hotel

92-94 High Street, Oxford, Oxfordshire, OX1 4BN, England

The original safe, too heavy to remove, now guards the wine cellar. The hotel is in the heart of old Oxford, flanked by colleges and cobbled streets. Rooms at the top have views across the fabled skyline – a sublime panorama of architectural splendour. Downstairs, the big old tellers' hall has been turned into a 'hip' bar and restaurant. In summer, eat on the deck at the back or in the shade of lime trees in a tiny private garden. Bedrooms are superb, stylishly clean-cut with the best linen, velvet and silk; some have big bay windows, all have 21st-century gadgetry.

- Radcliffe Camera.
- Bodleian Library.
- Christchurch College & Cathedral.
- Punting on Cherwell.
- Botanic Gardens.
- Museum of Modern Art.

rooms	42: 36 twins/doubles, 4 singles, 2 suites.
price	£160-£320. Singles from £140.
meals	Breakfast £8-£11. Lunch & dinner £8.75-£25.
closed	23-27 December inclusive.
directions	Cross Magdalen Bridge for city centre. Keep left through 1st set of lights; 1st left into Merton St. Follow road right, then 1st right into Magpie Lane. Car park 2nd right.

Jackie Wallis-Jones

tel	+44 (0)1865 799599
fax	+44 (0)1865 799598
e-mail	info@oldbank-hotel.co.uk
web	www.oxford-hotels-restaurants.co.uk

Hotel

Burford House

99 High Street, Burford, Oxfordshire, OX18 4QA, England

Burford House is a delight, full of elegant good taste and so relaxing. Small enough for Simon and Jane to influence every corner, which they do with ease and good cheer. Classical music and the scent of fresh flowers drift through beautiful rooms; oak beams, leaded windows, antiques, log fires and a little garden for afternoon teas. And there's an honesty bar, with home-made sloe gin and cranberry vodka. Hand-written menus promise ravishing breakfasts and tempting lunches, and they will recommend the best places for dinner. A perfect little find.

- Bicycles & maps available.
- Cotswold Wildlife Park.
- Blenheim Palace & Gardens.
- River Windrush walks (with maps).
- Oxford colleges.
- Burford & the Cotswolds.

rooms	8: 3 doubles, 2 twins, 3 four-posters.
price	£105–£140. Singles from £80.
meals	Light lunch & afternoon tea only. Dinner in Burford & nearby villages.
closed	2 weeks in January/February.
directions	Down hill from roundabout in centre of Burford, on right.

Jane & Simon Henty

tel	+44 (0)1993 823151
fax	+44 (0)1993 823240
e-mail	stay@burfordhouse.co.uk
web	www.burfordhouse.co.uk

Inn

map 18   entry 256

Dick Turpin's Cottage

Cockford Hall, Clun, Craven Arms, Shropshire, SY7 8LR, England

The luxurious eccentricity of it all – come to have your spirits lifted. The space is vast and generous: a long, light hall and huge sitting/dining room with terrific fireplace and all the logs you need. The fabrics on the chairs and great sofa are colourful and expensive, the views are deep and glorious, the 'welcome' pack is as large as a Harrods' hamper. Your bedroom has heavily patterned fabric wallpaper, like a Turkish carpet, and your shower is gargantuan. There's even a log path built into the hillside to make your walk flawless: Roger has thought of everything.

- Poetry & Play-writing: 1 mile.
- Bookbinding: 1 mile.
- Computers, Beginners & Advanced: 1 mile.
- Pottery & Sculpture: 5 miles.
- Art & Design: 15 miles.
- Guided Wildlife Walks: 15 miles.

rooms	1 twin/double.
price	£465–£595 per week.
meals	Self-catering. Restaurant 1 mile.
closed	Rarely.
directions	Take B4368 W to Clun. Left at fork towards Knighton on A488. Over bridge. Cockford is 1 mile from bridge, signed on left. House on right up drive.

Mr Roger Wren

tel	+ 44 (0)1588 640327
fax	+ 44 01588 640881
e-mail	cockford.hall@virgin.net
web	www.dickturpincottage.com

Self-catering

Porlock Vale House

Porlock Weir, Somerset, TA24 8NY, England

Exmoor National Park runs into the sea here, and headlands rise to meet the waves. This is an exceptional riding school, so come to jump, to brush up your dressage, or to hack across the moors. All levels (above 16 years) are welcome, so don't be shy. Or you can sit out on the terrace and watch the deer, or walk to Porlock Bay. Bedrooms are big, bright and comfortable; most have sea views. Make sure you see the beautiful Edwardian stables; you may find the blacksmith at work, and the smell of polished leather in the tack room is just fantastic. Smashing people.

- Horse-riding: from £19.
- Clay Pigeon & Game Shooting.
- Coastal & moor walking.
- Bicycle hire.
- Exmoor National Park.
- Golf, 15-minute drive.

rooms	15: 9 doubles, 5 twins, 1 single.
price	£100–£150. Singles from £45.
meals	Lunch from £5. Dinner from £25.
closed	Mid-week in January & early February.
directions	West past Minehead on A39, then right in Porlock, for Porlock Weir. Through West Porlock, signed right.

Kim & Helen Youd

tel	+44 (0)1643 862338
fax	+44 (0)1643 863338
e-mail	info@porlockvale.co.uk
web	www.porlockvale.co.uk

Hotel

map 17   entry 258

Wyndham House

4 Sea View Terrace, Watchet, Somerset, TA23 0DF, England

The Vincents have made the house 'smile' again – handsome and Georgian, it overlooks Watchet harbour and marina. Bedrooms are pleasing – the double has duck-egg blue walls and pretty floral curtains and looks down onto a Mediterranean courtyard; the twin, with blue chintz valances and matching curtains, has a sea view. Expect home-made cakes and biscuits and generous breakfasts. Relax in the garden within sight and sound of sea and steam railway, with palm trees, ponds and a revolving summerhouse. *Children and dogs by arrangement.*

- Cookery Demonstration: winter.
- Botanical Painting.
- Steam train at bottom of garden.
- Dunster Castle (NT) & village.
- Quantock Hills & Exmoor.
- Greencombe Gardens, Porlock.

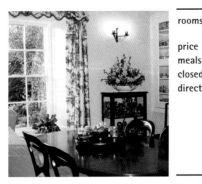

rooms	2: 1 twin; 1 double with private bathroom.
price	£55–£65. Singles from £28.
meals	Pub/restaurants a short walk away.
closed	Christmas.
directions	From railway station & footbridge in Watchet, up South Road (for Doniford). After 50yds, left into Beverly Drive. House 50yds on left.

Susan & Roger Vincent

tel	+44 (0)1984 631881
fax	+44 (0)1984 631881
e-mail	rhv@dialstart.net

B&B

Blackmore Farm

Cannington, Bridgwater, Somerset, TA5 2NE, England

Massive stone walls, heavy timbers, flagged floors and lack of fussiness give this Grade I-listed 15th-century farmhouse solidity and atmosphere. Explore the West Bedroom with timbered walls, ceiling open to the beamed roof and four-poster bed, and don't miss the oak-panelled Gallery Bedroom with recently uncovered secret stairway. Feel baronial while seated for breakfast beside the Great Hall's massive fireplace at the 20-foot oak table. There's a new stable room, too – although less architecturally stunning, it's perfect for wheelchair users.

- Horse-riding on Quantock Hills, 3 miles.
- Walking Quantock Hills, 3 miles.
- Golf courses, 1-3 miles.
- Fossil-hunting on Kilve Beach, 6 miles.
- Walking the Coleridge Way, 3 miles.
- Hestercombe Gardens, 10 miles.

rooms	6: 4 doubles, 1 family, 1 twin.
price	50–£70. Singles from £35.
meals	Pub 500 yds.
closed	Rarely.
directions	From Bridgwater, A39 west around Cannington. After 2nd r'bout, towards Minehead. 1st left after Yeo Valley creamery. 1st house on right.

Ann Dyer

tel	+44 (0)1278 653442
fax	+44 (0)1278 653427
e-mail	dyerfarm@aol.com
web	www.dyerfarm.co.uk

B&B

map 17   entry 260

Causeway Cottage

West Buckland, Wellington, Somerset, TA21 9JZ, England

Robert, an ex-restaurateur, is a South African and as easy-going as they so often are; Lesley's cooking gets heaps of praise from guests and she has run successful cookery courses for some years now. Causeway Cottage is a perfect Somerset home with an apple orchard and views across fields to the lofty church. The interior is utterly in keeping with its pine furniture, coir carpets, wooden beams and a warm sense of fun. Bedrooms are light, restful and simple, with white walls and old pine. All this, and such easy access to the M5. *Children over 10 welcome.*

- Cookery Demonstrations: £27.
- Cothay Manor.
- West Somerset Steam Railway.
- Hestercombe Gardens.
- Sheppy's Cider Farm & Museum.
- Knighthayes Court & Gardens (NT).

rooms	2: 1 double, 1 twin.
price	From £54. Singles from £44.
meals	Dinner from £17.
closed	Christmas.
directions	From M5 junc. 26 to West Buckland for 0.75 miles. 1st left just before Stone garage. Bear right; 3rd house at end of lane, below church.

Lesley & Robert Orr

tel	+44 (0)1823 663458
fax	+44 (0)1823 663458
e-mail	orrs@westbuckland.freeserve.co.uk
web	www.welcome.to/causeway-cottage

B&B

Brooke House

Thorne Coffin, Yeovil, Somerset, BA21 3PZ, England

Brooke House was built in 1690 of local hamstone, one of four farms in this conservation hamlet. With mullioned windows, it's furnished traditionally and comfortably: a big open fire in the drawing room is lit on cooler days; some of the pictures are watercolours painted by talented friends. The large south-facing double bedroom is decorated in peach and blue with views over the well-stocked rose garden, while the rose and green twin overlooks a paved area with a central pond. Both rooms have attractive American-style patchwork quilted bedspreads.

- Specialist Plants: 7 miles.
- Garden Itineraries.
- Car, tank & air museums.
- Montacute House (NT), 3 miles.
- Cider farm, smokery, willow centre.
- Cycle on the Somerset Levels.

rooms	2: 1 double; 1 twin with private bath.
price	From £62. Singles from £41. Reductions for 3 nights.
meals	Dinner £17–£20.
closed	Christmas & New Year.
directions	From A303, A37 to Yeovil, up hill to big r'bout, follow signs to Thorne. Right at r'bout, straight across at next 2 x-roads. 1st right to village; house 1st on right.

Jane & Iain Galloway

tel	+44 (0)1935 433396
fax	+44 (0)1935 475556
e-mail	jane@logspt.demon.co.uk

B&B

map 17   entry 262

Pennard Hill Farm

Stickleball Hill, East Pennard, Shepton Mallet, Somerset, BA4 6UG, England

Exquisite: Phoebe, a shepherd, sought the perfect home for her flock and she found it. Terracotta walls, rugs, flagstones and brick – stunning. The antique beds have handmade mattresses, good linen, fat pillows. The indoor swimming pool has a breathtaking view through a Gothic, arched window, and the house is a treasure box of decorative arts from the carved Dutch fireplaces to the Turkmen rugs. In the barn and cottages you have luxurious privacy. A magnificent place for a house party. *In conjunction with barn and cottages, 11 bedrooms in all.*

- Therapy Retreat, Counselling & Organic Food: £450-£700 per day full-board.
- Acupuncture, massage, reflexology, shiatsu, yoga available as part of retreat.
- Roman spa city of Bath, 22 miles.
- Wells Cathedral, 5 miles.
- Glastonbury Tor & Abbey, 5 miles.
- Hadspen, Montacute & Stourhead gardens, 5-15 miles.

rooms	5: 1 double, 1 suite with drawing room, 3 singles (only let to one party). Also 3 luxury serviced cottages.
price	£150-£200 per room or suite.
meals	Dinner from £25.
closed	Rarely.
directions	From Wells, A39 to Glastonbury. 0.5 miles on left for North Wootton, follow for West Pennard. Right onto A361. 1st left. 1 mile up hill. 1st drive to left at top.

Phoebe Judah

tel	+44 (0)1749 890221
fax	+44 (0)1749 890665
e-mail	phebejudah@aol.com
web	www.pennardhillfarm.co.uk

B&B & self-catering

Saltmoor House

Saltmoor, Burrowbridge, Somerset, TA7 0RL, England

So much to delight the eye… elegant Georgian lines, beautiful art, a 19th-century French mirror, French Empire chairs, a mixture of checked, striped and *toile de Jouy* fabrics – all existing in absolute harmony. This is one of the most stylish retreats that you'll find. There's comfort, too… thick bathrobes, warm towels, the fattest pillows. The house is 18th-century, Grade II-listed and Elizabeth's cooking is sublime. You are in the heart of the Somerset Levels, surrounded by mystical views and countryside of huge environmental significance.

- Local basket-makers' studios.
- Hestercombe Gardens.
- Somerset cider brandy distillery.
- Montacute House & Garden (NT).
- Wells & Glastonbury.
- Walks on the Somerset Levels.

rooms	3: 1 twin; 2 doubles, both with private bathroom.
price	£100–£120. Singles from £50.
meals	Dinner £20–£25.
closed	Rarely.
directions	From M5, junc. 24. 5 miles via Huntworth & Moorland. 2 miles after Moorland, house on right after sharp right-hand bend.

Crispin & Elizabeth Deacon
tel   +44 (0)1823 698092
e-mail   saltmoorhouse@amserve.net

B&B

map 17   entry 264

Hillview Cottage

Paradise Lane, Croscombe, Wells, Somerset, BA5 3RL, England

One of our favourites – the cosiest hillside cottage filled with the prettiest things. French-inspired bedheads and wardrobes made by a local craftsman, antique patchwork quilts and jolly china on the old Welsh dresser in the kitchen. And there's Catherine – warm, spirited, cultured; she'll make you fresh coffee, chat about the area, give you a guided tour of Wells Cathedral if you wish. The cottage is set in eight acres superb walking country. You can play tennis or croquet, and have your own pretty sitting room. Excellent value.

- Guided Tours of Wells Cathedral (emphasis on stained/painted glass): 2 miles.
- Wookey Hole Caves.
- Montacute House & Lytes Cary Manor (NT).
- Stourhead House & Gardens (NT).
- Glastonbury Abbey.
- Tyntesfield House - National Trust's newest acquisition.

rooms	2: 1 twin/double; 1 twin, for members of same party.
price	From £50. Singles from £30.
meals	Good pub 0.25 miles.
closed	Christmas & New Year.
directions	From Wells A371 to middle of Croscombe. Right at red phonebox, then immediately right into lane. House up on left after 0.25 miles. Drive straight ahead & park in signed field.

Michael & Catherine Hay

tel	+44 (0)1749 343526
fax	+44 (0)1749 676134
e-mail	cathyhay@yahoo.co.uk

B&B

Lower Farm

Shepton Montague, Wincanton, Somerset, BA9 8JG, England

The Good Life in the depths of Somerset: organic vegetables on an organic farm, home-made marmalade, own milk and eggs. The Dowdings had a Special Place – and have converted this old stone barn into a super self-contained apartment with a continental feel. Do your own thing – or have Susie cook breakfast and dinner for you (Charles grinds their own wheat for bread-making). Central to the oak-floored sitting room is a woodburner and bedrooms have oak floors, exposed beams, lime-washed walls and *toile de Jouy* curtains.

- Organic Vegetable Growing: in French & English, April & October, £30.
- Stourhead House & Gardens (NT), 8 miles.
- Hadspen Garden, 1 mile.
- Cadbury Hill, Camelot, 5 miles.
- Montacute House (NT), 15 miles.
- Organic farmland setting.

rooms	2: 1 double, 1 twin, with kitchenette.
price	£60. Singles from £35.
meals	Supper from £8.
closed	Rarely.
directions	From A303 at Wincanton, A371 for Castle Cary. Before Cary, right on A359 for Bruton. 2nd right for S. Montague. Over x-roads by inn. Round sharp bend, church on left. House on right; right into yard.

Charles & Susie Dowding

tel	+44 (0)1749 812253
e-mail	lowerfarm@clara.co.uk
web	www.lowerfarm.org.uk

B&B & self-catering

map 17 entry 266

Slab Bridge Cottage

Little Onn, Church Eaton, Staffordshire, ST20 0AY, England

The cottage takes its name from the nearby bridge on the Shropshire Union Canal (one of England's prettiest). Bedrooms have floral curtains and covers and all is spotless and cosy with open fire, antique furniture, lovely bathrooms, fresh flowers. Meals can be served outside on the terrace overlooking the canal and dinner can be arranged on board the narrow boat with a delightful trip along the canal. Diana makes her own bread, biscuits, cakes and jams and David provides fresh vegetables and salads from the garden. On a good day there are home eggs, too.

- Canal Boat & Lock Taster Tour.
- Peak District.
- Ironbridge.
- The Potteries.
- Shugborough Estate & Gardens (NT).
- Weston Park House.

rooms	2 doubles both with private bathroom.
price	£50–£55. Singles from £30.
meals	Dinner from £15.
closed	Christmas & New Year.
directions	From Stafford, A518 for Newport. 4 miles on, left at Haughton (opp. church) for Church Eaton. There, right along Main St. At end of village, left along Little Onn road. Over canal bridge & left after 300yds. Cottage on left.

Diana Walkerdine

tel	+44 (0)1785 840220
fax	+44 (0)1785 840220
e-mail	daviddiana@walkerdine.com

B&B

Wood Hall

Little Waldingfield, Nr. Lavenham, Suffolk, CO10 0SY, England

For breakfast on summer mornings, make your way to the terrace in the walled garden, for home-made marmalade, jams and fruit compotes; in winter, settle beside an arched Tudor brick fireplace in the dining hall. Janus-like, the house looks both ways, Georgian to the front, and richly-beamed, 1485 – Tudor behind. The bedrooms are elegant and very English: padded bedheads, thick curtains, armchairs, writing desks, candles and lots of books with which to settle down. Pretty and full of thoughtful touches. *Multi-lingual host.*

- Lavenham.
- Gainsborough's House, Sudbury.
- Long Melford.
- The Beth Chatto Gardens.
- Flatford Mill & Bridge Cottage, Dedham Vale.
- Cambridge.

rooms	2: 1 double; 1 twin with bath/shower & separate wc.
price	£65–£70. Singles from £35.
meals	Dinner from £15 (if staying more than one night). BYO.
closed	Christmas.
directions	From Sudbury B1115 for Lavenham for 3.5 miles. Right to Little Waldingfield. House on left, 200yds beyond The Swan.

Mrs Susan T. del C. Nisbett

tel	+44 (0)1787 247362
fax	+44 (0)1787 248326
e-mail	susan@woodhallbnb.fsnet.co.uk
web	www.thewoodhall.co.uk

B&B

map 18   entry 268

The Hall

Milden, Nr. Lavenham, Suffolk, CO10 9NY, England

The atmosphere is relaxed, and Juliet has masses of imaginative ideas: nature trails, local walks, bike rides (borrow a bike), tennis and car-free days out. The house is a glorious unspoiled 16th-century hall farmhouse, lived in and loved by the family for 300 years, with period furniture and good bedrooms overlooking a wildflower meadow and walled garden. The courses and Living History activites are geared for those staying in the 16th-century Tudor-style barn where you self-cater. Four-poster and truckle beds, oak banquet tables, even Tudor costumes!

- Historical, Environmental & Creative Activities - individually tailored.
- Drawing & Painting: summer.
- Trees, Woodland & Pond: summer.
- Farm Nature Trails: all year.
- Small Farm Museum.
- Family-friendly Activity Packs.

rooms	3: 1 family, 2 twins, all sharing private bathroom. Also self-catering barn.
price	£55-£75. Singles from £35.
meals	Dinner from £20.
closed	Christmas.
directions	From Lavenham, A1141 for Monks Eleigh. After 2 miles, right to Milden. At x-roads, right to Sudbury on B1115. Hall's long drive 0.25 miles on left.

Juliet & Christopher Hawkins

tel	+44 (0)1787 247235
fax	+44 (0)1787 247235
e-mail	gjb53@dial.pipex.com
web	www.thehall-milden.co.uk

B&B & self-catering

Butley Priory

Butley, Nr. Woodbridge, Suffolk, IP12 3NR, England

Wild marshes, deserted beaches – the area is silent but for the call of birds and the Augustinian monastery has been brought to life by Frances, an artist and musician. It is undeniably breathtaking and romantic. Decorative stonework clasps the windows, the vaulted dining room soars heavenwards. Steps lead to cascades of damask, huge stone-arched windows, beautiful beds with goose down duvets and embroidered linen and invigorating power showers. The magic is all around in seven acres. Beyond, wonderful walking and seafood restaurants.

- Tunstall & Rendlesham forest walks.
- Shingle Street beach, 2 miles.
- Orford Castle, 4 miles.
- Framlingham Castle, 10 miles.
- Aldeburgh & Snape concert halls.
- Sutton Hoo.

rooms	3: 1 double, 1 small double; 1 double with private bathroom (down small staircase).
price	£100-£130. Single occ. by arrangement.
meals	Pubs & restaurants nearby.
closed	Rarely.
directions	From A12 at Woodbridge, B1084 for Orford. In Butley at Oyster Inn, take Hollesley road for 1 mile to x-roads. Private entrance to Priory immed. right after x-roads.

Frances Cavendish

tel	+44 (0)1394 450046
fax	+44 (0)1394 450482
e-mail	cavendish@butleypriory.co.uk
web	www.butleypriory.com

B&B

map 18   entry 270

Lower Eashing Farmhouse

Eashing, Nr. Godalming, Surrey, GU7 2QF, England

A homely place with a lovely walled garden and super hosts. Multi-lingual Gillian welcomes guests from all over the world, yet she and David will make you feel like their first ever; their conversation is lively and informed. The house, 16th to 19th century, has exposed timber frames and bold colours – the dining room's red. The guest sitting room, with its log fireplace and piano, is hung with a collection of hats and ethnic treasures. In the walled garden the distant rumble of the A3 reminds you how well placed you are for Gatwick and Heathrow.

- London (45 minutes by train).
- Windsor Castle.
- Hampton Court Palace.
- Royal Horticultural Gardens, Wisley.
- Chessington World of Adventures.
- Portsmouth Historic Dockyard.

rooms	4: 1 twin/double; 1 twin/double with private bath/shower, 2 singles sharing shower room.
price	£60-£65. Singles from £35.
meals	Good pub 300 yds.
closed	Christmas & New Year.
directions	A3 south. 5 miles after Guildford, Eashing signed left at service station. House 150yds on left behind white fence.

David & Gillian Swinburn

tel	+44 (0)1483 421436
fax	+44 (0)1483 421436
e-mail	davidswinburn@hotmail.com

B&B

Easton House

Chidham Lane, Chidham, Chichester, Sussex, PO18 8TF, England

Lots of beams, charming bedrooms, a cosily cluttered drawing room with a Bechstein piano and comfortable armchairs... this is a haven for musicians – and cat-lovers. It has the feel of a well-loved and lived-in family home; Mary has lived at Easton House for over 30 years. The house looks out over the watery delight that is Chidham harbour, is just five minutes walk from the water's edge, the boats and the nautical delights – and is surrounded by great walking and bird-watching country. A lovely setting for a delightful house.

- West Dean College Courses: 7 miles.
- Fishbourne Roman Palace.
- Westgate Leisure Centre, Chichester.
- Chichester Cathedral.
- Weald & Downland Museum.
- West Dean Gardens.

rooms	3: 1 twin, 1 double sharing bathroom; 1 double with private bathroom.
price	£48–£56. Singles from £34.
meals	Excellent pub in village.
closed	Christmas.
directions	From Chichester for Portsmouth. Pass Tesco. Exit off r'bout to Bosham & Fishbourne. Follow A259 for 4 miles, pass Saab garage on right. Next left into Chidham Lane. Last on left, 1 mile down.

Mary Hartley

tel	+44 (0)1243 572514
fax	+44 (0)1243 573084
e–mail	eastonhouse@chidham.fsnet.co.uk

B&B

map 18   entry 272

South Paddock

Maresfield Park, Nr. Uckfield, Sussex, TN22 2HA, England

Both Graham and Jennifer have travelled extensively in the Army with The King's Own Scottish Borderers; their experience is reflected in a regimental 'museum' in the downstairs cloakroom. They are kind and dedicated hosts, who are happy to help you plan your day or book a table at the village pub. Visitors from 55 nations have enjoyed the comforts of this unspoilt, wisteria-clad 1930s bastion of old-Englishness. The garden is beautiful and the fruit and vegetable plot big enough to feed an army. Log fires in winter. *Children over 10 welcome.*

- Riding in Ashdown Forest, 3 miles.
- Bluebell & Lavender Line Steam Railways, 2-3 miles.
- St George's Vineyard & Barnsgate Manor Vineyard, 2-3 miles.
- Sheffield Park Garden, 3 miles.
- Glyndebourne, 8 miles (you may use kitchen to prepare picnic).
- Chartwell, 22 miles.

rooms	3: 1 double, 1 twin, both with private bathroom; 2nd twin available.
price	From £65. Singles from £44.
meals	Pub in village.
closed	Rarely.
directions	From M25, A22 to Maresfield. At mini-r'bout in centre of village, under stone arch opp. church & pub, & over 5 speed bumps. House 1st on left.

Graham & Jennifer Allt
tel   +44 (0)1825 762335

B&B

Jeake's House
Mermaid Street, Rye, Sussex, TN31 7ET, England

The gorgeous house has been many things – wool store, school and former home of poet Conrad Aiken; hard to believe the deep red dining room, full of busts, books, paintings and mirrors, was an old Baptist chapel. Jenny is engagingly easy-going and has created a lovely atmosphere. Rooms are traditionally furnished, with rich drapes, antique four-posters... there's a large attic room with beams, a book-lined bar, a mind-your-head stairway, a small library to keep away the rainy day blues. A smart retreat among Rye's cobbled streets and so much to see and do.

- Rye.
- Bodiam Castle.
- Gardens at Great Dixter.
- Sissinghurst Castle Gardens (NT).
- Leeds Castle & Gardens.
- Brighton.

rooms	12: 8 doubles; 1 single, sharing bathroom; 2 honeymoon suites.
price	£80–£120. Singles from £35.
meals	Many local restaurants.
closed	Rarely.
directions	From London, into centre of Rye on A268, left off High St onto West St, then 1st right into Mermaid St. House on left. Private car park, £3 a day for guests.

Jenny Hadfield

tel	+44 (0)1797 222828
fax	+44 (0)1797 222623
e-mail	jeakeshouse@btinternet.com
web	www.jeakeshouse.com

B&B

map 18 entry 274

The Hare on the Park

3 Emscote Road, Warwick, Warwickshire, CV34 4PH, England

Wow! Hot bedroom colours make a change from the usual creams and chintzes – one is vibrant blue with a red ceiling, another yellow with blue, and a further one a super burnt orange, all with original art. It's bold and vibrant, 'green' and fun – just like Prue. She's passionate about good food, too – organic and mostly vegetarian. Expect home-made bread, velvety egg puddings, succulent stuffed mushrooms and a fresh fruit platter drizzled with lime and honey dressing. The substantial blue-stone 1850s townhouse is opposite Warwick's park.

- Organic Gardening at Ryton: 10 miles.
- Warwick Castle, 15-minute riverside walk.
- Leamington Spa, 1.5 miles.
- Royal Shakespeare Theatre, Stratford-upon-Avon, 5 miles.
- Ryton Organic Garden, Coventry 10 miles.
- Birmingham.

rooms	3: 2 doubles, 1 twin.
price	£70–£80. Singles from £45.
meals	Dinner £20–£30.
closed	Rarely.
directions	On A445, 500yds past St John's Museum for Leamington, directly opp. entrance to St Nicholas' Park.

Prue Hardwick
tel	+44 (0)1926 491366
e-mail	prue@thehareonthepark.co.uk
web	www.thehareonthepark.co.uk

B&B

Hardingwood House

Hardingwood Lane, Fillongley, Nr. Coventry, Warwickshire, CV7 8EL, England

A theatrical home: dark wood, reds and pinks dominate and, in one bedroom, more theatre: plush velvet curtains open to the bathroom. The conversion of the 1737 barn is immaculate: the kitchen, with Aga and stone floors, gives onto a stunning patio, conservatory and drawing room; bedrooms and bathrooms are plush, big and comfortable. Denise, cheerful and kind, runs her B&B with careful attention to detail. Much rural charm, a large garden, excellent value and yet so close to Birmingham and the NEC.

- National Exhibition Centre (NEC) Birmingham, 8 miles.
- Golf, the Belfry & Forest of Arden, 8 miles.
- Ryton Organic Garden, Coventry, 10 miles.
- National Motorcycle Museum, 8 miles.
- Packwood (NT), 12 miles.
- Baddesley Clinton (NT), 12 miles.

rooms	3: 1 double, 2 twins.
price	£75–£85. Singles from £50.
meals	Pub 1 mile.
closed	Rarely.
directions	At M6 junc. 4, A446 for Lichfield. At sign to Coleshill South, get in right lane & turn off. From High St, turn into Maxstoke Lane. After 4 miles, 4th right. 1st drive on left.

Mrs Denise Owen

tel	+44 (0)1676 542579
fax	+44 (0)1676 541336
e-mail	denise@hardingwoodhouse.fsnet.co.uk

B&B

map 18   entry 276

Westcourt Bottom

165 Westcourt, Burbage, Wiltshire, SN8 3BW, England

Bill – who paints in oils and watercolours – has applied his considerable artistic talents to the renovation of this 17th-century cottage. The A-frame sitting room has bold Chinese yellow walls, three plump sofas, light wooden floor and books – it is unintimidatingly stylish. The bedrooms are in similar vein and Bill and Felicity are easy, cultured hosts. There's a heated swimming pool, which you can use, and a sunken Italianate garden whose borders are edged with clouds of lavender. Shelter on sunny days, colonial-style, under a tiled loggia. *Children by arrangement.*

- Drawing & Painting.
- Clay Sculpting.
- Horse-riding: 5 miles.
- Stonehenge, 16 miles.
- Avebury stone circle, 10 miles.
- Marlborough, 5 miles.

rooms	3: 1 double; 1 double, 1 twin, sharing bathroom.
price	£50–£60. Singles from £30.
meals	Dinner from £25.
closed	Rarely.
directions	From Marlborough, A346 Salisbury Rd south. At r'bout ending Burbage bypass, B3087 Pewsey Rd. Right at x-roads 0.3 miles on. 1st house on right.

Felicity & Bill Mather

tel	+44 (0)1672 810924
fax	+44 (0)1672 810924
e-mail	westcourt.b-and-b@virgin.net
web	www.westcourtbottom.co.uk

B&B

Hilcott Farm House

Hilcott, Marlborough, Wiltshire, SN9 6LE, England

A listed Georgian thatched farmhouse and a stylish B&B – Val and David moved out of London in search of peace and found it in the heart of crop circle and Stonehenge country. Val is an interior decorator who specialises in paint finishes and has stamped her elegant mark on every room: a gentle terracotta linen-effect in the guest sitting room; big yellow checks in the bathroom. A tranquil atmosphere pervades this home with its old rugs on wooden floors, log fires, crisp bed linen and plump pillows. The garden is charming and contains a 16th-century drover's rest.

- Special Paint Effects: minimum 5 people.
- Marlborough Summer School - courses for adults & children: 10 miles, July-August.
- Broadleas Garden, Devizes.
- Wilton House.
- The Courts Garden.
- Bowood House – gardens & adventure playground.

rooms	3: 1 double; 1 twin, 1 single, sharing bathroom.
price	£65-£75. Singles from £30.
meals	Lunch from £15. Dinner from £25.
closed	Rarely.
directions	From Marlborough, A345 through Pewsey. 3 miles on, at Woodbridge Inn r'bout, right to Hilcott. House 2nd on left over cattle grid. From M3/A303, Hilcott is 11 miles from Amesbury r'bout via Upavon & Woodbridge r'bout.

Val & David Maclay

tel	+44 (0)1672 851372
fax	+44 (0)1672 851192
e-mail	beds@hilcott.com

B&B

map 17 entry 278

Ridleys Cheer

Mountain Bower, Chipppenham, Wiltshire , SN14 7AJ, England

In a hamlet approached down meandering lanes, a small 18th-century cottage enlarged in 1989 by architect William Bertram. One addition was the large conservatory where summer guests can breakfast amid plumbago and jasmine. The bedrooms are bright, simple and cosy, with pale walls, pretty curtains and antique furniture, and the eye is drawn through the small windows to the glories below, which lead to an arboretum and wildflower meadow. Sue, a Cordon Bleu chef, cooks delicious meals served at a mahogany table.

- Garden Design & Plant Advice.
- Cookery Demonstrations & Tuition.
- Tennis court.
- Grade I-listed, part-Norman church.
- Corsham Court & Iford.
- Bath, 10 miles.

rooms	3: 1 double; 2 doubles, 1 twin, sharing bathroom.
price	From £70. Singles from £35.
meals	Lunch from £15. Dinner from £27.50.
closed	Rarely.
directions	M4 junc 17. At Chippenham, A420 for Bristol. After 9 miles, right at x-roads in hamlet, The Shoe. 2nd left, then 1st right into Mountain Bower (no sign). Last house on left; park on gravel drive opp.

Sue & Antony Young

tel	+44 (0)1225 891204
fax	+44 (0)1225 891139
e-mail	sueyoung@ridleyscheer.co.uk

B&B

The Yorke Arms

Ramsgill-in-Nidderdale, Nr. Harrogate, Yorkshire, HG3 5RL, England

The Yorke Arms is near perfection. Exquisite food from the foremost female chef in Britain, wonderful rooms and beautiful countryside make it irresistible. The interior is absolutely charming, with polished flagstone floors, low oak beams, comfy armchairs, open fires and antique tables; attention to detail is guaranteed. In summer, eat under a pergola near a burbling beck. Bill, affable and considerate, is a natural host. Wander from the hamlet of Ramsgill in the middle of the glorious Yorkshire Dales to nearby Gouthwaite reservoir. *Kennels for pets £5 per night.*

- Cookery with Frances Atkins.
- Michelin-starred restaurant.
- Fountains Abbey.
- Newby Hall.
- Stump Cross Caverns.
- Brimham Rocks.

rooms	14: 7 doubles, 3 twins/doubles, 3 singles, 1 cottage suite.
price	Half-board for two £190-£320. Single half-board from £95.
meals	Lunch from £6. Dinner from £28. Restaurant closed Sunday evenings to non-residents.
closed	Occasionally in Jan & Nov.
directions	From Ripley, B6165 to Pateley Bridge. Over bridge at bottom of High St, 1st right into Low Wath Rd to Ramsgill (4 miles).

Bill & Frances Atkins

tel	+44 (0)1423 755243
fax	+44 (0)1423 755330
e-mail	enquiries@yorke-arms.co.uk
web	www.yorke-arms.co.uk

Inn

map 17 entry 280

Millgate House

Richmond , Yorkshire, DL10 4JN, England

Prepare to be amazed. In every room of the house and in every corner of the garden, the marriage of natural beauty and sophistication exists in a state of bliss. The four Doric columns at the entrance draw you through the hall into the dining room and to views of the Swale Valley. Beds from Heals, period furniture, cast-iron baths, myriad prints and paintings. Tim and Austin, both ex-English teachers who share a love of their award-winning garden, have created something very special. Their sense of style will last long in the memory.

- Painting: £45 per day.
- Specialist Plant Days: Snowdrops/Clematis/Hostas: £45 per day.
- Italian, Beginners & Advanced: £45 per day.
- English Language.
- Georgian Theatre Royal, Richmond - recently restored.
- Richmond Castle.

rooms	3: 1 double, 1 twin; 1 double with private bath & sitting room.
price	£70-£90. Singles £45-£55.
meals	Lunch from £25. Dinner from £35.
closed	Rarely.
directions	Just off Richmond Market Place, house at bottom of square opp. Barclays Bank, next to Halifax. Look for green door with small brass plaque.

Tim Culkin & Austin Lynch

tel	+44 (0)1748 823571
fax	+44 (0)1748 850701
e-mail	oztim@millgatehouse.demon.co.uk
web	www.millgatehouse.com

B&B

Nether Underwood

By Symington, Kilmarnock, Ayrshire, KA1 5NG, Scotland

You'll quickly feel at home in this unusual, elegant 1930s-style home built by the original owners of the nearby big house. The large yellow drawing room with Adam fireplace has log fires in winter and on chilly summer evenings. Felicity serves delicious breakfasts at the refectory table – she is a former chef who specialises in Scottish fare and home baking. Antique furniture, rich, thick curtains, lovely cosy bedrooms – the twin has tartan and thistle motifs. Colour everywhere and, in the background, the gentle tick-tock of Austin's collection of longcase clocks.

- Wine Appreciation Weekends: November & February.
- Breadmaking.
- Celtic Connections, International Folk Festival (January), 40-minute drive.
- Racing at Ayr & Troon.
- Rennie Mackintosh Museum, Glasgow.
- Championship golf courses & 2004 Open at Troon.

rooms	4: 2 doubles; 1 twin with private bathroom; 1 double with bath/shower.
price	From £90. Singles from £55.
meals	Village pub 10-minute drive.
closed	Rarely.
directions	From Glasgow, A77 for Ayr. Pass Little Chef, left for Underwood. Left at T-junc., over bridge, past farm, down hill & left. Pass gates to Underwood House, then immed. left. At end of lane.

Felicity & Austin Thomson

tel	+44 (0)1563 830666
fax	+44 (0)1563 830777
e-mail	netherund@aol.com
web	www.netherunderwood.co.uk

B&B

map 19 entry 282

Minmore House

Glenlivet, Banffshire, AB37 9DB, Scotland

Amid this beautiful cattle-grazing land is Minmore, a great wee pad run with breezy good cheer by Victor and Lynne. Their kingdom stretches to nine spotless bedrooms and a suite that Lynne describes as "very zoosh". Guests swap highland tales in a pretty sitting room or, best of all, in a carved wooden bar, half-panelled, with scarlet chairs, a resident Jack Russell, the odd trophy and 104 malts. The garden is a twitcher's paradise, with lapwing, curlew and a rare colony of oystercatchers. Those with an iron constitution may fancy the unheated pool!

- Whisky tastings.
- Fly-casting.
- Guided trails.
- Bicycle trails.
- Walking trails.
- Golf at Ballindalloch Castle, 5 miles.

rooms	10: 4 doubles, 3 twins, 2 singles, 1 suite.
price	£120–£240. Singles from £45.
meals	Lunch from £15. Dinner £30–£40.
closed	November & February.
directions	From Aviemore, A95 north to Bridge of Avon; south on B9008 to Glenlivet. At top of hill, 400yds before distillery.

Victor & Lynne Janssen

tel	+44 (0)1807 590378
fax	+44 (0)1807 590472
e-mail	minmorehouse@ukonline.co.uk
web	www.minmorehousehotel.com

Hotel

41 Heriot Row

Edinburgh, Edinburgh, EH3 6ES, Scotland

High on Edinburgh's exalted Georgian escarpment, this light, bright eyrie mixes 19th-century elegance with Danish and Middle Eastern style. Brass beds, burnished pine floors, a vast hall with a stairway that floats regally above a magnificent sitting room, long views of the Firth of Forth from the airy twin. Erlend, an award-winning travel writer, creates gourmet feasts at breakfast. The Cloustons will meet you from the train, and help you carry your bags up the stairs. Relaxed, informative, fun. *Also available: cookery, golf fitness & hire of classic sports car.*

- Painting & Drawing.
- Chi Kung (Qi Gong).
- Guitar.
- English Language.
- Balloon Sculpting.
- Scottish Game Cookery.

rooms	2: 1 double, 1 twin.
price	£95–£120. Singles from £70.
meals	Available in Edinburgh.
closed	Rarely.
directions	Heriot Row parallel to Princes Street, 3 major blocks north.

Erlend & Hélène Clouston

tel	+44 (0)131 225 3113
fax	+44 (0)131 225 3113
e-mail	erlendc@lineone.net
web	www.wwwonderful.net

B&B

map 19   entry 284

The Witchery by the Castle

Castlehill, Royal Mile, Edinburgh, EH1 2NF, Scotland

Ornately Gothic in style and grandly exuberant, this should really be a theatre – it's a such magical and passionate setting. The two 16th-century tenements are full of sumptuous architectural bric-a-brac, from the medieval to the quasi-Byzantine. The suites are incredible: the Inner Sanctum has one of Queen Victoria's chairs, the Old Rectory's pillars came from London's Trocadero, and the Vestry has a fabulous *trompe l'œil* draped and swagged bathroom. Champagne is included, as is a continental breakfast in bed, and the three restaurants excel.

- Wine-tasting.
- Edinburgh Castle.
- Scottish National Gallery.
- Scottish Parliament.
- Palace of Holyrood House.
- Museum of Scotland.

rooms	7 suites.
price	From £225.
meals	Lunch from £9.95. Dinner from £35.
closed	Christmas Day & Boxing Day.
directions	Find Edinburgh Castle. Witchery 20 yards from main castle gate.

Mark Rowley

tel	+44 (0)131 225 5613
fax	+44 (0)131 220 4392
e-mail	mail@thewitchery.com
web	www.thewitchery.com

Restaurant with rooms

Kinkell

St Andrews, Fife, KY16 8PN, Scotland

An avenue of beech trees patrolled by guinea fowl leads to the house. If the sea views and the salty smack of St Andrew's Bay air don't get you, walk inside and have your senses tickled pink. The double-ended drawing room has two open fires, a grand piano, fine windows and its original pine floor – gorgeous. Sandy and Frippy both excel in the kitchen and all meals are a treat; dinner, served in the purple dining room, may be local crab or pheasant. From the front door head down to the beach, walk the wild coast or jump on a quad in the back field. Exceptional.

- 4x4 off-roading: from £30.
- Quad-biking: from £10.
- Golf courses.
- Scottish Fisheries Museum.
- Falkland Palace.
- Byre Theatre of St Andrews.

rooms	3: 1 twin,1 twin/double; 1 twin/double with private bathroom.
price	£60-£80. Singles £40-£50.
meals	Lunch from £7. Dinner from £25.
closed	Rarely.
directions	From St Andrews, A917 for 2 miles for Crail. Driveway in 1st line of trees on left after St Andrews.

Sandy & Frippy Fyfe

tel	+44 (0)1334 472003
fax	+44 (0)1334 475248
e-mail	fyfe@kinkell.com
web	www.kinkell.com

B&B

map 19   entry 286

Kinlochfollart

By Dunvegan, Isle of Skye, IV55 8WQ, Scotland

Donald looks after the garden, Rosemary cooks all the food, including her own bread, the loch starts at the end of the garden and the mountains rise beyond. This is Clan MacLeod territory: Skye is steelped in inter-clan rivalries stretching back 800 years, and its history is celebrated in poetry, music and song. Donald and Rosemary have introduced personalised four-day breaks to help you explore the different parts of this fascinating and varied landscape. The house is delightful with fine linen, a country-house feel and tremendously spoiling hosts.

- The Story of Skye - planned itineraries: Mon-Fri, £215 (4 days) full-board.
- Hill, loch & coastal walks from door.
- Archaeology, flora & fauna.
- Dunvegan Castle & Gardens, 2 miles.
- Talisker Distillery, Carbost, 18 miles.
- Calmac ferry to Outer Hebrides, 15 miles.

rooms	3: 2 twins/doubles; 1 single/small double with private bath/shower.
price	Four days: £215 p.p. full-board (includes laundry).
meals	Full-board Mon-Fri (or eat out Tues and/or Wed, £18/£36 reduction).
closed	Christmas & New Year.
directions	From Skye Bridge, for UIG to Sligachan Hotel. Left fork to Dunvegan. There, left (after Health Centre) for Glendale. 0.75 miles on.

Donald & Rosemary MacLeod

tel	+44 (0)1470 521470
fax	+44 (0)1470 521740
e-mail	klfskye@tiscali.co.uk
web	www.klfskye.co.uk

B&B

Lyne Farmhouse

Lyne Farm, Peebles, Peeblesshire, EH45 8NR, Scotland

Simple but freshly decorated and comfortable bedrooms, crisp, clean air and a silence disturbed only by wildlife combine to ensure a good night's sleep. Come if you love space, animals and the values of a hard working farm. The views make your heart soar and there are 1,300 acres to roam with sheep, cattle, horses. An excellent place for families: Arran, in spring, encourages children to bottle-feed lambs; she and John are open and friendly, the atmosphere is easy. Set off to explore the nearby Roman encampment, Lyne Fort. Good value.

- Jewellery & Silversmithing: 2 miles, end of August, £300 (3 days).
- Portrait Photography: 3 miles.
- Throw a Pot: 3 miles.
- Sculpture with Stone: 8 miles.
- Lyne Roman Fort.
- Pentland Hills' trekking on Icelandic horses.

rooms	3: 2 doubles, 1 twin, sharing 2 bathrooms.
price	£44-£48. Singles from £24.
meals	Lunch from £7. Dinner from £10.
closed	Christmas Day.
directions	4 miles west of Peebles on A72, signed on right-hand side of main road.

Arran & John Waddell

tel	+44 (0)1721 740255
fax	+44 (0)1721 740255
e-mail	awaddell@farming.co.uk
web	www.lynefarm.co.uk

B&B

map 19   entry 288

Mackeanston House

Doune, Trossachs, Perth & Kinross, FK16 6AX, Scotland

The fine organic garden gives fruit, the river yields salmon, the moors provide game in winter. An exceptionally welcoming family with a house in a rural setting that combines informality with luxury. There are gigantic beds and generous, sunny bathrooms. Colin, a piper, is a tour guide (juggling a mere three languages), while Fiona is a wine buff and talented cook (shortbread, ice-cream, jam and bread are home-made). Dinners are served in the conservatory with views to a floodlit Stirling Castle. You are 30 minutes from Gleneagles and Loch Lomond.

- Wine- & Whisky-Tasting & Aga Cooking Weekend.
- Stirling Castle & Trossachs Tour.
- Loch Lomond National Park.
- The Falkirk Wheel.
- The Famous Grouse Experience (malt distilleries), 40-minute drive.
- Doune Castle.

rooms	2: 1 double, 1 twin/double. Also 2 self-catering cottages.
price	£76-£80. Singles from £50.
meals	Dinner from £25.
closed	Christmas.
directions	From M9, north, junc. 10 onto A84 for Doune. After 5 miles, left on B826 for Thornhill. Drive on left after 2.2 miles, right off farm drive.

Fiona & Colin Graham

tel	+44 (0)1786 850213
fax	+44 (0)1786 850414
e-mail	enquiries@mackeanstonhouse.co.uk
web	www.mackeanstonhouse.co.uk

B&B & self-catering

Glenshian

Newton-of-Beltrees, By Loch Winnoch, Renfrewshire, PA12 4JL, Scotland

You'd hardly believe that you are 30 minutes from Glasgow. The hamlet used to house the furniture-makers of nearby Beith; each cottage is whitewashed and immaculate. Aileen loves her peaceful 1800s mini-manor and enjoys sharing house and garden; she's a Blue Badge guide and full of original travel ideas. The bedroom is under the eaves with chintz poppy curtains and bedspread and views: garden and fields one way, Loch Winnoch the other. Magazines and flowers, conservatory and drawing room, orchards and fields – a special retreat.

- Castle Semple Marina – watersports & bicycle hire.
- Muirshiel Country Park.
- RSPB bird reserve.
- Burrell Collection, Glasgow.
- Pollok House (NT), Glasgow.
- Culzean Castle (NT).

rooms	1 double with bath/shower.
price	£68. Singles from £40.
meals	At least 4 good pubs within 1-2 miles.
closed	Christmas & New Year.
directions	Glasgow-Irvine, A737, bypass village of Howwood, sign on left to riding stables & B&B. Follow road through stables & farm. Signed, 2nd on left.

Aileen Biggart

tel	+44 (0)1505 842823
fax	+44 (0)1505 842823
e-mail	sambiggart@aol.com

B&B

map 19   entry 290

East Lochhead

Largs Road, Lochwinnoch, Renfrewshire, PA12 4DX, Scotland

A substantial farmhouse built in 1886 from the local grey-cream stone. A log-burning stove glows in the huge living room with its big comfy chairs and piano. But the best thing is the view from the picture windows across the lovely garden to the spectacular lochs beyond. The alcove extension is like a garden room – a delightful spot in which to enjoy Janet's delicious meals. Capacious bedrooms upstairs with modern family paintings; stay in the twin for the 50-mile view of the lochs from the loo. A large downstairs room for wheelchair-users – or a big family.

- Art, Beginners to Competent: £90 (2 days).
- Mountain Biking: 10-minute drive, £12 (2 hours).
- Archery: 10-minute drive, £15 (2 hours).
- Guided Walks: 10-minute drive, £10 (3 hours).
- Sea fishing, 25-minute drive.
- Sailing, 20-minute drive.

rooms	3: 2 doubles, 1 twin.
price	£60–£70. Singles from £45.
meals	Lunch from £12. Dinner from £25.
closed	Rarely.
directions	M8 westbound junc. 28a; for Irvine on A737. Bear right when road divides. Right at r'bout to A760. Under 2 bridges, past bungalow, East Lochhead next house on left, behind trees.

Ross & Janet Anderson

tel	+44 (0)1505 842610
fax	+44 (0)1505 842610
e-mail	admin@eastlochhead.co.uk
web	www.eastlochhead.co.uk

B&B

Scarista House

Isle of Harris, Western Isles, HS3 3HX, Scotland

The landscape here is nothing short of magnificent... and the beach? Miles of pure white sand, hidden from the rest of the world. Patricia and Tim guide you to the island's secrets, and their old manse is the perfect retreat: shuttered windows, peat fires, rugs on bare oak floors, whitewashed walls. Bedrooms are lovely, with warm colours, old oak beds, maybe a writing desk facing out to sea. Food is delicious – they cook brilliantly. Kind island staff may speak in Gaelic, books wait to be read, the sunsets astound. Worth every moment it takes to get here.

- Painting.
- Obbe loch fishing.
- Boat trips to Taransay.
- Bike hire in village.
- Harris golf course.
- Callanish Stone Circle, 25 miles.

rooms	5: 3 doubles, 2 twins.
price	£125–£150. Singles from £75.
meals	Dinner from £32.50.
closed	Occasionally in winter.
directions	From Tarbert, A859, signed Rodel. House 15 miles on left, after golf course.

Patricia & Tim Martin

tel	+44 (0)1859 550238
fax	+44 (0)1859 550277
e-mail	timandpatricia@scaristahouse.com
web	www.scaristahouse.com

Hotel

map 19   entry 292

Chlenry Farmhouse

Castle Kennedy, Stranraer, Wigtownshire, DG9 8SL, Scotland

A comfortable, early-1800s ivy-clad farmhouse, Chlenry stands in its own glen by the Southern Upland Way. There are flowers, fresh fruit, bathrobes and biscuits in your bedroom, and you fall asleep to the sounds of the tumbling burn, retiring pheasants and sheep and the call of the owl. Bathrooms are large with deep old-fashioned tubs and everything that you may have left behind. The dining room is painted deep, warm red – it's flower-filled in summer and firelit in winter. Meals can be simple or elaborate, often with game or fresh salmon.

- Glen Luce Abbey.
- Castle Kennedy Gardens.
- Culzean Castle (NT).
- Southern Upland Way.
- Logan Botanic Gardens.
- Golf at Turnbury.

rooms	2: 1 twin, 1 double, 1 with private bathroom, 1 with shared.
price	From £60. Singles from £36.
meals	Picnic from £5. Dinner with wine from £26.
closed	Christmas & New Year.
directions	A75 for Stranraer. In Castle Kennedy, right opp. Esso garage. Approx. 1.25 miles on, after right bend, right for Chlenry. Down hill, 300yds on left.

David & Ginny Wolseley Brinton

tel	+44 (0)1776 705316
fax	+44 (0)1776 889488
e-mail	wolseleybrinton@aol.com

B&B

The Big Sleep Hotel
Bute Terrace, Cardiff, CF10 2FE, Wales

Cheap but groovy, this novel designer hotel is a perfect launch-pad from which to discover a regenerated Welsh capital. Retro 70s style and 90s minimalism blend to amazing effect inside a former office block near the station. Swimming-pool blues and stark white walls were inspired by 1950s architect Gio Ponti. Furry, formica rooms on the ninth floor are fun and the views are terrific, especially at night. Elsewhere: modular seating re-upholstered in white PVC, a colourful lobby and deep red 60s wallpaper in the busy bar. Novel and good value for a city hotel.

- Millennium Stadium Tours.
- Guide Friday Tours.
- Channel Cruises to Lundy.
- Cardiff Castle.
- Llanerych Vineyard.
- Museum of Welsh Life, St Fagan's.

rooms	81: 42 doubles, 30 twins, 7 family, 2 suites.
price	£45–£120. Singles from £45.
meals	Continental breakfast.
closed	Christmas Day & Boxing Day.
directions	M4, junc. 29, A48(M), for Cardiff East. 3rd junc., A4232 to city centre. At 1st r'bout, 2nd exit, 1 mile past Lloyds TSB, left at lights on A4160. Right at 3rd set of lights, under bridge. Hotel on left.

Cosmo Fry & Lulu Anderson

tel	+44 (0)2920 636363
fax	+44 (0)2920 636364
e-mail	bookings@thebigsleephotel.com
web	www.thebigsleephotel.com

Hotel

map 17   entry 294

The Old Barn

Esgairlygain, Llangynhafal, Ruthin, Denbighshire, LL15 1RT, Wales

The 15th-century wattle-and-daub house and former cow byre sit in a glorious position. The typical, honey-coloured barn has been sensitively converted for guests, keeping its low sloping ceilings, beams and small windows; you can still see the outlines of the original thick stone walls. The sitting room looks over the Vale of Clwyd and your jolly hosts will drop and collect you from Offa's Dyke walks. Irene's craft courses include creative canvas work and paper-making. Good value. *Self-catering possible. Children over 10 welcome.*

- Silk painting; bookmaking; textiles; creative canvas Work: taster or day/week courses.
- Several National Trust properties within 1-hour drive.
- Bodnant Gardens, 1-hour drive.
- Ruthin Craft Centre, 10-minute drive.
- Access to mountains.
- Informal cottage garden with views.

rooms	2: 1 double, 1 triple.
price	£42–£50. Singles from £25.
meals	Lunch from £8. Dinner at nearby inn.
closed	Rarely.
directions	A494 east from Ruthin. Left opp. Griffin Hotel onto B5429. After 0.5 miles, right to Llangynhafal. After 2 miles, Esgairlygain signed on right 100yds past Plas Draw. House left of courtyard.

Irene Henderson
tel   +44 (0)1824 704047
fax   +44 (0)1824 704047

B&B & self-catering

West Arms Hotel

Llanarmon Dyffryn Ceiriog, Denbighshire, LL20 7LD, Wales

A traditional inn in a gorgeous village where the road ends and the real country begins. Hear the sound of the River Cleriog through the open front door; sit in the half-glow of the warm and cosy bar. It's as a 16th-century inn should be; higgledy-piggledy with flagstones, beams, leaded windows, old Welsh colours, traditional furniture and inglenook fireplace. Bedrooms are clean and modest, some with oak beams and low ceilings; plainer ones at the back have pastoral views. Geoff and Gill are laid-back but dedicated, thoroughly at one with what they're doing.

- Landscape Painting: February, June, October, £225 (3 days) full-board.
- Flower Painting: June, £499 (6 days) full-board.
- Pony-trekking.
- Private fishing – 2 miles of river.
- Famous waterfalls, 7 miles.
- Chirk Castle, 10 miles.

rooms	15: 2 doubles, 2 twins, 9 twins/doubles, 2 suites.
price	£85–£138. Singles from £42.50.
meals	Lunch from £6. Dinner from £24.95.
closed	Rarely.
directions	From Shrewsbury, A5 north to Chirk, then left at r'bout on B4500, signed Ceiriog Valley, for 11 miles to Llanarmon DC. Hotel in centre.

Geoff & Gill Leigh–Ford

tel	+44 (0)1691 600665
fax	+44 (0)1691 600622
e–mail	lford@www.thewestarms.co.uk
web ·	www.thewestarms.co.uk

Hotel

map 17   entry 296

Erw

Llanfair, Harlech, Gwynedd, LL46 2SA, Wales

Trudie's quest for the last word in taste, style and comfort has ended here and bedrooms and bathrooms, with excellent lighting, jumbo towels and organic shampoos, are memorable. So are the sea and estuary views. Take advantage of Trudie's deep knowledge of Snowdonia and her personalised itineraries of what to see and where to go... enjoy the light, bright atmosphere of the place, the modern art and the sumptuous organic cookery from a hostess who is larger than life and full of fun. Glorious beaches, too.

- Themed Visits Connected to Historical Characters.
- Exploring antique shops.
- Discovering Snowdonia.
- Visits to Artists & Craftsmens Workshops.
- Ffestiniog Railway.
- Portmeirion, Harlech Castle & Bodnant Garden.

rooms	2: 1 double, 1 twin/double.
price	£100-£120. Singles from £75.
meals	Picnic from £5. Dinner from £25.
closed	Rarely.
directions	On A496 in Llanfair; entrance directly opposite signposted Slate Caverns.

Trudie Hunt

tel	+44 (0)1766 780780
fax	+44 (0)1766 781010
e-mail	erwharlech@waitrose.com
web	www.erwharlech.co.uk

B&B

Tan-y-Coed Isaf

Bryncrug, Tywyn, Gwynedd, LL36 9UP, Wales

The sort of retreat that has city dwellers vowing to leave for the country. There are valleys, mountains and beaches and the pretty terraced garden tumbles down from the house and merges with the scenery. Light-filled bedrooms have long views of the Welsh countryside and there are fresh flowers in each one. There's a guests' sitting room – beamed and warmed by the fire in the inglenook – and you'll be thoroughly spoiled if you decide to eat in. Jane is a professional Cordon Bleu chef and uses fresh local produce and home-grown vegetables whenever possible.

- Sculpture, Painting & Pottery: 0.25 miles.
- Horse-riding: 10 miles.
- Fishing - lake & sea: 5-8 miles.
- Golf, 8 miles.
- Mountain bikes on site.
- Walking at Cader Idris, 5 miles.

rooms	2: 1 double, 1 twin.
price	£50-£54. Singles from £25.
meals	Picnic from £5. Dinner from £12.95.
closed	Rarely.
directions	A487 from Machynlleth for Dolgellau. Left onto B4405, through Abergynolwyn. 2nd farmhouse on right after 1 mile.

Mrs J. Howkins

tel	+44 (0)1654 782639
fax	+44 (0)1654 782639
e-mail	tanhow@supanet.com
web	www.tanycoedisaf.co.uk

B&B

map 17   entry 298

The Old Vicarage

Moylegrove, Nr. Cardigan, Pembrokeshire, SA43 3BN, Wales

The guest book is full of praise for the food and the setting. David and Patricia go to great lengths to bring you the freshest, tastiest, most local produce, and there are good wines, too – even Welsh ones – and beer. Britain only has one Coastal National Park and the Old Vicarage is in it; the most challenging section of the path – a stunning bay and great cliffs – is just a mile away. Inland are woodland walks and the Preseli Hills. The Edwardian house, filled with books and family paintings, has an acre of lawned gardens and large bedrooms which drink in the coastal light.

- Pembrokeshire Coast National Park.
- Walking the coastal path & Preseli Hills.
- Reconstructed Iron Age fort, Castel Henllys, 5 miles.
- Pentre Ifan burial chamber, 7 miles.
- Welsh Wildlife Centre, 4 miles.
- Seals & dolphins off Ceibwr Bay.

rooms	3: 2 doubles, 1 twin.
price	£60-£65. Singles from £40.
meals	Picnic from £5. Dinner from £19.
closed	December-February.
directions	From Cardigan bypass towards Cardigan at southern r'bout. Left by Eagle Inn to St Dogmaels. Sharp right at end of High Street to Moylegrove. There, 1st left to Glanrhyd, then up hill. On right, past church.

Patricia & David Phillips

tel	+44 (0)1239 881231
fax	+44 (0)8701 362382
e-mail	stay@old-vic.co.uk
web	www.old-vic.co.uk

B&B

Trevaccoon

Llanrhian, St David's, Haverfordwest, Pembrokeshire, SA62 6DP, Wales

A decanter of port in your room, mints on your pillow: the sort of attention to detail that make a stay here so special. The Swedish-influenced décor echoes the serene west coast light – white floorboards, seagrass matting, pale antiques, original shutters. The Georgian house borders the National Park with its coastal path and all bedrooms have sea views. Hire bikes, play croquet, head off with a picnic (home-made, delicious) to unspoilt beaches. Caroline, a potter, offers tuition in her studios and a special garden for guests in wheelchairs is planned. A dream.

- Pottery.
- Fishing, Lobster & Crab: 1.5 miles.
- Horse-riding on Beach: 10 miles.
- Seal Watching: 8 miles, autumn.
- Pembrokeshire Coast National Park.
- Bikes for hire in St David's, 6 miles.

rooms	5: 3 doubles, 2 twins.
price	£60–£85. Singles from £40.
meals	Picnics from £4. Restaurants, pubs & café 1 mile.
closed	Christmas & very occasionally.
directions	From Fishguard A487. Right at Croesgoch x-roads, 6 miles from St David's. After 1 mile, left at Llanrhian x-roads. House on left, 0.5 miles on.

Caroline Flynn

tel	+44 (0)1348 831438
fax	+44 (0)1348 831438
e-mail	flynn@trevaccoon.co.uk
web	www.trevaccoon.co.uk

B&B

map 17   entry 300

Penpont

Brecon, Powys, LD3 8EU, Wales

Penpont is magnificent in its sweeping grounds on the River Usk and folded into the gentle Brecon Beacons' foothills. It has not a whiff of pretension yet a relaxed stateliness of its own: great one-table dining room, grand oak staircase and an oak-panelled drawing room. Large bedrooms (one with a tapestried wall) have stacks of atmosphere. An early 19th-century conservatory and two Victorian walled gardens are under restoration and a richly imaginative maze is being nurtured. Overflow into tents (£5), show off on the tennis court, borrow wellies and roam.

- Yoga.
- Painting.
- Writing.
- Grass-boarding centre in grounds.
- Fly-fishing: 1 mile.
- 40 acres with tennis, walled gardens & green man maze.

rooms	4: 1 twin; 1 double with private shower, 2 family both with private bath. Self-contained wing sleeps 14 in 6 bedrooms.
price	£70–£90. Singles from £45.
meals	Restaurants from 4 miles.
closed	Rarely.
directions	From Brecon, west on A40 through Llanspyddid. Pass 2nd telephone kiosk on left. Entrance to house on right. (Approx. 4.5 miles from Brecon.)

Davina & Gavin Hogg

tel	+44 (0)1874 636202
e-mail	penpont@clara.co.uk
web	www.penpont.com

B&B & self-catering

Llangoed Hall

Llyswen, Brecon, Powys, LD3 0YP, Wales

One of the most refined hotels in Britain, Llangoed is a fond tribute to the late Laura Ashley. Bedrooms are big and beautiful – Sir Bernard is redecorating with designs from his new fabric-printing company, Elanbach – and some have lovely views. There are corridors and rooms full of remarkable artefacts and curios from around the world, a maze big enough to get lost in and a private path to the River Wye for picnics on a small beach. Afternoon tea served on a silver tray is sheer indulgence. It's all done in house-party style and you're invited.

- Lifestyle Lunch with Aromatheraphy, Cookery Demo, Fabric Design: from £29.50.
- Wine-tasting & Gourmet Dinner at Llangoed Hall.
- Tennis & croquet.
- Maze & clay-pigeon shooting.
- Black Mountains.
- Golf course.

rooms	23: 20 twins/doubles, 3 suites.
price	£160–£380. Singles from £120.
meals	Lunch from £28.50. Dinner from £45.
closed	Rarely.
directions	From Brecon, A470 for Builth Wells for about 6 miles, then left on A470 to Llyswen. Left in village at T-junc. Entrance 1.5 miles further on right.

Sir Bernard Ashley

tel	+44 (0)1874 754525
fax	+44 (0)1874 754545
e-mail	101543.3211@compuserve.com
web	www.llangoedhall.com

Hotel

map 17   entry 302

The Felin Fach Griffin

Felin Fach, Brecon, Powys, LD3 0UB, Wales

The buzz of a smart city bistro mixed with the easy-going pace of good old country living. Make for three monster leather sofas around a raised hearth and settle in. Dine at a smartly-laid table, or opt for the rustic charm of the small backroom bar; the food has won rave reviews and there's usually a great atmosphere. Breakfast is served around one table in the morning room; make your own toast on an Aga. Bedrooms are done in a modern Scandinavian style, with a few designer touches. Charles and Huw, young and ambitious, host with aplomb.

- Brecon Beacons National Park.
- Pony-trekking.
- Mountain biking.
- Brecon Cathedral.
- Elan Valley.
- Hay-on-Wye.

rooms	7: 2 doubles, 2 twins/doubles, 3 four-posters.
price	£82.50–£92.50. Singles from £57.50.
meals	Lunch from £20. Dinner from £20. Restaurant closed Monday lunchtimes.
closed	Christmas Day, New Year's Day & occasionally.
directions	From Brecon, A470 for Builth Wells to Felin Fach (4.5 miles). On left.

Charles Inkin & Huw Evans-Bevan

tel	+44 (0)1874 620111
fax	+44 (0)1874 620120
e-mail	enquiries@eatdrinksleep.ltd.uk
web	www.eatdrinksleep.ltd.uk

Hotel

entry 303 map 17

Gliffaes Country House Hotel

Crickhowell, Powys, NP8 1RH, Wales

Gliffaes is a house for all seasons – not even driving rain could mask its beauty. Stroll along the rhododendron-flanked drive and wander the 33 acres of stunning gardens and woodland, or just sit and gaze at the River Usk 150 feet below. In winter, curl up by fires burning in extravagantly ornate fireplaces – one looks like the Acropolis. Tea is a feast of scones and cakes laid out on a long table at one end of a sitting room of polished floors and panelled walls. Bedrooms are excellent, the cooking British with Mediterranean flavours and a hint of the orient.

- Fly-fishing: June, £195 inc. B&B.
- Fishing: from 3 March.
- Local History: November & February.
- Falconery.
- Clay Pigeon Shooting.
- Horse-riding.

rooms	23: 6 doubles, 13 twins/doubles, 4 singles.
price	£69–£174. Singles from £60.
meals	Lunch from £4. Dinner from £28.
closed	1st two weeks in January.
directions	From Crickhowell, A40 west for 2.5 miles. Entrance on left, signed. Hotel 1 mile up winding hill.

James & Susie Suter

tel	+44 (0)1874 730371
fax	+44 (0)1874 730463
e-mail	calls@gliffaeshotel.com
web	www.gliffaeshotel.com

Hotel

map 17   entry 304

ireland

Photography by Tim Brook

ireland

Whitepark House

Whitepark Bay, Ballintoy, Co. Antrim, BT54 6NH, Northern Ireland

Whitepark House is in a superb position looking out across the Atlantic Ocean. On clear days you can see Rathlin lighthouse, Islay and the Paps of Jura. Entering the magnificent entrance is like stepping into a maharaja's villa in the Hindu Kush – were such a thing possible. This is an exotic, sensuous world teeming with indoor vegetation. Bob is a friendly and fastidious host who loves looking after folk. The bedrooms ooze splendour, especially the big double at the end of the corridor. Walk along the coast after breakfast by the big bay window.

- Giant's Causeway, 5 miles.
- Dunluce Castle, 8 miles.
- Rathlin Island Bird Sanctuary, 10 miles.
- Golf courses, 20-minute drive.
- Whitepark Bay.
- North Antrim Cliff Path from door.

rooms	3: 2 doubles, 1 twin, sharing bathroom & extra wc.
price	From £60. Singles from £35.
meals	Restaurants nearby.
closed	Rarely.
directions	From Bushmills, A2 coast road to Whitepark Bay. Entrance on right, 100yds past youth hostel.

Bob & Siobhán Isles

tel	+44 (0)28 2073 1482
e-mail	bob@whiteparkhouse.com
web	www.whiteparkhouse.com

B&B

Harmony Hill Country House

Balnamore, Ballymoney, Co. Antrim, BT53 7PS, Northern Ireland

Lounge and bar have the feel of a grand country house, full of restrained good taste, with aromatic turf fires and comfy seats to flop into with an aperitif. Peat fires too in the luxurious log cabin style bedrooms. The restaurant across a decked atrium has checked tableclothes that suggest rural France. Richard and Trish are serious about their food, using as much fresh and local produce as possible. Tantalising dishes, such as Beef Welly and Chocolate Orange Slider, jump off the menu. No surpise the restaurant has a big local following – book early.

- Own landscaped gardens.
- Drumaheghlis Marina, 1 mile.
- Bushmills Distillery, 10 miles.
- Golf courses, 3-10 miles.
- Beaches, 10 miles.
- On-site restaurant.

rooms	4 twins/doubles (3 with bunk beds).
price	From £65. Singles from £39.
meals	Sunday lunch from £10. Dinner from £20.
closed	Christmas & New Year.
directions	From Ballymoney, A26 for 1 mile. Left signed Balnamore, over r'way crossing. Left at T-junc. in village; 3rd right on tight bend, signed. House 400yds up gravel drive.

Trish Wilson

tel	+44 (0)28 2766 3459
fax	+44 (0)28 2766 3740
e-mail	webmaster@harmonyhill.net
web	www.harmonyhill.net

Restaurant with rooms

map 20   entry 306

Beech Hill Country House

23 Ballymoney Road, Craigantlet, Newtownards, Co. Down, BT23 4TG, Northern Ireland

Beech Hill was built by Victoria's grandmother along the one-storey lines of the house she grew up in as a child. Victoria is a natural hostess – you will be offered tea and delicious cakes in a sitting room with windows that look out onto a croquet lawn and fields with grazing cows. There is a lovely wooden conservatory with wicker furniture and hanging baskets filled with geraniums. The bedrooms are immaculate, with demure prints of Belfast on the walls. The house is a welcoming place and Victoria is chatty and friendly.

- Mount Stewart House & Garden (NT).
- Ulster Folk & Transport Museum.
- Golf courses.
- Yacht clubs.
- Castle Espie Wildlife Sanctuary.
- Somme War Museum.

rooms	3: 2 doubles, 1 twin.
price	£60-£64. Singles £40-£42.
meals	Restaurants in Holywood, 5 miles.
closed	Rarely.
directions	From Belfast, A2 for Bangor. Bypass Holywood, then right up Ballymoney Rd, signed Craigantlet. House 1.75 miles on left.

Victoria Brann

tel	+44 (0)28 9042 5892
fax	+44 (0)28 9042 5892
e-mail	info@beech-hill.net
web	www.beech-hill.net

B&B

Edenvale House

130 Portaferry Road, Newtownards, Co. Down, BT22 2AH, Northern Ireland

Exuberant, incredibly friendly and bursting with energy, Diane will quickly have you settled into this lovely 1780 Georgian house overlooking Strangford Lough. Gordon has a quick humour, too, and takes over welcome duties as the occasion requires. Relax in the beautifully furnished drawing room or in the bright sunroom with views of the Mourne Mountains. Large, immaculate bedrooms are well-proportioned, with luxuriously big beds. There is a lovely big flower garden and children will adore the horse and ponies. *Only 20 minutes from Belfast City Airport.*

- Birdwatching.
- Guided walks, Mount Stewart estate: 1km.
- Golf Tuition: 5km.
- Horse-riding: 6km.
- Grey Abbey village & monastery.
- Ulster Folk & Transport Museum.

rooms	4: 2 doubles, 1 twin, 1 family.
price	£60. Singles from £40.
meals	Restaurants in Bangor & Newtownards.
closed	Christmas & New Year.
directions	From Newtownards, A20 Portaferry road for 2 miles. Entrance on left up drive.

Diane & Gordon Whyte

tel	+44 (0)28 9181 4881
fax	+44 (0)28 9182 6192
e-mail	edenvalehouse@hotmail.com
web	www.edenvalehouse.com

B&B

map 20   entry 308

Clanmurry

16 Lower Quilly Road, Dromore, Co. Down, BT25 1NL, Northern Ireland

The big old house lies in six acres conveniently close to the A1. Once inside the grounds, the gentle atmosphere takes over. Sara and John speak thoughtfully and knowledgeably on a range of subjects – including the Latin names of plants in their truly wonderful garden. The bedrooms have lots of light and garden views and bathrobes are provided for the trip to your bathroom. This is the only B&B we know that serves coddled eggs for breakfast: Sara and John had their first coddled egg on an African honeymoon and they've been coddling each Sunday ever since!

- Golf: 8 miles.
- Mountains of Mourne, 20 miles.
- Rowallane Gardens, 12 miles.
- Belfast, 18 miles.
- Irish Linen Centre, Lisburn.
- Tours from Hillsborough.

rooms	2: 1 double, 1 twin, both with private bath.
price	From £60. Singles from £40.
meals	Restaurant 3 miles.
closed	Christmas & New Year.
directions	From Belfast, M1 south, then A1 south to Dromore for exactly 8 miles. 1st right after only road bridge over Dromore bypass. Entrance 1st on right.

Sara & John McCorkell

tel	+44 (0)28 9269 3760
fax	+44 (0)28 9269 8106
e-mail	mccorkell@btinternet.com
web	www.clanmurry.com

B&B

Drumcovitt House

704 Feeny Road, Feeny, Co. Londonderry, BT47 4SU, Northern Ireland

An intriguing old Georgian farmhouse on a hill, where many original features remain. Grand rooms have round bays, original pine flooring, gilded pelmets, dado rails, beehive door knobs and cornices circa 1796. Stairs sweep up to a wide, creaky, arched landing lined with old books. Visit the sandy beaches of Benone and Magillian, climb the glen to the reservoir; on misty mornings the highest peaks and the spire of Banagher church are still visible. Exceptional value and a favourite haunt for writers and poets. *Three self-catering cottages also available.*

- Angling.
- Hill-walking.
- Gliding.
- Pony-trekking.
- Archeological Tours.
- Giant's Causeway.

rooms	3: 1 twin, 2 family, sharing 2 bathrooms.
price	£42–£54. Singles £21–£27.
meals	Picnic from £5. Dinner £10–£20.
closed	Rarely.
directions	From Derry, A6 to Belfast for 10 miles; right on B74 to Feeny. Through village, house 0.5 miles on left.

Florence & Frank Sloan

tel	+44 (0)28 7778 1224
fax	+44 (0)28 7778 1224
e-mail	drumcovitt.feeny@btinternet.com
web	www.drumcovitt.com

B&B & self-catering

map 20   entry 310

Sherwood Park House

Ballon, Co. Carlow, Eire

The only rule Maureen seems to lay down is that you enjoy yourself; with her boundless generosity and Paddy's gift for hilarious one-liners, it is not hard. Approached through an original stone entrance, Sherwood is a fine example of early Irish-Georgian, with high ceilings and big, welcoming rooms. In the main hallway past the well-played piano is an elegant staircase that leads to bedrooms with half-testers and four-posters. Breakfast is served round a large dining table that must take weeks to polish. An enchanting house, and popular with Dubliners.

- Walks: 6km, includes drop-off, pick-up & packed lunch.
- Altamount Gardens, 0.5km.
- Ballykeenan Aviary & Pet Farm, 1.5km.
- Mount Wolseley Golf Club, 8km.
- Huntingdon Castle, 6km.
- Mount Leinster, 8km.

rooms	4: 1 double, 1 family, 2 suites.
price	€90–€120. Singles €55–€65.
meals	Dinner €35–€40.
closed	Rarely.
directions	From Naas, N9 south to Carlow, then N80 towards Wexford to Ballon. Through Ballon, up hill, then left at 2nd x-roads, signed to house.

Patrick & Maureen Owens

tel	+353 (0)59 915 9117
fax	+353 (0)59 915 9355
e-mail	info@sherwoodparkhouse.ie
web	www.sherwoodparkhouse.ie

B&B

Fergus View
Kilnaboy, Corofin, Co. Clare, Eire

Genuine Irish hospitality in a lovely family home close to The Burren, a unique lunar landscape of weathered limestone and prehistoric dolmens. A short walk in this beautiful wilderness is said to calm the most troubled mind. But first sample Mary's cooking: her simple lunch was exquisite, so imagine what dinner would be like. Everything is done well here. Bedrooms are compact and comfortable, with orthopedic beds. The garden stretches down to the River Fergus, hidden by a welter of colourful plants in summer. *Self-catering cottage next door, sleeps five.*

- Walking Tours: in English.
- Fishing: 0.8km-6.4 km.
- Archaeology, Flora & Fauna of the Burren: 3.2km.
- Clare Heritage Centre Museum, 3km.
- Traditional Irish music (July/ August), 3km.
- Cliffs of Moher, 32km.

rooms	6: 3 doubles, 1 twin/double, 1 family; 1 double sharing bathroom.
price	€ 66-€ 76. Singles from € 50.
meals	Dinner from € 23, Monday-Thursday only. Restaurants nearby.
closed	Last week October-March.
directions	From Shannon, N18 through Ennis to roundabout, for Ennistymon, for 3.2km, then right on R476 to Corofin & on to Kilnaboy. House on left after church ruins.

Mary & Declan Kelleher

tel	+353 (0)65 683 7606
fax	+353 (0)65 683 7192
e-mail	deckell@indigo.ie

B&B & self-catering

map 20   entry 312

Old Parochial House

Cooraclare, Kilrush, Co. Clare, Eire

Old Parochial House has the down-to-earth feel of being among friends. Alyson and Sean are a cheerful couple who make you feel immediately welcome. They did everything themselves in their lovely home, an 1872 former parish priest's house. Rich colours bring warmth to every room. Big bedrooms have post beds, fireplaces, corniced ceilings and wooden floors. Wake up to views of rolling countryside, then start the day with bacon rashers that have been voted the best by the whole family at an annual start-of-the-season tasting session!

- Dolphin Watching: 10km.
- Birdwatching: 10km.
- Flora & Fauna Field Trips: 10km.
- Nature Photography: 10km.
- Thalassotherapy: 15km.
- Sailing: 10km.

rooms	4: 2 doubles, 1 double/triple; 1 double/triple with private bath.
price	€ 70–€ 150.
meals	Pub within easy walking distance.
closed	October–April.
directions	From Ennis, N68 towards Kilrush for 28km, then right to Cooraclare, following signs. In village, right onto R483 at petrol station towards coast. 3rd house on left.

Alyson & Sean O'Neill

tel	+353 (0)65 905 9059
fax	+353 (0)65 905 9059
e-mail	oldparochialhouse@eircom.net
web	www.oldparochialhouse.com

B&B

Glenview House

Midleton, Co. Cork, Eire

Ken and Beth's enthusiasm is palpable and many guests have become good friends. The view in front of this 1780 Georgian house is exhilarating. Lawns dive into a wedge of pines to an unseen, gurgling river that asks to be discovered; quiet seclusion is yours among birds, horses and sheep. Large bedrooms have spectacular views through tall sash windows and big comfortable beds. One bathroom has a wonderful Heath-Robinson-like Victorian brass shower. *Two self-catering coach house cottages, one with full disabled facilities, sleep 2-6. Guide dogs welcome.*

- Birdwatching: 10km.
- Old Midleton Distillery, 5km.
- Fota House & Garden, Fota Island, 7km.
- Fota Wildlife Park, 7km.
- Barryscourt Castle, 6km.
- Golf course.

rooms	4: 3 doubles, 1 twin.
price	€ 127-€ 140. Singles € 79.
meals	Dinner € 32-€ 35.
closed	Rarely.
directions	Drive into Midleton. At large roundabout take L.35 to Fermoy. 4km onto T-junc., right. 0.5km on to next junction, Glenview signed to left. Entrance at top of hill on left.

Ken & Beth Sherrard

tel	+353 (0)21 463 1680
fax	+353 (0)21 463 4680
e-mail	info@glenviewmidleton.com
web	www.glenviewmidleton.com

B&B & self-catering

map 20   entry 314

Spanish Point Restaurant
Ballycotton, Co. Cork, Eire

Mary is an excellent host, happy to make time for you. This seafood restaurant perches on a small cliff looking over Ballycotton Bay; a small, rocky cove below is reached via a steep path. Rooms have low double beds and pink carpets; two have sea views. To the right is the harbour where John moors his trawler – his fish are cooked and prepared here. A place for foodies who want to eat the freshest seafood in unpretentious surroundings and for those who love to mull over the larger issues of life while gazing out to sea.

- Cookery, Breadmaking.
- Cookery, Fish.
- Cookery, Meat.
- Cookery, Soups, Stocks & Sauces.
- Cookery, Vegetables & Vegetarian.
- Cookery, Desserts.

rooms	5: 3 doubles, 2 family.
price	From € 80. Singles from € 50.
meals	Lunch from € 22. Dinner from € 39.
closed	Rarely.
directions	From Cork, N25 for Youghal. Right in Midleton to Ballycotton. Entering village, restaurant on left, signed.

John & Mary Tattan
tel	+353 (0)21 464 6177
fax	+353 (0)21 464 6179
e-mail	spanishp@indigo.ie

Restaurant with rooms

Rathcoursey House

Ballinacurra, Midleton, Co. Cork, Eire

The colour of dried apricots, the house sits at the end of an avenue on the brow of a hill. Owner and accomplished chef Beth has renovated the house exquisitely – and transformed the grounds, planting 3,000 trees and an orchard in the shape of a comet. She has even cleared a path through woodland to the local pub. Rooms are luxurious; the 'baptismal font' bathroom alone is incredible. Beth has a rare talent and it is to her credit that any praise offered is shrugged off with a graceful smile. A very special place – even ambassadors have pleaded to stay here.

- Mind, Body & Spirit - detox, relax & rejuvenate.
- Sailing, Kinsale & Crosshaven Yacht Clubs.
- Salmon fishing, Blackwater.
- Deep-sea fishing.
- Country walks & hill-climbing.
- Golf courses.

rooms	5 doubles, extra bathroom.
price	From €190. Singles from €100. Whole house, €725 per night.
meals	Lunch from €15. Dinner from €30.
closed	Rarely.
directions	From Cork, N25 to Midleton. At r'bout, Whitegate Rd for 1km, then right at x-roads to East Ferry. After 1km, look out for 1st arrow above 'Reduce Speed' sign, then follow arrows up bumpy lane.

Beth Hallinan

tel	+353 (0)21 461 3418
e-mail	beth@rathcoursey.com
web	www.rathcoursey.com

Hotel

map 20   entry 316

Maranatha Country House

Tower, Blarney, Co. Cork, Eire

On a hill surrounded by rhododendron, monkey-puzzle and giant redwood awaits a wonderful fantasy world. Lounge in palatial luxury amid fragrant flowers dreaming of Persia and the Orient as each room follows its own sumptuous theme. Beautiful fabrics frame window views of landscaped garden and secluded woodland; walks lead in all directions. Olwen and Douglas have a deep affection for the house and their enthusiasm rubs off on those who stay; many return. Breakfasts served in the conservatory are memorable. A wonderful place with a big heart.

- History of the Early-Irish Church: in English & German.
- Christian Studies.
- Relationship Studies.
- Blarney Castle & Blarney Stone.
- Golf, 5-minute drive.
- Pubs with live music.

rooms	6: 1 double, 3 four-posters, 2 family.
price	€53–€100. Singles €39–€75.
meals	Restaurants in Blarney.
closed	November-March.
directions	From Cork, N20, then R617 through Blarney. 1.km on, signed to house just after Tower village sign; right up hill.

Olwen & Douglas Venn

tel	+353 (0)21 438 5102
fax	+353 (0)21 438 2978
e-mail	info@maranathacountryhouse.com
web	www.maranathacountryhouse.com

B&B

Walton Court Country House

Oysterhaven, Co. Cork, Eire

There are not enough superlatives to describe what Paul and Janis have achieved here in six years. They removed 92 tons of soil from the hall, built an aquarium in the living room wall, filled the house with Africana from their time in Kenya. The house was built in 1645 by English smugglers. The view down to the harbour is perfect and the courtyard catches the setting sun; you eat in a conservatory which feels Mediterranean. The menu changes weekly. The place is gorgeous and the people are friendly and charming. *Also 3 self-catering cottages.*

- Spa & Yoga Weekends.
- Aromatherapy.
- Reflexology.
- Watercolours & Pottery.
- Own beach & slipway.
- Horse-riding, fishing, golf.

rooms	8 twins/doubles.
price	€ 108–€ 165. Singles from € 75.
meals	Lunch from € 18. Dinner from € 38.
closed	Christmas Day.
directions	From Kinsale, Cork road to Belgooly, then right at the Huntsman Bar, signed Oysterhaven. House on right, overlooking bay. 1st entrance (sharp right).

Paul & Janis Rafferty

tel	+353 (0)21 477 0878
fax	+353 (0)21 477 0932
e-mail	info@waltoncourt.com
web	www.waltoncourt.com

Hotel & self-catering

map 20   entry 318

Horseshoe Cottage

Horseshoe Harbour, Sherkin Island, Co. Cork, Eire

Folk down the centuries have been drawn to the peace and solitude of this beautiful little island. Horseshoe is three cottages rolled into one, built about 400 years ago. Downstairs is big and roomy with a wood stove, an eight-foot sofa, a small organ and hundreds of music tapes. Bedrooms are small and cosy, with wooden floors and extra blankets for those chillier nights. Steve and Chris are relaxed, hospitable souls. There are safe, sandy beaches, rocky headlands, a Franciscan friary, fields of wild flowers and masses of wildlife.

- English Language: 1km.
- Painting with Local Artist: 500m.
- Sailing: 10-minute drive.
- PADI Diving: 10-minute drive.
- Dolphin & Whale-watching Trips.
- Rock & Sea Angling.

rooms	3: 1 double, 1 twin, 1 single.
price	€60–€75. Singles €30–€38.
meals	2 pubs within easy walking distance.
closed	Christmas & New Year.
directions	Ferry from Baltimore (all year), or Schull (summer only). Up hill past abbey ruins, then left at telephone box. Cottage on right.

Steve & Chris Hayes

tel	+353 (0)28 20598 (Subject to change. See intro.)
fax	+353 (0)28 20980
e-mail	chris@sherkintefl.com
web	www.sherkinisland.ie

B&B

Grove House

Colla Road, Schull, Co. Cork, Eire

A sense of history drifts through Grove House like an unseen guest. Opening first as a hotel in the early 1900s, it became a popular haunt for many a distinguished visitor including Bernard Shaw and Irish painter Jack Yeats. With its big airy rooms and uninterrupted views over Schull harbour, it's easy to see what attracted them. Bedrooms are full of eccentric detail: panelled headboards salvaged from a bank, an original Victorian loo with a square wooden seat. Billy loves the *cráic* – there are some great pubs on the main street – and Mary's bacon is the best.

- English Language, Business & Conversation: one-to-one or small groups.
- PADI Diving with Qualified Instructor.
- Wildlife Discovery Tours.
- Schull Harbour.
- The Planetarium, Schull.
- Mizen Head Signal Station, Goleen.

rooms	5: 4 doubles, 1 twin.
price	€ 90–€ 120. Singles € 60–€ 75.
meals	Restaurants in Schull.
closed	November-February. Off season by arrangement.
directions	From Cork, N71 to Ballydehob, then R592 to Schull. Left opp. AIB bank. House 500m on right.

Billy & Mary O'Shea

tel	+353 (0)28 28067 (Subject to change. See intro.)
fax	+353 (0)28 28069
e-mail	info@grovehouseschull.com
web	www.grovehouseschull.com

B&B

map 20   entry 320

Frewin

Ramelton, Co. Donegal, Eire

Thomas and Regina have taken Irish hospitality to a new level in this lovely, relaxed house. The Victorian part was once a rectory and there's a fortified annexe behind that dates to 1698. Thomas, an antique collector and restorer of historic buildings, will tell fascinating tales about the house over a nightcap by the fire in the library. The bedrooms, elegant and uncluttered, have beautiful bathrooms and lush views. Regina's delicious food is served on a wonderfully-laid table, lit by a chandelier of candles. *Also a self-catering cottage, sleeps 2 + child.*

- Slieve League - Europe's highest cliffs, 80km.
- Golden beaches, 11km.
- Doon Rock - inland promontory fort.
- Glenveagh National Park, 24km.
- Golf courses, 8km.
- Dunfanaghy Workhouse.

rooms	4: 1 double, with private bath; 3 mini-suites.
price	€ 100–€ 126. Singles € 70–€ 86.
meals	Dinner from € 35. Restaurant 500m.
closed	24-27 December.
directions	From Letterkenny, R245 to Ramelton for 12km. Approaching Ramelton, right 600m after petrol station. House 300m on right.

Thomas & Regina Coyle

tel	+353 (0)74 915 1246
fax	+353 (0)74 915 1246
e-mail	flaxmill@indigo.ie
web	www.accommodationdonegal.net

B&B & self-catering

The Mill Restaurant

Figart, Dunfanaghy, Co. Donegal, Eire

The hostile beauty of the north-west of Donegal is manna to the artist. Acclaimed watercolourist Frank Egginton moved here in 1949, buying this 19th-century lodge on the shores of New Lake and now his granddaughter Susan and husband Derek have given it new life. Derek cooks with fabulous local ingredients – everything he uses is fresh and in season. Susan is charming, ensuring guests are well looked after; the pleasant bedrooms have Grandfather's paintings on the walls and lake views. The living room is full of his collection of antique oak furniture.

- Week-long Horse-riding Trail.
- Painting.
- Quilt-making.
- Golf: in village.
- Gallery, craft shop & heritage museum in village.
- Ferry to Tory Island to see fishermen artists.

rooms	6: 4 doubles, 2 family.
price	€ 76–€ 90. Singles from € 45.
meals	Dinner € 33–€ 45.
closed	Mondays.
directions	From Dunfanaghy, N56 Falcarragh road past gallery on right & down small hill. Entrance on right. House overlooks lake.

Susan & Derek Alcorn

tel	+353 (0)74 913 6985 / 913 6983
fax	+353 (0)74 913 6985
e-mail	info@themillrestaurant.com
web	www.themillrestaurant.com

Restaurant with rooms

map 20 entry 322

Ardnamona

Lough Eske, Co. Donegal, Eire

Deep in the rhododendron forest, logs crackle contentedly in the hearths at Ardnamona. You'll find Amabel in the kitchen with her two children, creating delicious morsels, while Kieran may be in the woods transforming a former arboretum to National Heritage status, or tuning a friend's piano. Ardnamona lends itself to long, cosy, convivial evenings. In the morning, wake up in cheerfully elegant bedrooms with white-painted furniture and patchwork quilts; some have window seats with views over Lough Eske to the heather slopes of the Blue Stack Mountains.

- Ancient Gaelic Songs & Ancient Irish Myths & Legends - recitals & stories.
- National Heritage Garden in 40 acres .
- Private lough shore, fishing & boating.
- Primieval oak forest next door.
- Walking country.
- Coast, 20-minute drive.

rooms	6: 3 doubles, 2 twins/doubles; 1 twin/double with private bath.
price	€140. Singles €80-€90.
meals	Dinner from €35; weekends only.
closed	Rarely.
directions	From Donegal, N15 to Letterkenny for 4km. Take small turning on left for Harvey's Point Hotel & Lough Eske Drive. On for 8km. Low wall, then white-gated drive on right.

Kieran & Amabel Clarke

tel	+353 (0)74 972 2650
fax	+353 (0)74 972 2819
e-mail	info@ardnamona.com
web	www.ardnamona.com

B&B

Portnason House

Portnason, Ballyshannon, Co. Donegal, Eire

Originally built as officers' accommodation for the British army in 1750, this Irish Georgian house down a beautiful sycamore-lined drive has been Madge's 'project' for some years; the results are striking. A mulberry staircase leads to bedrooms with pitch pine floors, original marble fireplaces and big brass beds, while bathrooms have claw-footed baths. The Georgian appetite for space and light is evident, the old practice of filling in windows to dodge heavy taxation being thankfully absent. White wooden shutters open onto beautiful views of the estuary.

- Art & Painting.
- Irish Language.
- Traditional Music.
- Birdwatching.
- English Language, Business & General.
- Corporate retreat.

rooms	5: 3 doubles, 2 twins.
price	From € 120. Single from € 80.
meals	Restaurant 1km.
closed	Christmas & New Year.
directions	From Donegal, N15 south to Ballyshannon. Through town, over bridge, then right at r'bout to Sligo. Entrance on right down tree-lined avenue by stone gate lodge.

Madge Sharkey

tel	+353 (0)71 985 2016
fax	+353 (0)71 985 2016
e-mail	portnasonhouse@oceanfree.net

B&B

map 20   entry 324

Aberdeen Lodge

53 Park Avenue, Ballsbridge, Dublin 4, Co. Dublin, Eire

Aberdeen Lodge is a refuge from Dublin city, yet the metro is close enough to catapult you back into the thick of things within minutes. Pat is a friendly professional with a quiet deferential manner – nothing is too much trouble. This modest Victorian villa has been cleverly converted into a variety of contemporary rooms with all mod cons. Rooms at the rear look onto a cricket pitch, an unusual sight in a country devoted to Gaelic football. Breakfast to piped classical music was revitalising. Ideal for those wanting the best of both worlds in this fair city.

- Dublin City Tour: 1km, € 12.50.
- Castle Tour: € 20.
- Scenic Country Tour: € 28 (transport from hotel).
- Golf tuition: € 45.
- Martello Tower.
- Trinity College.

rooms	17: 11 twins/doubles, 2 family, 2 triples, 2 suites.
price	€ 110–€ 160. Singles from € 95.
meals	Lunch from € 16. Dinner from € 25.
closed	Rarely.
directions	From city centre, Northumberland Rd to Merrion Rd, then left into Ailesbury Rd, signed to Sydney Parade Dart Station, then 1st left into Park Avenue. 500m on left.

Pat Halpin

tel	+353 (0)1 283 8155
fax	+353 (0)1 283 7877
e-mail	aberdeen@iol.ie
web	www.halpinsprivatehotels.com

Hotel

Fermoyle Lodge

Casla (Costelloe), Connemara, Co. Galway, Eire

Fermoyle Lodge lies in splendid isolation amid the rocky wilderness of Connemara's lakelands. It has an incredible view to the mountainous horizon of Connemara National Park. Dinner on the terrace at sunset has few equals. Jean-Pierre's French cuisine matches the occasion, with ingredients sourced locally and in season. Nicola is an impeccable hostess and a witty interlocutor. Bedrooms in the main house have the spectacular view and two big elegant rooms in a converted outbuilding look over the garden with its curious Victorian follies.

- Horse-riding.
- Walking.
- Golf Tuition: 20-minute drive.
- Fly-fishing.
- Coral beach, 20-minute drive.
- Ferry to Aran Islands, 10-minute drive.

rooms	6: 4 doubles, 2 twins.
price	€ 170-180. Singles from € 110.
meals	Dinner from € 40.
closed	November-mid-March. Groups off season by arrangement.
directions	From Galway, N59 to Oughterard. Left by Bridge Restaurant onto minor road to Costelloe; 16km on, entrance on right among trees.

Nicola Stronach & Jean-Pierre Maire

tel	+353 (0)91 786111
	(Subject to change. See intro.)
fax	+353 (0)91 786154
e-mail	fermoylelodge@eircom.net
web	www.fermoylelodge.com

B&B

map 20 entry 326

Railway Lodge

Canrower, Oughterard, Co. Galway, Eire

Carmel has returned to her native Galway to run a B&B on the family farm. This attractive modern house blends in well with its surroundings, and Carmel has done a wonderful job inside. Cottage-style bedrooms are pristine and cosy, with polished wooden floors, old Irish pine furniture, stitched bedspreads and Oxford pillowcases. There's a snug living room with log fire and comfy armchairs that feels old and settled, and a conservatory. Carmel's father breeds Connemara ponies and is the inspiration behind much of the railway memorabilia dotted about.

- Trout & salmon fishing on Lough Corrib.
- Golf, 3km–40km.
- Walk the Western Way from the door.
- Aran Islands, 20-minute drive to ferry.
- Kylemore Abbey & Victorian Gardens.
- Connemara National Park, 40-minute drive.

rooms	4: 3 doubles, 1 family.
price	€70–€80. Singles from €45.
meals	Restaurants within easy walking distance.
closed	Rarely.
directions	From Galway, N59 Clifden road to Oughterard. Through town, then left after Corrib House Hotel & immediately right. Follow signs to house.

Carmel Geoghegan

tel	+353 (0)91 552945 (Subject to change. See intro.)
e-mail	railwaylodge@eircom.net
web	www.railwaylodge.net

B&B

The Anglers Return

Toombeola, Roundstone, Co. Galway, Eire

Lynn gives you her absolute attention from the moment her cockerel ushers in another day. Fresh eggs, home-made breads, conserves, yogurt and organic cereals await you too. The ex-sporting lodge has whitewashed walls, wooden floors, antique furniture, fresh wild flowers, log fires and tasteful bedrooms with enchanting views of the tidal Ballynahinch River. A courtyard over-run with chickens leads to three acres of natural garden and a well-earned rest in a hammock. The pretty fishing village is the hub of life here, with an arts festival in June.

- Art Workshops: May & September, €320 (3 days) full-board.
- Irish Dance Workshops & Music Nights: no charge.
- Sea-fishing & Coastal Photography: 6.4km, in season.
- Golf links & 18-hole pitch & putt.
- Brown trout fishing on own lake.
- Connemara Garden Trail (14 gardens).

rooms	5: 1 double; 2 doubles, 1 twin, 1 family, sharing two bathrooms.
price	€72–€92. Singles from €50.
meals	Dinner €22–€30. Restaurant 3.2km.
closed	December-February.
directions	From Galway, N59 Clifden Rd; left R341 towards Roundstone for 6km. House on left, at Toombeola.

Lynn Hill

tel	+353 (0)95 31091
	(Subject to change. See intro.)
fax	+353 (0)95 31091
e-mail	lynnhill@eircom.net
web	www.anglersreturn.itgo.com

B&B

map 20   entry 328

Ballynahinch Castle Hotel

Recess, Connemara, Co. Galway, Eire

This beautiful estate with several thousand acres of fishing and shooting rights once boasted the world's longest driveway – its entrance was in Oughterard, 28 miles away. In 1924, a Maharaja bought the castle, landscaping the gardens to their present state. Today the house is back in the hands of the O'Flaherty family: Patrick is a dapper and welcoming presence in Irish tweed. Eric Clapton stayed and caught his first salmon here – it was probably paraded in the timeworn bar where fishermen bring their catch to be weighed. Rooms are luxurious and varied.

- Fly-fishing.
- Guided Walks through Twelve Bens.
- Salmon and Sea Trout Fishing, Ballynahinch River.
- Pony-trekking.
- Golf.
- Cycling.

rooms	40 twins/doubles.
price	From €187–€433. Singles from €112.
meals	Dinner from €47.
closed	Christmas week.
directions	From Galway, N59 Clifden road to Recess. 10km on, left down road, signed to hotel & Roundstone.

Hotel

Patrick O'Flaherty

tel	+353 (0)95 31006 (Subject to change. See intro.)
fax	+353 (0)95 31085
e-mail	bhinch@iol.ie
web	www.ballynahinch-castle.com

Dolphin Beach House

Lower Sky Road, Clifden, Co. Galway, Eire

Watch dolphins play in the bay from your bedroom window, then walk to a private sandy cove for a swim. This modified 19th-century farmhouse lies at the edge of Europe, surrounded by windswept scenery and the Atlantic ocean. Billy and Barbara belong to a family whose hotel pedigree is almost without equal in Ireland. Bedrooms are big and full of luxurious fun and eccentric detail and only seasonal local produce is used in the kitchen. After dinner, visit busy bustling Clifden by taxi; then return, and let the sound of the sea lull you to sleep.

- Kylemore Abbey, 10km.
- Connemara National Park, 7km.
- Connemara Golf Club, 9km.
- Inishbofin Island, 7km.
- Landing site of first transatlantic flight, 5km.
- Roundstone blanket bog, 5km.

rooms	8: 4 doubles, 3 twins/doubles, 1 single.
price	€ 130–€ 180. Singles from € 85.
meals	€ 35–€ 40.
closed	Mid-November–early March.
directions	From Clifden, Sky Rd for 3km to Y-junc., then left on Lower Sky Rd, signed. House on left after 2.5km, overlooking bay.

Billy & Barbara Foyle

tel	+353 (0)95 21204
	(Subject to change. See intro.)
fax	+353 (0)95 22935
e-mail	dolphinbeach@iolfree.ie
web	www.connemara.net/DolphinBeachHouse

B&B

map 20 entry 330

Delphi Lodge

Leenane, Co. Galway, Eire

Delphi is recommended by folk all over Ireland. Built in the 1830s by the Marquis of Sligo, the estate covers 600 acres of land and 1,000 acres of mountain, water and bogland. Guests dine together at a long table with Peter at the helm: lively conversation, local ingredients and a superb atmosphere make these occasions hard to beat. Most of the uncluttered bedrooms have a wonderful view of Fin Lough. Walk in unspoilt country before returning to friendly faces and a whiskey in front of a roaring fire. *Self-catering cottages also available.*

- Fly-fishing weekends: 5 times a year.
- Wine Weekends: winter.
- Wine & Food Gourmet Weekends: winter.
- Billiard room.
- Golf at Ballyconneely.
- Westport, 32km.

rooms	12 doubles.
price	€ 120-€ 240. Singles € 90-€ 135.
meals	Lunch € 15. Dinner € 45.
closed	Mid-December-mid-January.
directions	Turn north off N59 1.25km east of Leenane, signed to Delphi, towards Louisburgh for 10km. Lodge on left in woods 0.8km after spa/activity centre.

Peter Mantle

tel	+353 (0)95 42222 (Subject to change. See intro.)
fax	+353 (0)95 42296
e-mail	info@delphilodge.ie
web	www.delphilodge.ie

Hotel & self-catering

The Old Anchor

Main Street, Annascaul Village, Dingle Peninsula, Co. Kerry, Eire

The most unlikely things are likely to happen at the Old Anchor. Where other places have a view, a lovely garden or gorgeous antiques, here you meet the village. Within a few hours of arriving, the resident magician had shown me a few tricks, the keeper of folk tales had sung a hilarious song about lost love and a woman from Alabama had cooked us real southern fried chicken just the way her mom taught her. Marie is a quiet, considerate constant amid this social maelstrom. Comfortable bedrooms and a hearty breakfast set you up for a day's exploration.

- Watercolours: April-November.
- Ink Painting: August.
- Tapestry Weaving: August.
- Walking Tours: March-December.
- Surfing: 2km.
- Fungi the Dolphin, Dingle harbour, 10km.

rooms	8 twins/doubles.
price	From €64. Singles from €42.
meals	Lunch from €10. Dinner from €30.
closed	15 December-7 March.
directions	From Killarney, N72 to Castlemaine, left on R561 towards Dingle, then right on N86 towards Tralee. Annascaul 0.8km. House in middle of village, on right.

Marie Kennedy

tel	+353 (0)66 915 7382
fax	+353 (0)66 915 7382
e-mail	dropanchor@eircom.net
web	www.dingle-peninsula.ie/annascaul

B&B

map 20   entry 332

Tahilla Cove Country House

Tahilla, Co. Kerry, Eire

This quaint guesthouse tumbles down into a beautiful, secluded cove in Kenmare Bay, surrounded by 14 acres of landscaped gardens and mature woodland. James runs the place with his wife Deirdre, a local doctor, and his mother Dolly, a great character who will happily relate the whole history of this unique place. Old-fashioned bedrooms have modern comforts and most have sea views and a private balcony or terrace. Dinner is a relaxed house party affair. The family are upholding a fine tradition established more than half a century ago.

- Skellig Island.
- Garnish, Derreen & Muckross Gardens, 1-hour drive.
- Golf.
- Fishing – river, sea & lake.
- Walking the Kerry Way.
- Bike hire in village.

rooms	9: 2 doubles, 1 twin, 6 twins/doubles.
price	€ 120. Singles from € 80.
meals	Dinner from € 27, except Tuesdays & Wednesdays.
closed	Mid-October-March.
directions	From Kenmare, N70 towards Sneem for 17.5km. House left down drive, signed.

James, Deirdre & Dolly Waterhouse

tel	+353 (0)64 45204 (Subject to change. See intro.)
fax	+353 (0)64 45104
e-mail	tahillacove@eircom.net
web	www.tahillacove.com

Hotel

Coursetown House

Stradbally Road, Athy, Co. Kildare, Eire

The best mattresses, crisp linen and luxurious pillows ensure the soundest night's sleep at Coursetown; the softest towels and Gilchrist & Soames toiletries add to the luxury. Iris and Jim's early Victorian farmhouse is surrounded by one of the most well-looked after plots in the country, full of colour and scent. Bedrooms at the front overlook a small woodland garden that bursts into life in the spring. Over a slice of delicious home-made cake, ask about the sea-bean in the yard – Jim is a natural history enthusiast. Engaging company and a great advert for Ireland.

- Emo Court Gardens, 18km.
- Altamont Garden, Tullow, 38km.
- The Curragh & Punchestown Race Courses, both 22km.
- Russborough House & Art Collection, 35km.
- Stradbally Steam Museum, 10km.
- Golf courses, 2–32km.

rooms	4: 2 doubles, 2 twins/doubles, extra bathroom.
price	€ 100–€ 110. Singles € 60–€ 70.
meals	Restaurants in Athy.
closed	10 days at Christmas.
directions	From N78 at Athy, or N80 at Stradbally onto R428. House 3km from Athy & 9km from Stradbally, signed.

Jim & Iris Fox

tel	+353 (0)59 863 1101
fax	+353 (0)59 863 2740

B&B

map 20   entry 334

Ivyleigh House

Bank Place, Church Street, Port Laoise, Co. Laois, Eire

Dinah means it when she says you are going to get the best of everything in this 1850 Georgian-style townhouse. Every item has been carefully chosen for your greater comfort: the Italian Frette towels, the Piubelle linen, the pocket-sprung mattresses, the Mason tableware, the Newbridge silver cutlery, the Osborne & Little wallpaper and the lovely Chippendale double bed. Breakfast is more than a match – choose from a dizzying array of delicious alternatives. Dinah and husband Jerry are friendly, down-to-earth people who work hard to look after you.

- Golf, 3km.
- Angling, 10km.
- Museums, 23km.
- Slieve Bloom Park, 20km.
- Emo Court Gardens, 10km.
- Heywood Garden, 12km.

rooms	6: 2 doubles, 3 twins/doubles, 1 single.
price	€ 110–€ 120. Singles from € 80.
meals	Restaurant in Port Laoise.
closed	Christmas.
directions	Follow signs for Church Street, multi-storey car park. House 25m on right.

Dinah Campion

tel	+353 (0)502 22081 (Subject to change. See intro.)
fax	+353 (0)502 63343
e-mail	dinah@ivyleigh.com
web	www.ivyleigh.com

B&B

Ballaghmore Manor House & Castle

Borris-in-Ossory, Co. Laois, Eire

An extraordinary 16th-century house – one of the oldest in Ireland – with a 15th-century tower castle in its back garden and a remarkable owner who never seems to run out of stories. Grace, former gilder and restorer of Irish paintings, left the good life in Dublin for an even better life in the country. She has converted the castle into a medieval fantasy, where the sound of logs crackling in the hearth will catapult you back four hundred years. B&B bedrooms in the house are elegant and subtly-lit, and the smoked salmon and scrambled egg breakfasts are peerless.

- Monastic Midlands Tour: on site and up to 16km.
- Tour of Ancient Kingdom of Ossory.
- Hunting.
- Fishing.
- 5th-12th-century churches.
- Connemara ponies on estate.

rooms	5: 2 doubles, 1 twin, 1 single, 1 family. Also self-catering tower castle for 6.
price	€ 120-€ 160. Singles € 60. Self-catering € 1,500 per week.
meals	Restaurant 1.6km.
closed	Rarely.
directions	From Dublin, N7 Limerick road through Borris-in-Ossory towards Roscrea. Castle signed 1.8km after Borris. Entrance on right.

Grace Pym

tel	+353 (0)505 21453 (Subject to change. See intro.)
fax	+353 (0)505 21195
e-mail	gracepym@eircom.net
web	www.castleballaghmore.com

B&B & self-catering

map 20   entry 336

The Mustard Seed at Echo Lodge
Ballingarry, Co. Limerick, Eire

Named after a passage from the Bible, this impressive Victorian mansion has impeccable style. It's all down to Dan Mullane, whose cheerful, energetic presence makes the place sparkle. The bedrooms are all different and include two suites, with styles ranging from elegant Regency to warm and contemporary. In the evening the dining room takes centre stage, and the seven acres of grounds include herb and vegetable gardens, an orchard and unusual plants. A place with a big reputation.

- Horse-riding.
- Golf.
- Fishing.
- Shooting.
- Award-winning restaurant & organic kitchen garden.
- Adare village.

rooms	13: 6 doubles, 3 twins, 2 family, 2 suites.
price	€ 172–€ 320. Singles from € 110.
meals	Dinner € 48–€ 54.
closed	24–26 December.
directions	From Limerick, N21 through Adare. Left just after village, signed Ballingarry. Follow signs for 12.8km taking right at village x-roads to house.

Daniel Mullane

tel	+353 (0)69 68508 (Subject to change. See intro).
fax	+353 (0)69 68511
e-mail	mustard@indigo.ie
web	www.mustardseed.ie

Hotel

Ghan House

Carlingford, Co. Louth, Eire

This 18th-century house is enclosed within the walls of Carlingford, probably the best preserved medieval town in Ireland. Slieve Foy rises impressively behind, and the house looks over Carlingford Lough and the Mourne Mountains. Some guests prefer the bedrooms in the creaky timeworn atmosphere of the house, while others enjoy the peace and quiet of the converted dairyhouse. There are arched doorways, corbelled ceilings, a half-tester bed, proper bathrooms – impeccable. Dinners are just as special. The friendly Carrolls know what they are doing.

- Cookery: from €55.
- Wine-tasting: from €20.
- Oyster Farm Tour: 1km, from €25.
- Horse-riding: 10km, from €25.
- Guided Mountain Walks: from €30.
- Sailing, Canoeing & Yacht Charter: from €55–€200 (latter for yacht charter).

rooms	12: 2 doubles, 7 twins/doubles, 1 single, 2 family.
price	€150–€220. Singles from €55.
meals	Dinner, 5 courses, from €45.
closed	Christmas & New Year.
directions	From Dublin, N1 north for 84km, then right at 1st r'bout after Dundalk, signed Carlingford. House 1st on left entering village, 10m after 30mph sign.

Paul & Joyce Carroll

tel	+353 (0)42 937 3682
fax	+353 (0)42 937 3772
e-mail	ghanhouse@eircom.net
web	www.ghanhouse.com

Hotel

map 20 entry 338

Rosturk Woods

Rosturk, Mulranny, Westport, Co. Mayo, Eire

When you reach the end of the long wooded drive of Rosturk Woods, you realise how close the sea is. At high tide, it laps at the garden gate; at low tide, walk to an island. Along the headland, the turrets of a castle poke above trees. Double doors open onto a long veranda which looks straight onto Clew Bay, home to otters and a host of birdlife. Alan, who was born here, and Louisa are good company with a great sense of humour. A warm, family home full of laid-back style. *Self-catering also available with wheelchair access, sleeps 8.*

- Creative Writing: from May 2004, € 1,500 p.w. full-board.
- Tennis court.
- Walking trails.
- Boat trips.
- Golf course, 5km.
- Pony-trekking, 5km.

rooms	3 twins/doubles.
price	€ 90–€ 130. Singles from € 60. Self-catering € 500–€ 1,000 p.w.
meals	Dinner from € 45.
closed	December-February.
directions	From Newport, N59 Mulranny-Achill road for 11km. Big blue house sign on left.

Louisa & Alan Stoney

tel	+353 (0)98 36264 (Subject to change. See intro.)
fax	+353 (0)98 36264
e-mail	stoney@iol.ie
web	www.rosturk-woods.com

B&B & self-catering

The Cottages

Seabank, Bettystown, Co. Meath, Eire

Come to relax in a unique hamlet of luxurious thatched cottages next to miles of sandy beach on Ireland's east coast. Originally three cottages, built 300 years ago, now there are six, including Roger and Liz's wonderful seafront home where they run art and photographic courses. Every cottage makes ample use of oak and antique pine to create a bright, fresh feel; all are different. The quilted bedspreads, big baths that fit two, CD players, comfy sofas and fully-fitted kitchens guarantee comfort… there's even a thatched Wendy house for your children.

- Leisure Painting: spring & autumn, €400 (3 days), full-board & wine.
- Photography: spring & autumn, €400 (3 days), full board & wine.
- Golf Tuition: 2km, €50 per hour.
- Fishing.
- Walking trails.
- Garden on sandy beach front.

rooms	5 cottages: 1 for 2, 2 for 4, 1 for 5, 1 for 6.
price	€120 for two per day.
meals	Self-catering unless doing courses. Restaurant 2km.
closed	Rarely.
directions	From Dublin, N1 north to Julianstown, right on R150 to Laytown, left along seafront. 1.6km on right opp. Lis-maura Farmshop.

Roger & Liz Pickett

tel	+353 (0)41 982 8104
fax	+353 (0)41 982 7955
e-mail	info@cottages-ireland.com
web	www.cottages-ireland.com

Self-catering

map 20   entry 340

Ardtarmon House

Ballinfull, Co. Sligo, Eire

Walk the 500 yards to sand and crashing surf, then turn back and behold the wonderous mountains. Charles and Christa are a relaxed and friendly couple bringing up a young family. The property has been Charles's ancestral home since his great-grandfather bought the land in 1852. Enjoy hearty cooking in the dining room where golden sunsets bathe the room in beautiful light. The bedrooms are big and comfy, with garden views over a labyrinth of walls, tangled orchards and a giant cedar with a treehouse for children. *Five thatched self-catering cottages available.*

- Secluded mature grounds with tennis court.
- Coastal walks.
- Drumcliffe – grave of WH Yeats.
- Sligo.
- Lissadell House.
- Tree house for children.

rooms	4: 3 doubles, 1 family.
price	€70–€100. Singles from €43.
meals	Dinner from €25.
closed	Christmas & New Year.
directions	From Sligo, N15 north towards Donegal for 8km to Drumcliffe. Left for Carney for 1.6km. In village, follow signs to Raghley for 7.5km, left at Dunleavy's shop. Gate lodge & drive on left after 2.4km.

Charles & Christa Henry

tel	+353 (0)71 916 3156
fax	+353 (0)71 916 3156
e-mail	enquiries@ardtarmon.com
web	www.ardtarmon.com

B&B & self-catering

Coopershill House

Riverstown, Co. Sligo, Eire

Coopershill is one of the most handsome and distinguished examples of Irish Georgian in the country. Brian and Lindy greet you with a friendly smile before inviting you into the awesome grandeur of the stone-floored entrance hall. Everything here is exemplary: beautiful paintings, gilt-edged mirrors, *chaise longues* and amazing old beds. Top-floor bedrooms look over copper beech and croquet lawn to the River Unsin and the four-poster with huge corner windows is stunning. The 1900 canopied bath in its green-tiled grotto will knock your socks off.

- Tennis courts on site.
- Niland Art Gallery, Sligo.
- Seaweed baths, Strendhill & Enniserone.
- Lissadell House.
- Strokestown House & Famine Museum.
- Golf courses, 1-hour drive.

rooms	8: 4 doubles, 1 twin, 2 four-posters; 1 double with private bath.
price	€ 184–€ 198. Singles from € 111.
meals	Dinner € 40–€ 45.
closed	November–March.
directions	From Sligo, N4 towards Dublin for 17.6km, left at Drumfin x-roads, signed Coopershill. Entrance on left after 2km, before sharp turn.

Brian & Lindy O'Hara

tel	+353 (0)71 916 5108
fax	+353 (0)71 916 5466
e-mail	ohara@coopershill.com
web	www.coopershill.com

Hotel

map 20   entry 342

Temple House
Ballymote, Co. Sligo, Eire

Temple House is one of the most idiosyncratic places that you are ever likely to stay. Three ruins of previous Temple houses lie to the left of the long drive, but the present version, built in 1864, sits overlooking the lake. The house is full of antiquity and the huge bedrooms pulse with past grandeur – Sandy's family has been here since 1665. Relax in the sitting room before a wonderful communal supper which Deb ministers with reassuring ease. Sandy is seriously allergic to perfumed products and sprays so please don't arrive with them on.

- Irish Music & Dance: 15km, in English/Irish, 13-19 July.
- Yeats Summer School: 19km, 27 July-8 August, € 270-€ 490.
- Ballymota Heritage Weekend: 6km, 1-4 August.
- Landscapes & Legends: 9km, April-September.
- Pony-trekking: 9-32km, April-November.
- Fishing - salmon, trout & pike: 0-19km, April-November.

rooms	6: 1 double, 1 twin, 1 single, 2 family suites; 1 double with private bath.
price	€ 130-€ 140. Singles from € 95.
meals	Dinner € 30-€ 35.
closed	December-March.
directions	From Sligo, N4 for Dublin, then N17 for Galway. House signed left 0.4km south of Ballinacarrow.

Deb & Sandy Perceval

tel	+353 (0)71 918 3329
fax	+353 (0)71 918 3808
e-mail	guests@templehouse.ie
web	www.templehouse.ie

B&B

Ballycormac House

Aglish, Borrisokane, Co. Tipperary, Eire

After years of visiting Ireland and going home with yet another horse, John and Cherylynn decided it would be cheaper to move here. The building is a warren of tiny passages, low doorways and narrow staircases. Cottage-style bedrooms have big, solid beds, and bathrooms are entered through saloon doors. Cherylynn makes full use of home-grown organic fruit and vegetables in the kitchen; John provides liquid refreshment. Dine round a big table in a snug yet baronial dining room. John usually manages to cajole guests onto one of their many horses.

- Horse-riding.
- Shooting.
- Fishing: 8km.
- Golf: 9km.
- Water-skiing: 8km.
- Walks from door.

rooms	6: 2 doubles, 1 twin, 1 twin/double, 1 family; 1 single with private bath.
price	€ 90–€ 120. Singles € 45–€ 60.
meals	Lunch from € 12. Dinner from € 32.
closed	Rarely.
directions	From Nenagh, N52 for Portumna, then right 0.4km after Borrisokane, signed to house, down long straight road. Left at T-junc, right in Aglish, following signs.

John & Cherylynn Lang

tel	+353 (0)67 21129
	(Subject to change. See intro.)
fax	+353 (0)67 21200
e-mail	ballyc@indigo.ie
web	www.ballyc.com

B&B

map 20   entry 344

Buggy's Glencairn Inn

Glencairn, Co. Waterford, Eire

A small pub, a small restaurant and a small B&B – small but perfectly formed. Dump your stuff on a wonderful double bed, soak in a hot bath, then slip downstairs for a pint of Guinness by a log fire in a snug, wooden pub. Dinner is in the even cosier restaurant next door with stone floors, country artefacts and check tablecloths. Food is utterly delicious. After coffee, amble back to the bar for a few nightcaps and a chat with Ken if he is around – his wry observations are hilarious. Both he and Cathleen are great company and have many entertaining tales to tell.

- Duke of Devonshire's Garden, 3km.
- Golf course, 3km.
- Salmon & trout fishing next door.
- Granary Museum, Waterford - Waterford's treasures.
- Curraghmore House & Gardens, Portlaw.
- Ardmore High Cross - 4th-century Christian settlement.

rooms	4: 3 doubles, 1 twin.
price	€ 110–€ 120. Singles from € 70.
meals	Dinner from € 36.
closed	Christmas Day & Good Friday. Open weekends only November-February.
directions	From Lismore, N72 for Tallow for 1.2km, right at Horneybrooks car showroom, signed Glencairn. House 3.2km on right in village, opposite T-junction.

Ken & Cathleen Buggy

tel	+353 (0)58 56232 (Subject to change. See intro.)
fax	+353 (0)58 56232
e-mail	info@lismore.com
web	www.buggys.net

Inn

Mornington House

Mornington, Multyfarnham, Nr. Mullingar, Co. Westmeath, Eire

Seclusion here is absolute. You approach Mornington through a gap in a barrier of trees, the manifold guardians of the property that protect it on all sides. Most of the bedrooms are large, with big bathrooms, brass beds and delightful views. Downstairs, carpets fade as they approach long ranks of park-facing windows and a huge potted lime tree in the dining room catches the sunlight in the morning. Warwick and Anne are genuinely dedicated hosts and produce the most delicious meals, using home-grown produce from the walled garden behind the house.

- Horse-riding: 20km, April-October.
- Clonmacnoise - early Christian sites.
- Fore Abbey & ancient ruins of Fore.
- Belvedere House.
- Locke's Distillery Museum.
- Cairns of Lough Crew.

rooms	4: 1 double; 1 twin/double; 2 doubles both with private bath.
price	€ 120. Singles from € 80.
meals	Dinner from € 38.
closed	November-March.
directions	From N4/Mullingar bypass, R394 for Castlepollard for 8km. Left at Wood Pub in Crookedwood, then 2km to 1st junc. Right, house 1.6km on right, down long drive.

Anne & Warwick O'Hara

tel	+353 (0)44 72191 (Subject to change. See intro.)
fax	+353 (0)44 72338
e-mail	info@mornington.ie
web	www.mornington.ie

B&B

map 20   entry 346

Glendine Country House

Arthurstown, Co. Wexford, Eire

Glendine sits on a hill in 50 acres of farmland with beautiful landscaped gardens and views over the Barrow estuary. Tom and Annie have put a huge amount of effort into the splendid renovation of this 1830 ancestral dower house, adding comfort without compromising the period style. Large bedrooms have Victorian bedsteads, pitch pine floors and original wooden shutters. This is a lively household run by a relaxed and friendly couple who will thoroughly look after you. Gourmet breakfasts use organic produce wherever possible.

- Cookery: €60–€100 per session. See www.cookingireland.com.
- Cookery: 2.4km, €60–€100 per session.
- Ballyhack, Tintern & Dunbrody castles, 3–5km.
- Waterford Crystal, 11km (take car ferry).
- Safe beaches, 16km.
- Hook Lighthouse.

rooms	5: 1 double, 2 twins/doubles, 2 family. Also 2 self-catering cottages for 5.
price	€90–€100. Singles €55–€75. Cottages €350 p.w.
meals	Hotel opposite; pubs a walk.
closed	Christmas.
directions	Rosslare, N25 north for 8km, left at 1st r'bout, left at 2nd r'bout on R733 for Wellington Bridge for 32km. Entrance on right as road dips into Arthurstown.

Tom & Annie Crosbie

tel	+353 (0)51 389258 (Subject to change. See intro.)
fax	+353 (0)51 389677
e-mail	glendinehouse@eircom.net
web	www.glendinehouse.com

B&B & self-catering

Kilmokea Country Manor & Gardens

Great Island, Campile, Co. Wexford, Eire

Georgian Kilmokea with its beautiful heritage garden and long history is one of those rare places that is hard to fault. Mark and Emma are gracious, welcoming and ever so helpful. The bedrooms are decorated with luxurious good taste: thick carpets, smart antiques and big bath towels. Before dinner, meet other guests over a drink. Everyone is introduced before sitting down in the formal dining room; couples can eat *à deux* if they wish. Much of the food comes from the walled kitchen garden – one small but integral part of the botanical treat in store.

- Cookery: 4km.
- Horse-riding: 5km.
- Fishing: 7km.
- Art: 8km.
- Aromatherapy Treatments.
- Irish pottery, art & craft shop.

rooms	6: 3 doubles, 1 four-poster, 1 family; 1 twin with private bath.
price	€ 140-€ 250. Singles from € 90.
meals	Lunch from € 10. Dinner from € 38.
closed	November-March.
directions	Waterford to Passage East, then R733 north, past Dunbrody Abbey. After 2.4km, road swings sharp right; straight on, for Great Island, then left at T-junc. 2km, on left.

Mark & Emma Hewlett

tel	+353 (0)51 388109 (Subject to change. See intro.)
fax	+353 (0)51 388776
e-mail	kilmokea@indigo.ie
web	www.kilmokea.com

Hotel

map 20 entry 348

Woodbrook House

Killanne, Enniscorthy, Co. Wexford, Eire

This enigmatic 1770s Georgian house lies in a setting worthy of an Old Master. You sweep down a long drive to a pillared entrance flanked by marble lions. So far, so Anglo-Irish, but walk inside and the mood changes: Alexandra has used paint techniques picked up in Rome and painted furniture from Rajasthan to give a distinctive style. The house also has Ireland's only 'flying staircase' – it quivers as you climb. Giles is a seasoned character with strong convictions and a wry humour, while Alexandra and their children lend youth and vitality to this memorable home.

- English Language: May-August.
- Landscape & Architectural Painting: May-August.
- Blackstairs Mountains.
- Kilkenny.
- Dunbrody Famine Ship, New Ross.
- JFK Arboretum, New Ross.

rooms	4: 2 doubles, 1 twin; 1 family with private bath.
price	From € 120. Singles from € 75.
meals	Dinner from € 25.
closed	November-May. Groups off season by arrangement.
directions	From Enniscorthy, R702 to Kiltealy, through village towards Rathnure for 2.7km then left down small lane with tall trees. Entrance 300m on left down drive.

Giles & Alexandra FitzHerbert

tel	+353 (0)54 55114
	(Subject to change. See intro.)
fax	+353 (0)54 55671

B&B

Barraderry House

Kiltegan, Co. Wicklow, Eire

A bucolic setting. The farmhouse, Georgian with Victorian additions, is approached along a drive that dips and curves through an avenue of trees. Olive decided to spruce up the place after the last of six daughters left home; she has done a wonderful job. The large hallway, spare of ornament and warm in colour, leads to a dining room where breakfast is served around a huge oval table. In the unfussy bedrooms are pretty bedspreads, good prints on the walls and the odd fireplace. Olive is so friendly and easy-going and John has been known to sing at the piano.

- Horse-riding, 6km.
- Hill-walking.
- Ten golf courses within 24km.
- Wicklow Garden Festival (May-August).
- Russborough House – Beit Art Collection.
- Angling & shooting (in season).

rooms	4: 1 double, 1 twin, 1 twin/double, 1 single.
price	From €80. Single from €45.
meals	Restaurant 6.4km.
closed	Mid-December–mid-January.
directions	From Dublin, N81 Blessington to Baltinglass for 56km, then left on R747 Kiltegan road. Entrance on right just before village.

Olive & John Hobson

tel	+353 (0)59 647 3209
fax	+353 (0)59 647 3209
e-mail	jo.hobson@oceanfree.net
web	www.barraderrycountryhouse.com

B&B

map 20   entry 350

WHAT'S IN THE BACK OF THE BOOK?

• Ask all about the things that are important to you before you go, and you'll get more out of your holiday that you ever imagined.

USEFUL VOCABULARY

Before arriving

Do you have a room free tonight?
Avete (disponibile) una camera per questa sera?
¿Tiene una habitación libre para hoy?
Tem um quarto para esta noite?
Avez-vous une chambre disponible pour cette nuit?

How much does it cost?
Quanto costa?
¿Cuánto cuesta?
Quanto custa?
Quel est le prix?

We'll be arriving at about 7pm.
Arriveremo verso le sette.
Vamos a llegar sobre las siete.
Nós chegaremos por volta das sete da tarde.
Nous arriverons vers 7 heures du soir.

We're lost.
Ci siamo persi.
Estámos perdidos.
Estamos perdidos.
Nous sommes perdus.

We'll be arriving late.
Arriveremo tardi.
Vamos a llegar tarde.
Vamos chegar tarde.
Nous arriverons tard/plus tard que prévu.

We'd like to have dinner.
Vorremmo cenare qui.
Queremos cenar.
Queríamos jantar.
Nous aimerions dîner.

On arrival

Hello! I'm Mr/Mrs X.
Buon giorno mi chiamo Signor X; mi chiamo Signora X.
¡Hóla! Soy Señor/Señora X.
Olá! eu sou o Senhor/Senhora X.
Bonjour! Je suis Monsieur X; Madame X.

We found your name in this book.
Abbiamo trovato la vostra struttura in questa guida.
Le hemos encontrado en este libro.
Encontramos o seu nome neste livro.
Nous vous avons trouvé dans ce guide.

● Italian ● Spanish ● Portuguese ● French

USEFUL VOCABULARY

Do you have an extra pillow/blanket?
Ha un cuscino/una coperta in più?
¿Podría dejarnos otra almohada/manta?
Você tem uma outra almofada/um outro cobertor?
Avez-vous un oreiller/une couverture de plus?

A light bulb needs replacing.
C'è una lampadina fulminata.
Es necesario cambiar una bombilla.
É preciso mudar uma lampada.
Il faut remplacer une ampoule.

The heating isn't on.
Il riscaldimento non è acceso.
No está encendida la calefacción.
O aquecedor não está ligado.
Le chauffage ne marche pas.

Can you show us how the air-conditioning works?
Potrebbe mostrarci come funziona l'aria condzionata.
¿Nos puede enseñar como funciona el aire?
Como funciona o ar condicionado?
Comment fonctionne la climatisation?

There is no hot water.
Non c'è acqua calda.
No hay agua caliente.
Naõ ha aqua quente.
Il n'y a pas d'eau chaude.

We have a problem with the plumbing.
Abbiamo un problema con il impianto idraulica.
Tenemos un problema de fontanería.
Temos um problema com a canalização.
Il y a un problème de plomberie.

Could we have some soap, please?
Possiamo avere del sapone per favore?
¿Hay jabón por favor?
Queriamos sabonete por favor?
Nous pouvons avoir du savon s'il vous plaît?

When does breakfast begin?
A che ora è la colazione?
¿A partir de qué hora dan el desayuno?
A que horas começa a servir o pequeno almoço?
On peut prendre le petit déjeuner à partir de quelle heure?

● Italian ● Spanish ● Portuguese ● French

USEFUL VOCABULARY

We'd like to order some drinks.
Vorremo ordinare qualche bevande, per favore.
Queremos tomar algo, por favor.
Queríamos tomar algumas bebidas, por favor.
Nous aimerions commander quelquechose à boire.

Where can we get some petrol?
Dov'è una stazione di vifornimento per favore?
¿Dónde hay una gasolinera?
Onde fica a próxima estação de serviço?
Nous cherchons une station de service / de l'essence.

We need a doctor.
Abbiamo bisogno di un medico.
Necesitamos un médico.
Precisamos dum médico.
Il nous faut un médecin.

Can you recommend a good restaurant?
Potrebbe raccomandare un buon ristorante per favore?
¿Podría recomendar un buen restaurante?
Onde há um sítio onde se coma bem?
Pouvez-vous nous recommander un bon restaurant?

Can you recommend a good walk?
Potrebbe raccomandare una bella passeggiata?
¿Podría recomendar algun paseo bonito?
Pode me recomendar um belo paseira?
Pouvez-vous nous recommander une belle promenade?

What time must we vacate our room?
A che ora dobbiamo lasciare la camera?
¿A qué hora tenemos que dejar libre nuestra habitación?
A que horas temos de libertar / deixar o quarto?
A quelle heure faut-il quitter la chambre?

We'd like to pay the bill.
Vorremmo pagare il conto.
Queremos pagar.
Queríamos pagar a conta.
Nous aimerions regler l'addition.

We've really enjoyed our stay.
È stato un soggiorno veramente divertente.
Nos ha gustado mucho nuestra estancia.
Tivemos uma estadia muito agradável.
Nous sommes ravis / es de notre séjour.

● Italian ● Spanish ● Portuguese ● French

USEFUL VOCABULARY

What is today's set menu?
Che cos' è il menu di oggi?
¿Qué tienen hoy de menú?
Qual é o menu para hoje?
Quel est le menu du jour?

What's that person eating?
Che cosa mangia quella persona?
¿Qué está comiendo aquel hombre?
O que é aquella pesoa esta a comer?
Qu'est-ce qu'il/elle mange, cette personne?

We'd like something with no meat in it.
Vorremmo mangiare qualcosa senza carne per favore.
Queremos comer algo que no tenga nada de carne.
Queremos a comer um prato sem carne.
Nous aimerions quelquechose à manger sans viande.

We'd like to see the wine list.
Vorremmo vedere la liste dei vini per favore.
Queremos la lista de vinos, por favor.
Queremos a ver a lista do vinhos.
Nous aimerions voir la liste des vins.

This food is cold!
Questo pasto è freddo!
¡Esta comida está fría!
Esta comida está fria.
Ce plat est froid.

Where are the toilets?
Dovè il bagno per favore?
¿Dónde están los servicios?
Onde ficam as casas de banho?
Où sont les toilettes?

It was a delicious meal.
Era un pasto delizioso.
Estaba muy rica la comida.
Foi uma óptima refeição.
Le repas était délicieux.

I'd like a white/black coffee.
Vorrei un caffè latte/caffè nero/espresso.
Un café con leche/un café solo.
Queria um café com leite/café simples.
J'aimerais un café noir/crème.

● Italian ● Spanish ● Portuguese ● French

WHAT IS ALASTAIR SAWDAY PUBLISHING?

Twenty or so of us work in converted barns on a farm near Bristol, close enough to the city for a bicycle ride and far enough for a silence broken only by horses and the occasional passage of a tractor. Some editors work in the countries they write about, e.g. France; others work from the UK but are based outside the office. We enjoy each other's company, celebrate every event possible, and work in an easy-going but committed environment.

These books owe their style and mood to Alastair's miscellaneous career and his interest in the community and the environment. He has taught overseas, worked with refugees, run development projects abroad, founded a travel company and several environmental organisations. There has been a slightly mad streak evident throughout, not least in his driving of a waste-paper-collection lorry for a year, the manning of stalls at jumble sales and the pursuit of causes long before they were considered sane.

These books owe their style and mood to Alastair's miscellaneous career and his interest in the community and the environment

Back to the travel company: trying to take his clients to eat and sleep in places that were not owned by corporations and assorted bandits he found dozens of very special places in France – farms, châteaux etc – a list that grew into the first book, *French Bed and Breakfast*. It was a celebration of 'real' places to stay and the remarkable people who run them.

The publishing company grew from that first and rather whimsical French book. It started as a mild crusade, and there it stays – full of 'attitude', and the more appealing for it. For we still celebrate the unusual, the beautiful, the individual. We are passionate about rejecting the banal, the ugly, the pompous and the indifferent and we are passionate too about 'real' food. Alastair is a trustee of the Soil Association and keen to promote organic growing and consuming by owners and visitors.

It is a source of deep pleasure to us to know that there are many thousands of people who share our views. We are by no means alone in trumpeting the virtues of resisting the destruction and uniformity of so much of our culture – and the cultures of other nations, too.

We run a company in which people and values matter. We love to hear of new friendships between those in the book and those using it, and to know that there are many people – among them farmers – who have been enabled to pursue their decent lives thanks to the extra income our books bring them.

FRAGILE EARTH SERIES

This fascinating new series has been praised by politicians, academics, environmentalists, civil-servants - and 'general' readers. It has come as a blast of fresh air, blowing away confusion and incomprehension

It is now widely accepted that the 'environment' is the main 'issue' of the new century. But it is awesomely complex; how on earth can the average mortal begin to understand the links between Fishing, Debt, War, Economics, Agriculture - and so on? Read these (it doesn't take long) and begin to understand - and be inspired.

The Little Earth Book £6.99
The Little Food Book £6.99

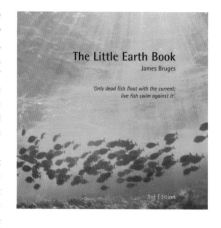

The Little Earth Book
James Bruges

'Only dead fish float with the current; live fish swim against it'.

3rd Edition

The Little Food Book
An explosive account of the food we eat today

Craig Sams

Also from
Alastair Sawday Publishing

Six Days

Links the story of the creation as told in 'Genesis' with the original story behind the creation of Chester Cathedral Millennium window.

Published June 2003 £12.99

SIX DAYS

The story of the making of the Chester Cathedral Millennium Window

Created by
Rowland Grimshaw

PAINTON COWEN

ORDER FORM UK

All these books, are available in major bookshops or you may order them direct. **Post and packaging are FREE within the UK.**

		Price	No. copies
French Bed & Breakfast	Edition 8	£15.99	
French Hotels, Inns and Other Places	Edition 2	£11.99	
French Holiday Homes	Edition 1	£11.99	
Paris Hotels	Edition 4	£9.99	
British Bed & Breakfast	Edition 7	£14.99	
British Hotels, Inns and Other Places	Edition 4	£12.99	
Bed & Breakfast for Garden Lovers	Edition 2	£14.99	
British Holiday Homes	Edition 1	£9.99	
London	Edition 1	£9.99	
Ireland	Edition 4	£12.99	
Spain	Edition 5	£13.99	
Portugal	Edition 2	£9.99	
Italy	Edition 2	£11.95	
Europe	Edition 1	£15.99	
The Little Earth Book	Edition 3	£6.99	
The Little Food Book	Edition 1	£6.99	
Six Days		£12.99	

Please make cheques payable to   Total £
Alastair Sawday Publishing

Please send cheques to: Alastair Sawday Publishing,
The Home Farm Stables, Barrow Gurney, Bristol BS48 3RW.
For credit card orders call 01275 464891 or order directly
from our web site **www.specialplacestostay.com**

Title   First name

Surname

Address

Postcode   Tel

ORDER FORM USA

All these books are available at your local bookstore, or you may order direct. Allow two to three weeks for delivery.

		Price	No. copies
Spain	Edition 5	$19.95	
Ireland	Edition 4	$17.95	
French Bed & Breakfast	Edition 8	$19.95	
Paris Hotels	Edition 4	$14.95	
British Holiday Homes	Edition 1	$14.95	
British Hotels, Inns and other places	Edition 4	$17.95	
French Hotels, Inns and other places	Edition 2	$19.95	
British Bed & Breakfast	Edition 7	$19.95	
London	Edition 1	$12.95	
Italy	Edition 2	$17.95	
French Holiday Homes	Edition 1	$17.95	
	Total $		

Shipping in the continental USA: $3.95 for one book, $4.95 for two books, $5.95 for three or more books.
Outside continental USA, call (800) 243-0495 for prices.
For delivery to AK, CA, CO, CT, FL, GA, IL, IN, KS, MI, MN, MO, NE, NM, NC, OK, SC, TN, TX, VA, and WA, please add appropriate sales tax.

Please make checks payable to:
The Globe Pequot Press

Total $

To order by phone with MasterCard or Visa: (800) 243-0495, 9am to 5pm EST; by fax: (800) 820-2329, 24 hours; through our web site: **www.GlobePequot.com**; or by mail: The Globe Pequot Press, P.O. Box 480, Guilford, CT 06437

Date

Name

Address

Town

State

Zip code

Tel

Fax

WWW.SPECIALPLACESTOSTAY.COM

Britain

France

Ireland

Italy

Portugal

Spain...

all in one place!

On the unfathomable and often unnavigable sea of online accommodation pages, those who have discovered www.specialplacestostay.com have found it to be an island of reliability. Not only will you find a database full of trustworthy, up-to-date information about all the Special Places to Stay across Europe, but also:

• Links to the web sites of all of the places in the series

• Colourful, clickable, interactive maps to help you find the right place

• The opportunity to make most bookings by e-mail – even if you don't have e-mail yourself

• Online purchasing of our books, securely and cheaply

• Regular, exclusive special offers on books

• The latest news about future editions and future titles

The site is constantly evolving and is frequently updated with news and special features that won't appear anywhere else but in our window on the worldwide web.

Russell Wilkinson, Web Producer
website@specialplacestostay.com

If you'd like to receive news and updates about our books by e-mail, send a message to newsletter@specialplacestostay.com

REPORT FORM

Comments on existing entries and new discoveries

If you have any comments on entries in this guide, please let us have them. If you have a favourite house, hotel, inn or other new discovery, please let us know about it.

Existing Entry:

Name of property _____

Book title: _____

Entry no: _____ Edition no: _____

New recommendation:

Name of property: _____

Address: _____

_____

_____

Postcode: _____

Tel: _____

Comments: _____

_____

_____

_____

Your name: _____

Address: _____

_____

_____

Postcode: _____

Tel: _____

Please send the completed form to:

Alastair Sawday Publishing,
The Home Farm Stables, Barrow Gurney, Bristol BS48 3RW
or go to www.specialplacestostay.com and click on 'contact'.

EUR

Thank you.

ITALIAN BOOKING FORM

All'attenzione di:
To:
_____

Date:
_____

Egregio Signor, Gentile Signora,

Vorrei fare una prenotazione in nome di:
Please could you make us a reservation in the name of:
_____

Per		*notte/notti*	*Arrivo: giorno*	*mese*	*anno*
For	night(s)		Arriving: day	month	year
			Partenza: giorno	*mese*	*anno*
			Leaving: day	month	year

Si richiede :		*camera/e sistemazione in:*
We would like		rooms, arranged as follows:

Doppia/e	*Due letti*	
Double bed	Twin beds	
Tripla/e	*Singola/e*	
Triple	Single	
Suite	*Appartamento*	
Suite	Apartment	

Si richiede anche la cena per . ... persone il ....
We will also be requiring dinner for ...... person on .... (date)

Per cortesia inviarmi una conferma della mia prenotazione al mio indirizzo in fondo pagina.
Please could you send us confirmation of our reservation to the address below.

Nome: Name:
_____

Indirizzo: Address:
_____

Tel No: _____ E-mail: _____

Fax No: _____

Scheda di Prenotazione — Special Places to Stay: Europe

SPANISH BOOKING FORM

Atencion de:
To:
_____

Date:
_____

Estimado Señor / Estimada Señora,

Le(s) rogamos de hacernos una reserva en nombre de:
Please make the following booking for (name):

_____

Para	*noche(s)*	*Llegando día:*	*mes*	*año*
For	night(s)	Arriving: day	month	year
	Saliendo	*día:*	*mes*	*año*
	Leaving:	day	month	year

Necesitamos   *habitacíon(es):*
We would like   rooms, arranged as follows:

Doble	*Dos camas individuales*	
Double bed	Twin beds	
Triple	*Individual*	
Triple	Single	
Tipo Suite	*Apartamento*	*o otro*
Suite	Apartment	or other

Requeriremos también la cena:	*Si*	*No*	*Para*	*persona(s)*
We will also be requiring dinner	yes	no	for	person(s)

*Les rogamos de enviarnos la confirmacíon de esta reserva a la siguiente
dirección:(esta misma hoja o una fotocopia de la misma con su firma
nos valdrá).*

Please could you send us confirmation of our reservation to the address
below (this form or a photocopy of it with your signature could be used).

Nombre: **Name:**
_____

Dirección: **Address:**
_____

_____

Tel No: E-mail:
_____

Fax No:
_____

Hoja de Reserva – Special Places to Stay: Europe

PORTUGUESE BOOKING FORM

Á Atençèo de:
To: _____

Date: _____

Estimado Senhor / Estimada Senhora,

Agradeciamos que efectuassem uma reserva em nome de:
Please could you make us a reservation in the name of:

_____

Para	*noite(s)*	*Chegada a: dia*	*mês*	*ano*
For	night(s)	Arriving: day	month	year
		Partida a: dia	*mês*	*ano*
		Leaving: day	month	year

Desejamos   *quarto,*
We would like   rooms, arranged as follows:

Duplo	*Camos seperadas*
Double bed	Twin beds
Triplo	*Individual*
Triple	Single
Suite	*Apartamento*
Suite	Apartment

Também desejamos jantar: *Sim*   *Não*   *Para*   *pesisoas*
We will also be requiring dinner   yes   no   for   person(s)

Agradeciamos que nos enviassem confirmação desta reserva para o endereço acima mencionado. (Pode utilizar este formulário ou uma fotocópia do mesmo com a sua assinatura.)

Please could you send us confirmation of our reservation to the address below (this form or a photocopy of it with your signature could be used).

Nome: Name: _____

Endereço: Address: _____

_____

Tel No: _____ E-mail: _____

Fax No: _____

FRENCH BOOKING FORM

À l'attention de:
To:

Date:

Madame, Monsieur
Veuillez faire la réservation suivante au nom de:
Please make the following booking for (name):

Pour	*nuit(s)*	*Arrivée le jour:*	*mois*	*année*
For	night(s)	Arriving: day	month	year
		Départ le jour:	*mois*	*année*
		Leaving: day	month	year

Si possible, nous aimerions   *chambres, disposées comme suit:*
We would like   rooms, arranged as follows

À grand lit	*À lits jumeaux*
Double bed	Twin beds
Pour trois	*À un lit simple*
Triple	Single
Suite	*Appartement*
Suite	Apartment

Nous sommes accompagnés de   *enfant(s) âgé(s) de*   *ans.*
Avez-vous un/des lit(s) supplémentaire(s), un lit bébé; si oui, à quel prix?
We are travelling with   children, aged   years. Please let
us know if you have an extra bed/extra beds/a cot and if so,
at what price.

Nous aimerions également réserver le dîner pour   *personnes.*
We would also like to book dinner for   people.

Veuillez nous envoyer la confirmation à l'adresse ci-dessous:
Please send confirmation to the following address:

Nom: **Name:**

Adresse: **Address:**

Tel No: E-mail:

Fax No:

INDEX BY TOWN NAME

INDEX BY TOWN NAME

INDEX BY TOWN NAME

INDEX OF COURSES
& ACTIVITIES

INDEX OF COURSES & ACTIVITIES

INDEX OF COURSES
& ACTIVITIES

INDEX OF COURSES & ACTIVITIES

INDEX OF COURSES & ACTIVITIES

INDEX OF COURSES & ACTIVITIES

INDEX OF COURSES & ACTIVITIES

INDEX OF COURSES & ACTIVITIES

INDEX OF COURSES
& ACTIVITIES

INDEX OF COURSES
& ACTIVITIES

INDEX OF COURSES
& ACTIVITIES

INDEX OF COURSES & ACTIVITIES

INDEX OF COURSES
& ACTIVITIES